Everyday V

Praying to a Mighty God

Second Edition

How Prayer Actually Works

John Harris

Dedication

To my wonderful wife, Penny, the one with whom I have become one. I don't remember what it was like to be two. God has blessed us richly!

And to my children and grandchildren, what a blessed surprise that love created so much more love. You are proof that God is good every day!

Everyday Wisdom for the Child of God

Praying to a Mighty God

Second Edition

How Prayer Actually Works

John Harris

Author of
Discourage the Pastor, Torpedo the Church…
A 31-Day Devotional Journey to a Faith-Filled Life in Christ!
and
How Prayer Actually Works, First Edition

Book Site
www.Facebook.com/Everyday.Wisdom.for.the.Child.of.God

Podcasts and Studies
www.Facebook.com/High.BandWidth.Word.Studies
www.Facebook.com/ImpactGraceMinistries
www.YouTube.com/@GraceTeachingToday
www.YouTube.com/@GraceBibleTeaching
www.YouTube.com/@Praying to a Mighty God

Pastor John Harris, Ph.D.
Pastor, Impact Grace Ministries
President, *Things to Come Mission, USA Board* https://tcmusa.org/
Professor Emeritus of Engineering, *Saint Francis University, Loretto, PA*

Copyright © 2025

by

Pastor John Harris, Ph.D

How Prayer Actually Works; First Edition, October 2023

ISBN: 979-8266832558

All rights reserved. No part of this book may be reproduced, copied, broadcast, stored, or shared without written permission, except for brief quotations in articles and reviews.

> For information, write Pastor John Harris,
> japjharris@gmail.com
> Impact Grace Ministries Church

All Scripture quotations in this book are from the *"Scofield Study Bible"* 1909, 1917, 1937, 1945, 1996 by Oxford University Press, Inc. -- Authorized King James Version.

Published 2025 by
Pastor John Harris, Ph.D.

Imprint: Independently published; Amazon Kindle Direct Publishing

Other Books:
Discourage the Pastor, Torpedo the Church... A 31-Day Devotional Journey to a Faith-Filled Life in Christ! by Pastor John Harris, PhD; Amazon; 2024
ISBN: 979-8336826265
ISBN: 979-8343607802

Previous edition:
How Prayer Actually Works, by Pastor John Harris, PhD; Amazon; 2023
ISBN: 979-8859737826
ISBN: 979-8864579008

Second Edition

After much prayer, I have changed the name of this Second Edition from "**How Prayer Actually Works**" to "**Praying to a Mighty God.**" The purpose of this book is to help God's children rise up to redeem the time in which we live. Ephesians 5 explicitly calls us to "Arise from the dead", walk cautiously, and "redeem the time." We live in dangerous times! We need to wrestle our families, our neighbors, our friends, our government, really every detail and aspect of our lives out of the arms of the enemy. Prayer is the means by which we can change this world and our lives. We are literally going to the throne of grace, seeking our mighty God's hand in transforming tomorrow. And He is a faithful God, always producing good in the believer's life.

This and the previous edition powerfully challenge the reader to engage in a faithful prayer life, bringing about change in their life by relying on God more deeply and prayerfully. The former title is descriptive of what is inside the cover, providing a clear understanding of prayer and our relationship with God, as well as how prayer and God's will are intertwined and how prayer actually works. It is presented clearly and solidly supported with Biblical truth. However, the former title fails to convey the book's greater purpose and thrust, which is to transform lives for Jesus Christ. This is the primary driving purpose behind my writing of this book on prayer. Our prayer in the hands of a mighty God transforms our tomorrow!

There are substantial changes. I have incorporated additional ideas and thoughts throughout the work to emphasize further the truth that prayer is effective and life-changing. Some are subtle, others more extensive. I added a chapter entitled "God is for us, so pray!" I also conducted a significant rewrite of the chapter "What is Good?" and added some impactful descriptive diagrams. I changed the title of the chapter, "Final Thoughts on Prayer," to "Commanded to Pray" to be more descriptive of its content and align it with significant changes and updates that draw out our purpose and God's will for us. I also moved one chapter, which addresses a doctrinal error some have concerning prayer, out of the main flow of the book to the appendix, as it is more of an add-on or bonus material. The chapter on "Am I a Child of God" remains, since without Christ in a person's life, nothing else matters. Throughout the book, I have tightened up language in numerous places and clarified some ideas as well. There are some additional updates regarding recent changes in my life to keep the work current with my current situation.   Blessings – **John**

Contents

Acknowledgments viii
Introduction   How did I Get Here? ix
Chapter 1   Introductory Thoughts on Prayer 1
Chapter 2   Fundamental Life-Changing Truths About Prayer 7
Chapter 3   What Can Prayer Do? 35
Chapter 4   Prayer and Worship 45
Chapter 5   Prayer and Spiritual Warfare 51
Chapter 6   What, When, and Whom Should We Pray For? 65
Chapter 7   How Do I Pray 89
Chapter 8   Prayer is a Dispensational Subject 105
Chapter 9   Pray Without Ceasing 129
Chapter 10   God is For Us…So Pray! 137
Chapter 11   Our Situation: A Difficult Truth to Accept 143
Chapter 12   Can Prayer Change What is Going to Happen?....... 153
Chapter 13   Prayer and the Will of God 163
Chapter 14   What is Good? 171
Chapter 15   The Will of God Revisited 187
Chapter 16   God's Answer to Your Prayer 203
Chapter 17   Commanded to Pray 213
Chapter 18   Am I a Child of God? 219
Appendix   Praying Only for Spiritual Things??? 225

Acknowledgments and Special Thanks

In every effort of life that means something, some walk the walk with you. Special thanks to my wife, Penny, my co-laborer in Christ and partner in life, without whom I could do little, for her love, support, and organizational skills. Special thanks to my family - Stephanie, Joshua, Elizabeth, and Aaron- for their faithfulness to the Lord, their support, and especially their partnership in the ministry. And to my grandchildren - Sophia, Matthias, Ava, Blake, Evanna, and Nolan, for their extraordinary love, and six reasons why I write.

I thank Joshua McClelland, Pastor Aaron Harris, Brandon Greenleaf, Kaitlyn Maxwell, Sharon Reynolds, Bruce Hostler, Nathan Bullock, and David Kinkead, who read drafts and gave valuable comments, suggestions, and encouragement. Special thanks to Sarah Kinkead for her many hours of editing and thoughtful recommendations.

Life would be bland and empty without Christian friendships and a supportive, loving family.

May your days be filled with good things. Our God is good.

Blessings in Christ,

Pastor John Harris, Ph.D.

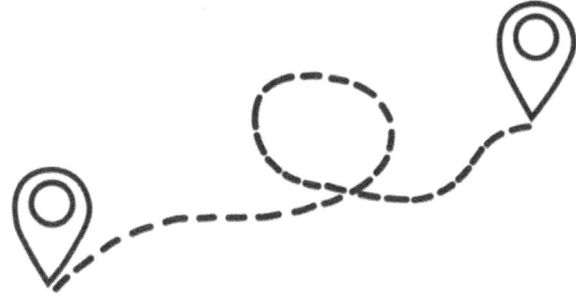

Introduction

How Did I Get Here?

I am a born-again believer in the Lord Jesus Christ, saved at an early age. Like many who are saved as a young child, it took a while before the Lord could penetrate my complacency and shake me into action. I irregularly attended church from childhood to my late teens, but was fortunate to have sat under the teaching of Pastor Henry F. Kulp, founding pastor of Altoona Bible church. His passion for the Lord Jesus Christ, the gospel of the Grace of God, and the Word of God was hard to ignore and had a profound impact on me. Having met my future wife after my first year in college, I felt a greater responsibility to know God's Word. I began taking my spiritual life more seriously by reading my Bible regularly and attending church more consistently.

As a diligent student, I discovered that I learn best and retain information more effectively by taking notes. This was also true in my church life, where I filled many notebooks with messages taught from God's Word.

Upon graduating from Saint Francis University with majors in Mathematics and Chemistry, I entered graduate school as a student pursuing a Ph.D. in Nuclear Engineering at Pennsylvania State University. My wife, Penny, and I were married at the Altoona Bible Church after my first year in Graduate school. By this time, we had begun attending every worship service, being fed from the Word of God, and growing. Neither of us was active in any ministries, but we were growing. As a married person, I chose to live at home and commute to Penn State every day. At that time, the trip was 75 minutes each way on a good day. The church had messages from Pastor Kulp dating back to the early 1960s on cassette tapes (yes, this was in the 1980s). I listened to two to three messages daily while commuting to and from the University. I learned a great deal during the two years I commuted to school.

When Penny and I had our first child, our daughter, Stephanie, I took on the responsibility of being a spiritually led dad. I began to study independently, reexamining what I had been taught, confirming and expanding my understanding. I drove to Penn State less often since my advisor had left the University to work at Sandia National Laboratories in New Mexico. Instead, I was working from home with a personal computer connected to supercomputers at Lawrence Livermore Laboratories in California via a government network, a precursor to today's Internet. (No WWW at that time, all text.)

Two or three times a year, I would fly to New Mexico or to a meeting on the West Coast to meet my advisor, discuss research, work on papers, and present at conferences and workshops. But at other times, I was working from home on my research and having the most blessed experience of being Mr. Mom, taking care of our daughter Stephanie. Penny worked during the day to support us. Life was filled with school, work, travel, our daughter Stephanie, and going to church. I also discovered Cornelius Stam of the Berean Bible Society at this time. I listened to him on the radio and bought and read as many of his books as I could afford.

In the Fall of 1986, Penny and I discovered we were expecting another child. By this time, God had me where He wanted me. At the annual Fall Bible conference in 1986, I was fully convicted, and I gave my life to the Lord, praying, "Father, I will do whatever you want me to do." And I meant it! Unexpectedly, nothing happened.

I was perplexed. I am unsure what I expected would happen, but there was only silence. I was in church, learning, growing, and waiting for God to show me what He wanted me to do. In early April 1987, Penny went into labor a full six weeks early. Eleven anxious hours passed, then God blessed us with a boy, Aaron. He was just a tad over 5 lbs. but healthy.

Penny was still on parental leave in June when Alex, the Assistant Pastor, announced that Daily Vacation Bible School (DVBS) would start the next day, and they needed more volunteers to help. I spoke to Penny that night about the two of us going to help with DVBS. When we arrived the next day, I approached the Assistant Pastor, Alex, and told him that I was there to help and that Penny could assist in the Nursery. He did not know what to do. No one ever just shows up! He fumbled a bit and then introduced me to Ruth Lockwood. Ruth was the administrative assistant to Pastor Henry F. Kulp for many years before his death, and now she taught the Junior High class at DVBS. Ruth was stern and strict, but her love for the kids was clear to everyone. I learned a great deal about ministry during the two weeks I spent with her at DVBS.

Eight months had passed since I gave my life to the Lord, and the floodgates opened. By the end of the year, I had become the church treasurer, sang in the choir, and, most impacting to me, taught a Sunday school class for adults. There are numerous "God wink" stories concerning these ministries (perhaps I will write an autobiography on God's faithfulness and work in the life of His child).

So, why did the floodgates open now, over eight months after I committed my life to the Lord and earnestly told Him I would do whatever He wanted me to do? It boils down to one thing: a simple step of faith. I chose to walk through an open door, not knowing what was on the other side. I had been waiting for God to push me through the door! But He was waiting for me, by faith, to step through the door by my own free will. I chose to serve, to minister. I answered a simple call for help and found what God had been preparing me to do for years.

Suddenly, many new ministries I had never considered were on my doorstep. He called me, and I answered. A simple step of faith changed my life and that of my family. I quit standing at the open doors and went through by faith, trusting the God who opened those doors. I could not see what was on the other side of the door, but He knew, so I trusted Him. But it started with one simple step of faith.

God had called me to serve in the local church. He had just given me the responsibility of leading an adult Sunday school class of 20-plus individuals, made me treasurer of the church, and encouraged me to reach beyond myself and love others. Upon graduating with my Ph.D. in Nuclear Engineering, I turned down a research position at Sandia National Laboratories without another job prospect. I knew the Lord wanted me and my family here in the local church. I sent out over a hundred job inquiries in an 80-mile radius (long before the days of searching online for a job) and received the same number of rejection letters. Too qualified, not hiring, looking for a different background, etc. It was now in the middle of summer, some six months into the job search, and I began considering teaching at the collegiate level. I had never thought of teaching before. However, I loved teaching the Bible in Sunday School; maybe I would like to teach in the secular arena.

I wrote a letter of inquiry to several regional universities. My undergraduate alma mater, Saint Francis University, replied and requested that I visit for an interview. A lead chemistry and mathematics department faculty member had left the University two weeks earlier without notice. The faculty knew me, so the interview was more of a reunion. I signed a contract for an assistant professor position the same day and went home. If I had thought about writing that letter of inquiry three weeks earlier, my letter would have ended up in the round file. This was no accident. Being a university professor gave me great flexibility to be in the ministry. I enjoyed the secular classroom and the numerous ministries in which I became involved at our church. I was a tentmaker, a self-supporting, full-time ministry worker for the Lord. After 33 ½ years in academia, I retired early to pursue full-time ministry, receiving my ordination for gospel service in March 2022.

In an exciting turn of events, a group of dedicated and faithful individuals and I have struck out to establish a new gospel work, Impact Grace Ministries Church. So, in addition to my writing, I also serve as a pastor and minister to a wonderful group of God's children in my church. The road has not been easy, but our Lord continues to renew our strength daily, and we press on.

I have studied many truths of Scripture over the years, taught them in Sunday School, Youth Retreats, at our church Camp, VBS, and in filling pulpits. I have had a burden for some time to write and share what God has given me through the years. I have books in the works, but I never seem to find the time to complete them. Now, I am writing and podcasting, still walking through open doors.

My hope and prayer is to teach challenging, impactful truths that change lives and build faith, and to provide practical, biblical resources about God's Word in a way that is easy to understand and apply in the daily walk of a child of God. Many of these truths are not understood or even taught. And if they are taught, frankly, they are taught or understood poorly. This world needs men, women, girls, and boys who have strong faith, love the Lord and His Word, and actively pray for and minister to others.

This book, *"Praying to a Mighty God,"* aims to equip the child of God with the prayer tools necessary to be effective in redeeming the time for Christ. God's children waking up and engaging in this spiritual conflict that we all find ourselves in can impact each individual's life, the lives of others, and the cause of Christ. Although much has been written on prayer, there remains a significant lack of good, Biblically based resources concerning prayer. Not understanding truths concerning prayer has led to crippled spiritual lives and or confusion about God and our relationship with Him.

In reality, many believers have an anemic prayer life. I've been there, and sometimes, life gets in the way. Life is so fast, with so many things vying for our attention and time, that unless we make time for prayer, it will end up a victim of neglect. Our relationship with God begins to wane and languish. We find ourselves less thankful and less aware of God's hand in our lives. The closeness and the "experience" of God in our lives seem to dim, and we start to meander through our days on our own until we find ourselves lost and finally cry out for help. But if we understand the true impact of prayer, how much our God cherishes our coming to Him in prayer, and how we worship God when we pray, we will perhaps prioritize prayer in our lives. Tomorrow can be changed when we go to God in prayer.

So, you now have this book in your hands on prayer, and you know a little about me and how I got here. I do pray that you will be challenged and convicted to engage in a prayer-filled life. God bless you and keep fighting the good fight of faith.

Pastor John

Chapter 1
Introductory Thoughts on Prayer

The Simplicity and Complexity of Prayer

Prayer is a fascinating and exciting topic to study and understand. You must think so, too, since you picked up this book. Why? We all yearn to know more about God and inherently understand that prayer is one way to connect with Him. Prayer is, at the same time, both simple and complex. No unique methods or techniques are necessary to learn to pray, which makes prayer simple. How does prayer work? Does prayer change things? Does God hear me? How do prayer and God's will work together? These questions are a bit more complex, so some study will be needed. We will examine these and many other questions as we journey together to understand how prayer works.

It is not the focus of this book to simply provide an intellectual understanding of prayer. The intent is to encourage you to be driven to your knees in a consistent and powerful prayer life for the cause of Jesus Christ and to effect change in your personal life and the world in which we all live. Exercising prayer in your daily walk is life-changing. Are you ready to experience what a prayer-driven life can be? As God's children, let us be engaged in the transformative power of praying to a mighty God.

The topic of prayer is an area of the Christian life in which there is much confusion. Finding a solid, doctrinally sound discussion on the subject is challenging. There are myriads of "self-help" style prayer books with prayers for this and prayers for that, filled with seemingly magical sets of words that get the attention of God. You could fill an arena with books on prayer promises and how to make those promises yours. There may be value in some of these. However, they miss the mark and often leave the reader feeling empty and unfilled.

To understand prayer, we must realize that it is central to the heart of God and His relationship with His children, with you. That may be why there is so much confusion concerning prayer everywhere. Satan has muddied the water and drawn the focus away from our relationship with the Lord to cursory elements such as words, semantics, styles, and methods. The Devil has further used doctrinal error to cause individuals to stumble and lose their confidence in God, weakening their relationship with Him.

If the Body of Christ were to wake up tomorrow and exercise the privilege of coming before the throne of grace in prayer, tomorrow would be very different. Our God is a great God, and He is listening, waiting for you to open your heart to Him. Pray.

This excursion into prayer will be different from most other books on prayer. Understanding how prayer works will be a considerable undertaking. We can follow two paths to seek answers to our questions. The first path involves examining the writings of men and women on the subject of prayer. An enormous number of books on prayer exist, approaching prayer from nearly every conceivable angle. However, these generally present an individual's perspective concerning prayer and not what God necessarily says about prayer. The alternate path, which is the one we will take, is to seek what God says about prayer from the source—the Word of God.

The Bible is meant to be read, meditated on, memorized, studied, and lived. We will compare scripture with scripture and focus on God's Word explicitly directed to the Body of Christ.[1] My hope and prayer are to give you a broad, usable understanding of prayer, dig deep where necessary, and challenge you, the child of God:

- to pray with intention and knowledge.
- to grow in your relationship with God.
- to become engaged on the battlefield of life in prayer.
- and to find a sense of peace and power in your life that only exists for the praying child of God.

I know I have been challenged in ways I never thought possible in undertaking this work. And I have been blessed and want to share those blessings with you. This is not a theological treatise for the seminary student, although it would be valuable as such. However, it is for you to exercise God's will in your life and have prayer as an active part of your life and relationship with God. I have sought to cover the subject of prayer in a clear and helpful manner so that you can make maximum use of the truths uncovered and become engaged in seeking God's hand in the details of your daily walk.

What is Prayer?

Prayer is a profoundly personal experience between you, the believer, and God. Our God wants us to be continuously in prayer with Him, building a loving and trusting relationship with Him. In conjunction with His Word, we become increasingly like Him, changed into His image[2] as we spend time with Him[3]. This will finally be accomplished on that blessed day when our Lord and Savior, Jesus Christ, returns for His children. This is our Blessed Hope[4], the Rapture.

> "For the Lord himself shall descend from heaven with a shout, with the voice of the archangel, and with the trump of God: and the dead in Christ shall rise first: Then we which are alive and remain shall be caught up together with them in the clouds, to meet the Lord in the air: and so shall we ever be with the Lord." *1 Thessalonians 4:16-17*

We will not need to pray after the Rapture, as we will be with Him forever, and then we will speak to our Savior face-to-face. However, until that day, we are commanded to pray.

> "Be careful for nothing; but in everything by prayer and supplication with thanksgiving let your requests be made known unto God. And the peace of God, which passeth all understanding, shall keep your hearts and minds through Christ Jesus." *Philippians 4:6,7*

> "Pray without ceasing. In everything give thanks: for this is the will of God in Christ Jesus concerning you." *1 Thessalonians 5:17-18*

> "Continue in prayer, and watch in the same with thanksgiving;" *Colossians 4:2*

What we pray for considers all aspects of life as we are commanded "in everything" and, at all times, to be in prayer. We are to pray for every detail of our lives: physical, emotional, and spiritual. This includes our health, our well-being, and that of others. We are to pray for our homes, families, travel, government, growth, local church, jobs, and, yes, everything that crosses our hearts and minds. And not only can we pray for everything, but in truth, we should pray for everything. And we are to pray without ceasing, that is, be in a prayerful state of communion with our God. God is with us all the time and is for us, working things together for good. As we face challenges or experience good things throughout the day, an open heart to God will lead us to praise Him or call out to Him in need. Continuing in prayer means being in an open dialogue with our Lord. Our first expression of need or thankfulness should go to Him. Thank you, Lord; Amen, Lord; Watch over me, Lord; Help; Thanks! These simple expressions can flow from our hearts to Him. Fortunately, God does all the heavy lifting when we pray. We call out to God, and He takes care of everything else.

Prayer should be a heartfelt conversation with our God, who loves us deeply and wishes to commune with us just as he did with Adam and Eve in the garden. In Genesis 3, God calls out to Adam in the cool of the evening, seeking to commune with them. But Adam and Eve had sinned, and that sweet fellowship was broken. God made a way for communion to be reestablished by the sacrifice of a sinless animal to provide coverings for them. Even after they were driven from the garden, as found in Genesis 4, mankind had access to the Lord through offering a proper sacrifice, and the Lord met with them. He makes the way open; He wants us to come to Him.

Today, those who have trusted Christ as their Savior are reconnected with God, and that communion has been reestablished. We are accepted in the beloved and have access to His grace in which we stand. As His child, God still truly desires to commune with you. So, go to Him in prayer.

Good Communication

Good communication is necessary for a good relationship. In our human interactions, the lack of good communication often causes relationships to fall apart or causes problems to arise. Relationship building is a significant need in our associations with one another.

Communication is a critical factor in a successful relationship, whether it is between spouses, parents and their children, dating couples, coworkers, or friends. Why would it be different in our relationship with God?

Are you communicating to Him all that is on your heart and mind? Are you sharing all your needs, concerns, wants, fears, blessings, thanks, anger, joy... everything with Him? He is listening and asking you not to hold back from Him. He is ready to answer and help in your time of need. If you are holding back in your relationship, won't this hinder your relationship with Him? Are you listening to Him as well? What are you doing with His communication to you? Are you reading His Word? Are you meditating on it, memorizing it, studying it? What are you doing with God's communication to you, or is it one-sided?

When you are consistent in your prayer life to God and regularly engage with God's Word, letting it speak to you, your relationship with the Lord grows. Be sure to communicate effectively and develop a full relationship with Him. Prayer and God's Word, when combined, will promote that relationship.

Thankfulness

Thankfulness in our lives is tied closely to how engaged we are in prayer. Thanksgiving and prayer go hand in hand and are dynamically linked in the believer's relationship with our God. The three verses just examined show this truth:

> "Pray without ceasing. **In everything give thanks...**"
> *1 Thessalonians 5:16-18*

> "...but in everything by prayer and supplication **with thanksgiving** let your requests be made known..."
> *Philippians 4:6-7*

> "Continue in prayer, and watch in the same **with thanksgiving;** ..." *Colossians 4:2-3*

The prayerful Christian should be a thankful Christian, and vice versa. It is as natural as water flowing downhill. As we see God's hand in our lives and the lives of others and understand that our God works all things together for good to those who love God and are called according to His purpose[5], we can say thanks. In prayer, we can thank our God for all He has done and is doing in our lives.

So, with this introduction, let us delve into the subject in earnest and begin our journey to understanding prayer in a new and richer way. This journey will call you to pray, challenge you to pray, and engage you in your life and the lives of others in a fuller and richer way than you ever thought possible.

Chapter 1 Reference List

[1] 2 Timothy 2:15
[2] 2 Corinthians 3:17,18
[3] Ephesians 1:4
[4] Titus 2:13
[5] Romans 8:28

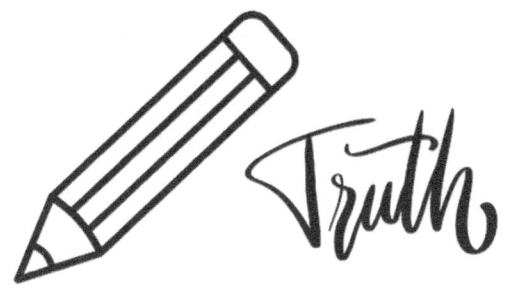

Chapter 2
Fundamental Life-Changing Truths About Prayer

Which of Your Prayers Does God Answer?

Have you ever wondered why some prayers seemingly go unanswered? Is God listening to you? Where are you, God? Questions like these have crossed the minds of every believer at some point in their life. So, as a child of God, which of your prayers does God answer? Is there a special type of prayer, a method, a particular set of words, or a unique framework needed? Perhaps you must have your eyes closed, be on your knees, or pray for a certain amount of time. And if you get the right combination, words, and length, then God responds and answers your prayer. It seems complex, and many people make it so. However, in reality, it is pretty simple: **God hears and answers every prayer of His children; yes, every prayer.**

It is true; let me explain. You see, He is a loving God who absolutely loves and desires what is best for all His children. It is His divine nature. As John states in 1 John 4:8, "He that loveth not knoweth not God; **for God is love.**" The truth is that God is love and chooses to love His children, responding to them every time they speak to Him in prayer.

To grasp this concept, consider the following counterarguments to the above statement. If God does not hear and answer every one of His children's prayers, then that means our God must be doing one of the following four things:

- God only listens to us with no response or answer.
- God listens to all our prayers, answers some, and ignores others.
- God selectively listens to some of our prayers, answers some, and ignores others.
- God outright ignores all our prayers and answers nothing.

First, does God only listen, that is, hear the words we pray, without response or answer to His children? What this means is that He hears your heart and concerns. He feels for you because He loves you, but that is the extent of it. No response whatsoever. No answer, no action. He hears us, but it does not move Him to any action. All our prayers receive no consideration or thought from God. However, if He only listens and does not respond to and answer your prayer, He is not caring or loving, which is contrary to His nature.[6] You cry out to God, and perhaps He says in His heart, I hear you, but He never lets you know or moves to action. Where is the love? Where is the giving of self and putting others first that is at the core of love, 'agape' love?

This failure to respond does not match the God of the Bible. His Word states, "He that spared not His own Son, but delivered Him up for us all, how shall He not with Him also, freely give us all things."[7] And again, in this verse: "But God commendeth His love towards us, in that while we were yet sinners, Christ died for us."[8] The truth is that God cannot simply listen without some response.

To solidify this thought, here is a further example from life. If my children talked to me and I stood there stone-faced without response or, even worse, continued to do whatever I was doing and ignored them completely, how loving would that be? My children beg me to listen to them, calling my name, but I stare off into the distance, not answering or showing that I even heard them. Would I be a loving father in such a circumstance? You see, I must answer my children in some fashion, perhaps only with a nod, a glimpse of my eye, or even better, a verbal response. Why? Because there is a loving relationship, one bathed in grace, because they are my children. The truth that "God is love" requires Him to respond to and answer our prayers. We are calling out to our Heavenly Father.

> "For ye have not received the spirit of bondage again to fear; but ye have received the Spirit of adoption, whereby we cry, Abba, Father." *Romans 8:15*

> "And because ye are sons, God hath sent forth the Spirit of His Son into your hearts, crying, Abba, Father." *Galatians 4:6*

The word here, "Abba," implies a profoundly personal relationship with our heavenly Father, like a child to his dad. God's love is expressed to each of us as His children.

Let us examine the other three counterarguments. **The second and third considerations above, which are similar in that He answers some of your prayers while ignoring others, seem more compelling. However, God's ignoring His children at any time would also contradict His nature of absolute "agape" love. Therefore, these are** not the case as described above.

And finally, the worst of the four is that God outright ignores all the prayers of His children and answers nothing. This is the brass sky concept, where God does not even hear us or respond. He is too busy for us. The God who cannot lie could never do such a thing. His inspired Word repeatedly admonishes us and encourages us to pray in everything, for everything, and without ceasing. If God ignores our prayers, what a fruitless and ridiculous waste of time it would be. He has a deaf ear to us in such a case. This is so far from the heart of our God, who is love and sent His Son to die for us to redeem us from all iniquity and deliver us from this present evil world. Therefore, by necessity and the simple fact that God is love, our God must answer all our prayers. It is a natural outcome of His divine nature of love.

Our God is love and manifests perfect love. He is our loving heavenly Father. He has a personal stake in us and deeply cares for us.

> "What? Know ye not that your body is the temple of the Holy Ghost which is in you, which ye have of God, and ye are not your own? For ye are bought with a price: therefore glorify God in your body, and in your spirit, which are God's." *1 Corinthians 6:19-20*

> "What shall we then say to these things? If God be for us, who can be against us? He that spared not his own Son, but delivered him up for us all, how shall he not with him also freely give us all things? Who shall lay any thing to the charge of God's elect? It is God that justifieth. Who is he that condemneth? It is Christ that died, yea rather, that is risen again, who is even at the right hand of God, who also maketh intercession for us. Who shall separate us from the love of Christ? shall tribulation, or distress, or persecution, or famine, or nakedness, or peril, or sword? As it is written, for thy sake we are killed all the day long; we are

accounted as sheep for the slaughter. Nay, in all these things we are more than conquerors through him that loved us. For I am persuaded, that neither death, nor life, nor angels, nor principalities, nor powers, nor things present, nor things to come, nor height, nor depth, nor any other creature, shall be able to separate us from the love of God, which is in Christ Jesus our Lord." *Romans 8:31-39*

His investment in us is the reality of God the Son, Jesus Christ, dying for our sins, demonstrating His love for us.[9] He desires that we be in conversation with Him, as He calls us to pray without ceasing, to give thanks in everything, to be careful for nothing, and to make our requests known to God through prayer and supplication.[10] He is always listening and responding to every prayer that we make.

Now, before we get carried away, note, as will be studied in the rest of this book, that **God's answer is not always "Yes"** but can be **"No"** or something else. But He does answer every prayer of His children and for His children. His answers are not always as we might think they should be, but they will be perfect. They will be for our best. Frankly, it is a blessing and best not to get a "Yes" answer to everything we pray about, for "We do not know what we should pray for as we ought."[11] Remember, our Heavenly Father knows tomorrow, and we do not. Just because we do not see or perceive an answer does not mean God has not answered our prayer. Sometimes, we do not see God's answer until much time has passed. If you are like me, dull of head and heart sometimes, we can finally see the hand of our loving God when time clears the way of the clutter of life.

We must grasp this truth and understand how big our God is and how powerful He is! **He answers every prayer of his children, every one! And His answers are perfect.** We need to get on our knees and get busy! He is waiting for you.

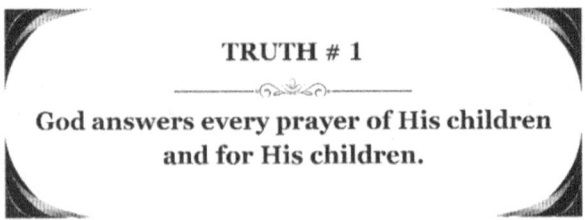

TRUTH # 1

God answers every prayer of His children and for His children.

10 Praying to a Mighty God

What about the Prayers of Those Who Are Not God's Children?

God answers every prayer of His children, as we have concluded from His Word. What about prayers that are not from His children? Ephesians 2 talks about these children. These children are called the "children of disobedience," who walk according to the course of this world. They are dead in trespasses and sins and are, by nature, the children of wrath who fulfill the desires of the flesh and mind. These are not lovely children, and they are not God's children. They have another father, the Devil. The Apostle Paul says that is who we used to be, but we had a miraculous change.

We became children of God by faith in Christ Jesus, saved by grace through faith. We were made new, alive in Christ, delivered from the power of darkness, and translated into the Kingdom of His dear Son.[12] Ephesians 2:10 tells us that we are the workmanship of God, created in Christ Jesus unto good works, and we should walk in them. We are now children of God, an expression of His love. We are saved to do good works, but not saved by good works; instead, we are saved by grace through faith.

So, what about those who are not His children? First, by His sovereign choice and nature, God is only committed to answering prayer for one group of people, His children. He has a relationship with His children. Note the following:

> "Then came the Jews round about him, and said unto him, How long dost thou make us to doubt? If thou be the Christ, tell us plainly. Jesus answered them, I told you, and ye believed not: the works that I do in my Father's name, they bear witness of me. But ye believe not, because ye are not of my sheep, as I said unto you. **My sheep hear my voice, and I know them, and they follow me:** And I give unto them eternal life; and they shall never perish, neither shall any man pluck them out of my hand. My Father, which gave them me, is greater than all; and no man is able to pluck them out of my Father's hand." *John 10:24-29*

> "The sacrifice of the wicked is an abomination to the LORD: but the **prayer of the upright is his delight.**" *Proverbs 15:8*

> "The LORD is far from the wicked: but **he heareth the prayer of the righteous.**" *Proverbs 15:29*

"For the eyes of the Lord are over **the righteous, and his ears are open unto their prayers:** but the face of the Lord is against them that do evil." *1 Peter 3:12*

God's children have an inside track into the presence of Almighty God; the unsaved (the lost, the children of wrath) do not. The Lord can answer their prayer if He chooses, but He is not obligated to respond. However, He always chooses to answer His children. The moment you trusted Christ as your Savior, His Holy Spirit indwelt you, and you were positionally placed into Christ. It is your standing, your position. You are found in Christ, you are standing in His grace, and you now have access by faith into this grace in which you stand. Part of that access is that you are free to boldly enter the throne of grace with your praise, thanksgiving, supplications, intercessions, and requests at any time.[13] The Lord knows you by name, and you are His![14]

> **NOTE:**
>
> **Not sure if you are a child of God, see the chapter entitled "Am I a Child of God?" It is the most important question of your life.**

Those who are not in Christ are not saved. They have not trusted the Lord Jesus Christ as their Savior, and they are not part of God's family or one of His children. Jesus Christ is the way to God the Father; He is the only way.

> "Jesus saith unto him, **I am the way**, the truth, and the life: no man cometh unto the Father, but by me." *John 14:6*

> "For ye are all the children of God by faith in Christ Jesus." Galatians *3:26*

Those without Christ have no access to God and no Holy Spirit intervening on their behalf. There is no free access to the throne room of God. Ephesians 2:1-3 expounds this truth:

> "And you hath he quickened, **who were dead in trespasses and sins; Wherein in time past ye walked according to the course of this world, according to the prince of the power of the air,** the spirit that now worketh in the children of

disobedience: Among whom also **we all had our conversation in times past in the lusts of our flesh, fulfilling the desires of the flesh and of the mind; and were by nature the children of wrath**, even as others." *Ephesians 2:1-3*

Before coming to Christ, we were also dead in trespasses and sins. Dead to the things of God. We had no relationship with the Lord, driven by the world and the Devil (the prince of the power of the air). We found ourselves driven by the lust of our flesh and had condemnation as our future. We were separate from God and all that He is. But then we believed what Christ did for us on the cross, and we were made alive; he quickened us with Christ. We became children of God and were blessed beyond our comprehension in this life and the next. We now have access to God anytime, but those not in Christ have no access.

Consider the following example: if the neighbor's child comes to your door and asks you for $100, you might not answer the door at all, and if you do, you might say, "Who are you? What relationship do I have with you?" However, if your child asks you for $100, the response is much different. There is a real relationship. You still might say no, but there is a loving obligation to listen and answer in some fashion. Our God always listens to you and me, and He always answers. And we can come to our God anytime with any care or thanksgiving of our hearts.

Now, the truth that God is love does reach those who are lost. The cross shouts to the highest hills, "...Christ Jesus came into the world to save sinners..."[15] God loves the whole world. John 3:16 states, "For God so loved the world, that He gave His only begotten Son, that whosoever believeth in Him should not perish, but have everlasting life." And Romans 5:8 declares, "But commendeth His love towards us, in that, while we were yet sinners, Christ died for us." Our God does love the lost with a love that transcends their sin and their wicked ways.

Consider the example I just shared about the neighbor's child who comes to your door and asks for money. As you look and listen to that child, your heart might go out to that child, even though she is not yours. You see her need and heart, so you respond with a gift, not being bound to do so but out of love. Our God can do the same. He sees their real heart and needs and can respond to their prayer if He wills. He knows everything, so he always hears prayers, even of the lost, but He is under no obligation or commitment to answer those prayers. But He can, and if He wills, He does. Not by way of a relationship and free access, but because He is God and is love. Our God can easily see the blackness of their heart and nature and choose to ignore their prayer as well because there is no relationship. They are of their father, the Devil.[16]

Thus, let us be prayer warriors for those about us. Pray for the lost, for the unsaved. Pray for all those in authority. Make your prayer requests known to God. As a child of God, you have the inside track to His throne of Grace. You have a blessed and loving relationship with the ruler of the Universe. (It is all in who you know.) God is waiting for you to pray. Help somebody today. Pray for them!

TRUTH # 2

Not everyone's prayer is always answered by God, just those that are uttered by His children.

The Exception that's Not an Exception.

On the surface, there appears to be one exception, yes, one instance in which God always answers an unsaved person's prayer. That is when they call out in belief and faith to God for salvation. When a person comes to understand and believe, to see the light that Satan has blinded them from seeing, that Jesus Christ is God and that He died for their sin and rose again for their justification, and then they call out to God in belief, God hears and answers "Yes!". Remember, salvation is not a result of someone working to please God. Ephesians 2:8-9 states that salvation is a gift of God that one receives by grace through faith in what Christ did on the cross for them. We cannot earn it, and we do not deserve it. However, because of God's great grace and that Jesus Christ died for our sins and His blood freely justifies us by the redemption in Christ Jesus, God's Word declares, "Whosoever shall call upon the name of Lord shall be saved."[17] Our Heavenly Father hears and always says yes to this prayer!

An example of "faith" is recorded in the book of Romans concerning faithful Abraham when he was about 100 years old. God told him that he would have a son with his wife, Sarah, who was well past childbearing age.

> "He **staggered not at the promise of God through unbelief;** but was **strong in faith**, giving glory to God; **And being fully persuaded that, what he had promised, he was able also to**

perform. And therefore it was imputed to him for righteousness. Now it was not written for his sake alone, that it was imputed to him; But for us also, to whom it shall be imputed, **if we believe on him that raised up Jesus our Lord from the dead; Who was delivered for our offences, and was raised again for our justification."** *Romans 4:20-25*

Impute means to place on an account. Abraham received righteousness when he was fully persuaded and believed (trusted) that God was able to do what He said, regardless of what his eyes and body told him. It was by faith. Today, Almighty God tells us that Jesus Christ died for our sins, was buried, and rose again on the third day for our justification. If you are fully persuaded that God did what He said He did for you, then God imputes righteousness to your account; you are saved and become a child of God. "For ye are all children of God by faith in Christ Jesus."[18]

Therefore, pray for those in your life who need Jesus Christ as their Savior. Pray that they will hear the gospel and understand God's good news for them. Pray for open doors to share the ways God has worked in your life. Share the gospel with someone today.

What if you find yourself not sure about your eternal destiny? You are not sure if you are a child of God. You can take care of that right now if you believe that Jesus Christ is Lord of all and that He died for you, yes, you, to pay the wages of sin for you.[19] His blood that He shed on the cross paid for that sin. He is risen and alive and offering the gift of salvation to you if you believe. Call on His name. What are you waiting for? Call on the name of the Lord in belief and receive the gift of salvation. He is listening. He will hear you. He will save you.

However, as stated at the opening of this section, this exception is not an exception. The truth is that salvation, the gift of eternal life, is a matter of faith.

> "For by grace are you saved by faith and that not of yourselves, it is the gift of God, not of works, lest any man should boast." *Ephesians 2:8-9*

> "...(righteousness) it shall be imputed, if we believe on him that raised up Jesus our Lord from the dead; Who was delivered for our offences, and was raised again for our justification." *Romans 4:24-25*

> "In whom ye also trusted, after that ye heard the Word of truth, the gospel of your salvation: in whom also after that ye believed, ye were sealed with that holy Spirit of promise," *Ephesians 1:13*

Thus, the moment a person, by faith, understands that Jesus Christ is Lord and God Himself, and that He died for their sins personally, was buried, and rose again, and trusts in Christ for their eternal destiny, they are saved. It is by grace, through faith, not by any work. God, the Holy Spirit, indwells them and seals them. They have believed in the truth of Christ's redemptive work for them. By trusting Him, they have called on the name of the Lord in faith and are saved.

So why encourage a person to pray and call on the name of the Lord? Well, salvation is a gift of God, so saying thanks would be proper and a good thing to do. Additionally, praying to God to thank Him for what He has done creates a set point in the new believer's life, marking the first time they prayed to God in belief. This can help the person later in life when their faith is challenged. Thus, when a person prays to God for salvation, it is in response to the faith that they just exercised by believing the truth and are just saying thanks to God. They are formally acknowledging to God what they already believe and affirming their faith to God, but they were saved and indwelt by the Holy Spirit of God the moment they believed. So, they are praying as a child of God, and God answers every prayer for His children. So, in summary, it is not an exception because, by the time an individual prays to God, they are already saved.

Confession with thy mouth?

Some might argue with me concerning Romans 10:9-10, which talks about confession with thy mouth and, later in verse 13, calling on the name of the Lord. Let us look at the passage in its slightly broader context, Romans 10:8-13.

First, Romans 10:8, which describes the overarching context for the text that follows, clearly states that this is the "Word of Faith which we preach." Therefore, this is faith, not some work or action that must be performed.

> "But what saith it? The word is nigh thee, even in thy mouth, and in thy heart: that is, **the word of faith, which we preach**;" *Romans 10:8*

Okay, what is this "Word of Faith" that we preach? Answer: Romans 10:9.

> "That **if thou shalt confess with thy mouth the Lord Jesus**, and shalt believe in thine heart that God hath raised him from the dead, thou shalt be saved." *Romans 10:9*

Is this saying that you need to tell others that you accepted Christ, or you are not saved? No matter how small that might be, the requirement to tell others would be a work and not just faith. The apostle Paul says it is just "**grace**" or "**works**." It cannot be both. Salvation by faith alone is trusting in God's grace.

The mistaken conclusion of Romans 10:9 is that this is a confession to man, or perhaps confessing one's sins. However, this confession is not made to people but to God. There is a tendency to elevate the importance of man, making man have some part in his salvation. But any elevation of man in the work of salvation would demean Christ's work, which was complete and fully satisfied almighty God.

> "For all have sinned, and come short of the glory of God; Being justified freely by his grace through the redemption that is in Christ Jesus: Whom God hath set forth to be a **propitiation**[20] through faith in his blood, to declare his righteousness for the remission of sins that are past, through the forbearance of God; To declare, I say, at this time his righteousness: that he might be just, and the justifier of him which believeth in Jesus." *Romans 3:23-26*

Salvation is a personal experience with God, where the individual is confronted with the reality of their sin and their total lack of ability to fix the problem. The individual sees Christ as the only remedy, believing He is God and has paid for their sin. His confession is directed to the Lord with the acknowledgment that He is the Lord and has authority over all. When one sees their need and that the work of Christ is the answer, their very thoughts are that confession to the Lord Jesus. It is not confessing one's specific sins either, but acknowledging that they are a sinner with no escape except through Jesus Christ.

What about "confess with thy mouth"? Doesn't that mean you must say it out loud with your lips? To understand this, we must recall the absolute truths at play here. Salvation is by grace through faith; it has never been by works, or individuals could boast in the presence of God, declaring themselves righteous apart from God's work. Doing anything, even lifting a finger or whistling, or the requirement that you audibly say something, would be a work, even something as simple as confessing with your mouth.

So, how do we understand what this means? Examining the entire verse and its context raises another question that will shed some light.

> "That **if thou shalt confess with thy mouth** the Lord Jesus, **and shalt believe in thine heart** that God hath raised him from the dead, thou shalt be saved." *Romans 10:9*

Do you believe in your heart? That is what the second part of this verse says. Let me say it this way: Can your heart believe in something? The answer is that it cannot. The truth is that you believe in your mind. Your heart is a vital muscle, for sure, but it cannot believe or think. "Believe in your heart" is an idiom, a set of words, or a phrase that has a meaning beyond the literal meaning of those words. "Believe in your heart" means that what you believe deeply affects your emotions and thoughts. The "with thy mouth" here is used in the same fashion. When you think to yourself, words are formed in your mind. You can have an entire conversation without vocalizing one word. When someone reads a book, we sometimes criticize those who move their lips while reading and advise them to read it to themselves. We understand that we can speak within our minds. That is the meaning of the context here, not using the literal mouth (although one can audibly talk with God, but does not have to). Hence, in our minds, we are convicted and acknowledge that Jesus Christ is Lord and God has raised Him from the dead, and God knows. He hears our very thoughts. God equates our faith in Him and His work on the cross with righteousness, which He gives us along with eternal life in Christ when we believe. The Holy Spirit indwells us, and we are sealed until Christ returns for us. All of this can happen without uttering an audible word.

Romans 10:10 sums it up. "For with the heart man believeth unto righteousness; and with the mouth confession is made unto salvation." In both cases, the heart and mouth refer to the mind and our thinking. The passage below in Romans is a beautiful account of Abraham's faith and God's gift of salvation through which we can better understand "With the heart man believeth unto righteousness."

> "And **being not weak in faith**, he considered not his own body now dead, when he was about an hundred years old, neither yet the deadness of Sara's womb: **He staggered not at the promise of God through unbelief; but was strong in faith**, giving glory to God; And **being fully persuaded that,**

what he had promised, he was able also to perform.** And therefore it was imputed to him for righteousness." *Romans 4:19-22*

Abraham believed in God with a deep and fully trusting faith. Abraham knew that the one true God could do anything He said He would, and God gave him righteousness. Abraham believed in his heart and was saved.

And finally, we read Romans 10:13: "**For whosoever shall call upon the name of the Lord shall be saved.**" This is just a summary of the verses before it and what we have already discussed. It gives us the imagery of one who is drowning, going down for the last time, calling for help to the only one who can rescue the perishing. He will answer the call, and He will save you. The amazing truth here is that anyone, anywhere, any place is a "whosoever." Salvation is available to all. Call on the name of the Lord. Believe that Jesus Christ is God Himself. Believe that He is the Lord Jesus Christ, and He loved you so much that He went to the cross of shame and died for your sins. His blood paid for the sins of you and all mankind. He was buried and rose again on the third day to live eternally. And now He invites you, by His grace, to receive the free gift of salvation and eternal life by simple faith. Will you accept what Christ has done for you? Will you realize that you have a desperate need and call on the name of the Lord?

For it is Sanctified by the Word of God and Prayer

The following truth is significant as well as profound. You do not want to miss this! Consider what God's Word says in 1 Timothy.

> "For every creature of God is good, and nothing to be refused, if it be received with thanksgiving: **For it is sanctified by the Word of God and prayer.**" *1 Timothy 4:4-5*

Here, we find an absolute and powerful truth: everything is sanctified to God by the Word of God and Prayer. What does this mean? First, let us see how sanctified is used in the following three verses to get a breadth of understanding of the meaning of sanctified.

> "And God blessed the seventh day, **and sanctified it:** because that in it he had rested from all his work which God created and made." *Genesis 2:3*

"Sanctified" in this verse speaks of making the day a special, holy day to God.

> "Now mine eyes shall be open, and mine ears attent unto the prayer that is made in this place. For now have I chosen and **sanctified this house**, that my name may be there forever: and mine eyes and mine heart shall be there perpetually." *2 Chronicles 7:15-16*

"Sanctified" in these verses speaks of something special with the characteristic of personal ownership and attention. There is additionally the idea of separation from the world to God. It is His place now.

> "Unto the church of God which is at Corinth, to them that are **sanctified in Christ Jesus**, called to be saints, with all that in every place call upon the name of Jesus Christ our Lord, both theirs and ours:" *1 Corinthians 1:2*

This final verse speaks of believers being sanctified in Christ Jesus. "Sanctified" in this sense involves the earlier ideas of separation from the world, God's personal possession and ownership, with the uniqueness of being holy and special to God. God's eyes and heart are with the believer in Christ, and He has chosen to dwell in us.[21] This is our position in Christ as a child of God. The "called to be saints"[22] command involves the believer's walk. A call to behave like the child of God that you are positionally, because God has redeemed you and made you a new creature in Jesus Christ, with a new life and the indwelling Holy Spirit.[23] You are now the temple of the living God!

The previous three verses have the following usages of the word sanctified:

- Holy
- Special
- Separated for God's use
- His Personal Possession.

Thus, something or someone that is sanctified becomes holy, separate from the world, and God considers it His special and personal possession. There is so much truth here to understand, but we will focus our discussion on prayer.

Therefore, 1 Timothy 4:5 - **"For it is sanctified by the Word of God and prayer"** teaches that the Word of God and Prayer set apart what we pray for to God, and He takes ownership of them. Our prayer requests become His personal possession. He becomes engaged in taking care of what we have given Him, and it has become His. God has chosen, in His sovereignty, to do this as part of His loving relationship with His children. Since God has taken ownership and is at work on what we have prayed for, we can be thankful and rest in His grace. God's peace can take over in our lives as we acknowledge that our God is a great God who loves us and works all things together for good. No wonder God can produce in our lives a peace that passes understanding.[24]

Furthermore, the Word of God is closely tied to prayer in this sanctification process, as it dictates God's response. His actions will be in accordance with His perfect will and His Word. Additionally, the Holy Spirit is aware of the Father's will and intercedes with our prayers in alignment with God's will and the Word of God. We examine these truths in detail later in our text.

Consider this example to firmly establish the point in our minds. Under the Law, the nation of Israel was called by God a holy nation, a peculiar people, a sanctified people unto God, a nation set apart to God. They were God's people, His personal possession. Today, in the Body of Christ, it is also true for each of us. We are sanctified to God, and we are God's personal possession. Notice these verses:

> "What? know ye not that your body is the temple of the Holy Ghost which is in you, which ye have of God, and ye are not your own? For **ye are bought with a price:** therefore glorify God in your body, and in your spirit, which are God's." *1 Corinthians 6:19-20*

> "And such were some of you: but ye are washed, **but ye are sanctified,** but ye are justified in the name of the Lord Jesus, and by the Spirit of our God." *1 Corinthians 6:11*

> "Unto the church of God which is at Corinth, **to them that are sanctified in Christ Jesus,** called to be saints, with all that in every place call upon the name of Jesus Christ our Lord, both theirs and ours:" *1 Corinthians 1:2*

Since each of us in Christ is His child, we are His personal possessions bought with the precious blood of the Lord Jesus Christ. He takes ownership of our prayer requests, intercessions, and supplications, which become sanctified to God. He is a loving heavenly Father. When we pray, we give God our requests, cares, concerns, and supplications. We can leave them with Him and let go because we can trust that He will be at work on everyone, for He is faithful. God cannot lie. In praying, we are seeking God's hand in transforming our tomorrow. And when we pray, it is fitting and glorifying to God to be always thankful.

> "Rejoice evermore. Pray without ceasing. In everything give thanks: for this is the will of God in Christ Jesus concerning you." *1 Thessalonians 5:16-18*

When we give our requests unto Him, He takes them and is at work at once. How amazing is our God!

This truth should drive us to our knees, calling on our Father God with prayers, supplications, and requests with thanksgiving! When we pray, God takes our prayer requests, and they become His. We give them; He takes them. Can't you feel the burdens lifting as you give them all to Him? And He wants us to free ourselves and give them all to Him. He will work all things together for good. He will give us the peace of God that passes understanding. He will do exceedingly abundantly above all that we ask or think.[25] He is God, and there is nothing too hard for Him. Share your heart. He is waiting.

TRUTH # 3

God makes what we pray for His own personal possession. He takes ownership of the things we pray for, they become His.

We Ought to Pray by Faith

God's Word proclaims in Romans,

> "Therefore being justified by faith, we have peace with God through our Lord Jesus Christ: By whom also **we have access by faith into this grace** wherein we stand, and rejoice in hope of the glory of God." *Romans 5:1-2*

To access the grace we (every believer) stand in, we must do it by faith. We are surrounded by the grace of God, which is His unmerited favor. His desire to shower us with grace (favor) is ever-present and real. But we need to seek that grace, that favor by faith.

Earlier, we saw that faith is being fully persuaded that what God says, He is able to do. He is God, the creator of all things and all flesh. We see in Romans 10:17 that faith comes by hearing, and hearing by the Word of God. As we pray, we should pray by faith, knowing whom we are praying to —the Creator God of all things. He is our heavenly Father, who loves us and sent His Son to Earth to die for our sins.

> "**But God commendeth his love toward us,** in that, while we were yet sinners, Christ died for us." *Romans 5:8*

> "What shall we then say to these things? **If God be for us, who can be against us?** He that spared not his own Son, but delivered him up for us all, **how shall he not with him also freely give us all things?**" *Romans 8:31-32*

We should boldly enter the throne of grace and trust our heavenly Father to do what He says, which will always be good. Hebrews 11:6 states, "**But without faith it is impossible to please Him: for he that cometh to God must believe that He is, and that He is a rewarder of them that diligently seek Him.**" When we pray, we are (by definition) coming to God and seeking Him as the one true God who can do all things. This does not mean our Heavenly Father will give us everything that we pray for. We are not God, nor can we see tomorrow. But He will answer every prayer perfectly and with what is best. Sometimes, that answer is "No," and sometimes, that answer is something completely different than what we thought was best. Sometimes, we cannot see the answer until we are on the other side of the problem or even years later. And sometimes, we do not understand the answer and will not until we get to glory, when it will all make sense. When we get to heaven, we will have a lot of "ah-ha" moments as the difficulties and hardships of this life suddenly become clear in reason and purpose. Ah ha, I understand now.

On praying with faith, some think that God the Father will ignore our prayer if we are wavering in faith, have doubt, or do not have enough faith. I have heard numerous (not-so-edifying) individuals say over the years something like, "Well, your prayers didn't get answered because you didn't have enough faith." The accusing person often referred to a lack of healing or physical problems that a believer was experiencing. Nothing is worse than tearing down someone who is already hurting and spiritually frustrated. You do not need friends like that in your life. Job had three of them. We will discuss these concerns and questions in the upcoming chapters.

At this point, however, please note two facts. First, the Holy Spirit is active in our prayer life, interceding on our behalf and "fixing" our prayers to align with the will of God the Father.[26] And second, when we pray, it pleases God and glorifies our God when we engage our prayer life in faith. Trusting Him and knowing that He can do what we ask in prayer and will do what is best for us glorifies our God. So, let us seek God, trust God, and pray to God in faith. We are told in Ephesians 3:20 something incredibly amazing:

> **"Now unto him that is able to do exceeding abundantly above all that we ask or think**, according to the power that worketh in us." *Ephesians 3:20*

Our God is able to do far more than you can possibly ask or think. Let that sink in. This is the God to whom we pray. Nothing is too hard for Him, and He wants to do exceedingly abundantly above what we ask or think. Thanksgiving should flow from us like water over a waterfall with this realization.

> "Ah Lord GOD! behold, thou hast made the heaven and the earth by thy great power and stretched out arm, and **there is nothing too hard for thee:**" *Jeremiah 32:17*

> "Behold, I am the LORD, the God of all flesh: **is there anything too hard for me?**" *Jeremiah 32:27*

These verses from God's Word should challenge us to get busy praying. There is no time like the present.

> **"I will therefore that men pray everywhere,** lifting up holy hands, without wrath and doubting." *1 Timothy 2:8*

> **"Be careful for nothing**; but in everything by prayer and supplication with thanksgiving let your requests be made known unto God. **And the peace of God, which passeth all understanding, shall keep your hearts and minds through Christ Jesus."** *Philippians 4:6-7*

> "Rejoicing in hope; patient in tribulation; **continuing instant in prayer;**" *Romans 12:12*

> **"Continue in prayer and watch in the same with thanksgiving;"** *Colossians 4:2*

> **"Pray without ceasing."** *1 Thessalonians 5:17*

"Likewise **the Spirit also helpeth our infirmities: for we know not what we should pray for as we ought**: but the Spirit itself maketh intercession for us with groanings which cannot be uttered." *Romans 8:26*

> **TRUTH # 4**
>
> **Pray in faith. You are praying to the God of the Universe who loves you completely!**

So, pray! What are you waiting for? Make a list of people, needs, and concerns that need God's hand on them… that is truly everything in life. Do it right now. Pray about it. Nothing on your list is too hard for our God.

> **TRUTH # 5**
>
> **Our God is able to do exceeding abundantly above all that we ask or think.**

Just a Little Talk…What is Prayer?

Prayer is talking to God; it is part of a relationship, a conversation. It is an integral and vital component of worshipping God. Prayer can take many forms and aspects as we converse and commune with God our Father. In praying, there are the very heartfelt worship aspects of thanksgiving and praise, as well as the requests, supplications, and intercessions. Our prayer requests, supplications, and intercessions are given with thanksgiving and praise. Below are a few verses to highlight this:

> "Be careful for nothing; but in everything by **prayer** and **supplication with thanksgiving** let your **requests** be made known unto God. And the peace of God, which passeth all understanding, shall keep your hearts and minds through Christ Jesus." *Philippians 4:6-7*

> "**Pray** without ceasing. In everything **give thanks**: for this is the will of God in Christ Jesus concerning you." *1 Thessalonians 5:17-18*

> "**Praying** always with all **prayer** and **supplication** in the Spirit, and **watching** thereunto with all perseverance and **supplication** for all saints;" *Ephesians 6:18*

> "I exhort therefore, that, first of all, **supplications, prayers, intercessions, and giving of thanks**, be made for all men; For kings, and for all that are in authority; that we may lead a quiet and peaceable life in all godliness and honesty." *1 Timothy 2:1- 2*

Let's review the various forms of prayer found in God's Word, along with an explanation of each.

Prayer:

This is the general talking that we do that is addressed to God in recognition of who He is, as God our Father, the creator of all things. It is a worshipful discourse, thankfully acknowledging Him and His authority over all things. Scripture has many examples of this type of prayer as individuals lifted their hearts to God in praise, worship, and thanksgiving. For example, consider Psalm 8 from the heart of David:

> "O LORD our Lord, how excellent is thy name in all the earth! who hast set thy glory above the heavens. Out of the mouth of babes and sucklings hast thou ordained strength because of thine enemies, that thou mightest still the enemy and the avenger. When I consider thy heavens, the work of thy fingers, the moon and the stars, which thou hast ordained; What is man, that thou art mindful of him? and the son of man, that thou visitest him? For thou hast made him a little lower than the angels, and hast crowned him with glory and honour. Thou madest him to have dominion over the works of thy hands; thou hast put all things under his feet: All sheep and oxen, yea, and the beasts of the field; The fowl of the air, and the fish of the sea, and whatsoever passeth through the paths of the seas. O LORD our Lord, how excellent is thy name in all the earth!" *Psalm 8:1-9*

When we praise Him in our prayers, we are truly thankful for His goodness and grace; we give Him the glory due His name; we express our faith that He can do all things and that He made us and loves us…this is prayer—a worshipful acknowledgment of who God is. The command to pray without ceasing shows that we should maintain a continuous, worshipful discourse with God, acknowledging Him throughout each day. We need to open our eyes to the activity of God in our lives and the lives of those around us. Part of our regular experience should be that we look for (and see) God's hand at work about us and in us. It should be commonplace to see God working in our lives. We must tune our vision to see His hand of grace and love.

Here are some places where we can start looking to see God at work in our lives and begin to grow in our worshipful prayer to our God ("praying without ceasing"):

1. **God never ceases to work and produce good in the believer's life, in your life.**

    "And we know that all things work together for good to them that love God, to them who are the called according to his purpose." *Romans 8:28*

    "Being confident of this very thing, that he which hath begun a good work in you will perform it until the day of Jesus Christ." *Philippians 1:6*

    "For it is God which worketh in you both to will and to do of his good pleasure." *Philippians 2:13*

God works all things together for good, even the hard things, even the things that happen in our lives that make no sense. How can that be? He is God. What more needs to be said? He began a good work in your life when He saved you. He is not going to let that work go to waste. He will continue to work on you until you enter His presence. God is good, and He makes good happen in our lives and the lives of His children.

> **Look for the Good.**

2. **God never ceases to work in the life of His Child.** He watches over us, filtering through the difficulties of life, enabling us to work through the hard things with victory. His grace is sufficient, and He strengthens us in life's challenges. Our God is a great God, deserving of praise.

    "And he said unto me, My grace is sufficient for thee: for my strength is made perfect in weakness. Most gladly therefore will

> I rather glory in my infirmities, that the power of Christ may rest upon me. Therefore I take pleasure in infirmities, in reproaches, in necessities, in persecutions, in distresses for Christ's sake: for when I am weak, then am I strong."
> *2 Corinthians 12:9-10*

> "There hath no temptation taken you but such as is common to man: but God is faithful, who will not suffer you to be tempted above that ye are able; but will with the temptation also make a way to escape, that ye may be able to bear it."
> *1 Corinthians 10:13*

Temptation here refers to a trial, a tribulation, or a difficulty that lasts for a season, whether short or long. The word "suffer" here means "to allow"; thus, God does not allow you to be tempted – tested – tried above what you can handle. He does not eliminate or remove the testing, but makes a way to escape through it. With Christ in your life, you can bear and endure it. The heat of any tribulation will not harm you because He is with you. The part that would destroy you, God does not allow.

In the context of this verse in God's Word,[27] God lists time after time when Israel in the wilderness faced a trial or temptation, and instead of trusting God by faith, they complained, murmured, blasphemed, and more. However, all they needed to do was trust. God was right there with them, but they did not see Him. They did not worship and praise Him. Instead, they forgot that He was there and that He was God, the Creator of all things, who had delivered them from Egypt just a few days before. In life's trials, remember that God is with you. Pray to Him and trust Him. Recall Daniel's friends in the fiery furnace.[28] God did not rescue them from the fire but stood with them in the flame, carrying them through. In life's difficulties, your God will stand with you and help you bear them. You see, His grace is sufficient for you, and you can also do all things through Christ, who strengthens you!

> "Not that I speak in respect of want: for I have learned, in whatsoever state I am, therewith to be content. I know both how to be abased, and I know how to abound: everywhere and in all things I am instructed both to be full and to be hungry, both to abound and to suffer need. I can do all things through Christ which strengtheneth me." *Philippians 4:11-13*

> Look for Him. Look for that grace.
> Look for that strength and thank Him.

3. **Our God is for us and supplies all our need in Christ Jesus.**
   Everything that the Lord does in your life is for you. He knows what we especially need and provides that as well. Sometimes we confuse "want" with "need," don't we?

   > "What shall we then say to these things? If God be for us, who can be against us? He that spared not his own Son, but delivered him up for us all, how shall he not with him also freely give us all things?" *Romans 8:31-32*

   > "For all things are for your sakes, that the abundant grace might through the thanksgiving of many redound to the glory of God." *2 Corinthians 4:15*

   > "But my God shall supply all your need according to his riches in glory by Christ Jesus." *Philippians 4:19*

Many children of God live as if God is far off, even though they theologically know that God is with them. They hear the truth of God being with them, in fact, indwelling them, and even that they are the temple of God,[29] but their lives are relatively empty of joy and peace. This is an unnecessary situation for any child of God. Oddly, we are saved by grace through faith,[30] we are declared to be children of God by faith in Christ Jesus[31,] and God's children are even called believers; yet what we lack in our daily lives is faith in God. Romans 10:17 tells us that our faith grows as we dig into the Word of God. God's Word effectually works in everyone who believes,[32] transforming us by renewing our minds to live godly lives.[33]

Our God becomes more real to us as our faith grows. Mix that faith with prayer, and our relationship with God grows. It becomes a two-way conversation, a real relationship. God uses His Word to speak to us and us to pray to Him. When God becomes more real to us and we understand that God is for us and that we stand in His grace, it is a game-changer in our lives. Not only is He working on the big things in our lives, but also the little things. God is love, and so He is a giver. Our God wants us to pray and bring all our requests to Him because He is for us and wants to give and give. He wants us to be engaged in our tomorrow today.

> **Look for God's bounty. Look for His comfort and care. Look for His joy and peace in your life and praise Him for it.**

Prayer, the expression of thanksgiving and worship to our God, should readily flow from our hearts, minds, and lips as we truly perceive how much our God loves us and is engaged in the details of our daily lives. When I think of this continuous discourse of prayerful praise and worship, my Uncle Ernie Csato comes to mind. He and his wife, Lillian (my mom's sister), loved the Lord - literally out loud. They were in full-time ministry, engaged in pastoring and rescue mission work for most of their lives. They were living examples of individuals who saw God's hand at work all around them - "Thank you, Lord" and "Praise the Lord" passed Ernie's lips nearly as often as you or I breathe. Whether I was helping him with some tasks at the Mission or we were fishing at the lake, his heart was always thankful, and he was expressive of that thankfulness all the time. One evening, in preparation for a day of fishing, I remember "pulling" nightcrawlers with him (using a flashlight and our hands), and his excitement about the bounty of worms we gathered was continuously directed to God. "Amen," "Thank you, Lord," "Praise the Lord" still rings in my mind. They never had much money, but they were full of joy and rich beyond measure.

We, too, ought to open our eyes to see our God involved in the infinite details of life, and to see His hand (as readily as my uncle and aunt did) and be prayerfully thankful. Doing so would take our eyes off the worrisome details of life and place them on the God who has those details in His hands. Praise the Lord!

Supplication:

Supplications involve addressing God (asking/entreating) for our needs and wants. Supplications are the "pray for" things of prayer. Supplications, by necessity, come from a humble recognition that we are needy people and that our God and His grace are sufficient for our needs. As Philippians 4:6 says, "Be careful for nothing," which many will say means not to be anxious or worried. But actually, God is saying not to restrict yourself in prayer. Do not hold back what you would like to pray for – don't "choke off" prayer. Let your wants and needs be known. God, our Father, wants us to pour out our hearts, our cares, our fears, our needs, and our wants and give them to Him. And as we have already learned, they become His personal possession. He is at work on them from the very moment you utter them…our God is a mighty God!

Additionally, "Be careful for nothing" is in the imperative mood, which means it is a command, and yes, a command from God. God is commanding us to pray for everything in our lives without limitation. In theological circles, there is some variance in what some say you can pray for, but scripture is clear that we are to pray for everything in our lives. God's Word trumps man's word every time. Scripture does not tell us to first determine what should be considered worthy of prayer, weeding out the lesser things. Instead, the Scriptures tell us to let our hearts overflow to Him in prayer without reservation. God does not require us to become some spiritually led giant in the faith before entering the throne of grace in prayer. But we are to boldly enter the throne of grace because we are worthy through the blood of Christ. We have access by faith into His grace in which we stand! We can pray for all aspects of life, whether spiritual matters, emotional issues, or physical things.

Requests:

Requests are precisely that, addressing to God our petitions, asking for specific things. God encourages us and commands us to present our particular requests to Him, to let our requests be known. These are the specific requests of life, the "pray that" aspect of prayer. There is nothing too small or too large for our God. If it is on your heart, then share it with Him. I would be remiss not to remind you that God is not a "genie in a bottle" looking to give you everything that you ever dreamed of, but He is a God who will supply everything you genuinely need. Later in this study, I will share details from the Word of God on how God answers our prayers, and He does answer each one. But what you want and what you need may well be opposite entities. God knows what you can handle, what would be good for you, and what would not be good for you. And in love, He answers every one of our prayers. His perspective is on what is eternally beneficial to you and thus answers our prayers with what is best for us in that light. This is why it is sometimes hard to see God's answer to our prayers, as we are finite beings and only grasp so much. Our God is infinite, and His answers are complete, perfect, and good. They transcend time and space, working in the here and now but reaching into eternity for our eternal benefit. Our God is omniscient and omnipotent. Amen.

Intercessions:

Intercessions are giving to God supplications and requests for others. A child of God who is walking with the Lord should have a full prayer life. A prayer life that not only examines their personal needs but also focuses on the needs of others: family, church family, friends, neighbors, all in authority, and all men. Spiritual people should pray for others because Christ also died for them. Without question, we all make intercessions for our families and friends. We love them, so we pray for their physical, emotional, and spiritual needs. Note Job 1:5 and Job's concern for his ten children.

> "And it was so, when the days of their feasting were gone about, that Job sent and sanctified them, and rose up early in the morning, and offered burnt offerings according to the number of them all: for Job said, It may be that my sons have sinned, and cursed God in their hearts. Thus did Job continually." *Job 1:5*

Job interceded on behalf of his children continually, as we are all called to do. We are to watch with all "perseverance and supplication for all saints."[34] Our prayer for others sanctifies them to God, that is, sets them apart unto God; they become His personal possession along with your requests and supplications for them, and He will work on them for what they need.

In our families and friends, we know of certain temptations that an individual is undergoing or sins that have ensnared them. In their walk, prayer is most likely not a regular part of their daily diet if they are caught up in such things. Many will only cry out to God when things get so bad that they are on the ground in grief or great remorse. They have suffered much because of bad choices—no joy, no peace, no love, no fruit of the Spirit active in their life. And in many instances, physical and emotional hurt has been inflicted on themselves and others. Their sin has created a great divide from experiencing God's blessings and goodness. And yet God will hear their prayer when they cry out because He loves them. In some cases, they may be unsaved, and praying to God is, frankly, ineffective.

So, concerning our families and friends, at all times and especially when their walk is far from God, it is imperative for the standing saint, the spiritually mature child of God, to watch over them in perseverant prayer. We need to pour out to our God prayer and supplications for them since they are not where they ought to be in their walk with God. In this way, they are sanctified to God, and He is working diligently in their lives because of you and in response to your prayer. It is our responsibility to watch over those that we love and pray for them, making intercessions on their behalf.

It is also true that we are to pray for all men and for all who are in authority. When we pray for the unsaved, we look to God to reach them with the gospel. We ask God to convict them and create circumstances in which they can hear and believe. We are asking God to remove obstacles and the blindness that Satan has brought into their lives. Sometimes, God will reach your heart and convict you to reach them with the gospel. Paul prayed for open doors and for boldness to be that one who reaches the lost. We should entertain the same in our prayer life as well. On another note, if you have an unsaved person in your life, pray for them, since your God will listen and answer you. They need Christ most of all, so be sure to pray for that as well.

And we are to pray for all those in authority so that we might be able to lead a quiet and peaceable life in all godliness and honesty. Governments affect our lives in so many ways. We need to pray "for" those in authority, that they make godly decisions, and that God raises up godly individuals to lead or counsel those in power. Governments, the powers that be, are ordained of God,[35] and we need to pray for the people in those positions of authority that God will convict them with truth and that they might be moved to make good and godly decisions.

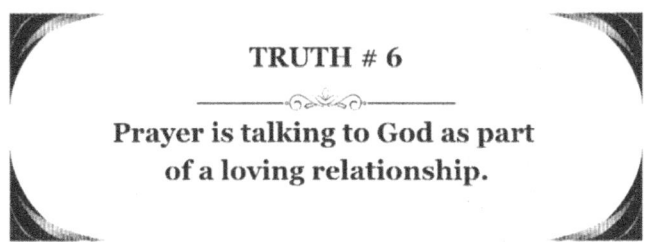

TRUTH # 6

Prayer is talking to God as part of a loving relationship.

Fundamental Life-Changing Truths About Prayer 33

Chapter 2 Reference List

[6] 1 John 4:8,16
[7] Romans 8:32
[8] Romans 5:8
[9] Romans 5:8
[10] I Thessalonians 5:17-18; Philippians 4:7-8
[11] Romans 8:26
[12] Colossians 1:13
[13] Romans 5:1,2; Hebrews 4:16; I Corinthians 12:12, 13; Galatians 2:20
[14] 2 Timothy 2:19
[15] I Timothy 1:15
[16] John 8:44
[17] Romans 10:8-9,13
[18] Galatians 3:26
[19] Romans 6:23
[20] Propitiation – a fully satisfying sacrifice
[21] Galatians 2:20
[22] Saints – a child of God, a believer, someone that has believed the gospel. They are in Christ and the Bible refers to them as saints – holy ones, called out ones.
[23] I Corinthians 6:19-20
[24] Philippians 4:6-7
[25] Ephesians 3:20
[26] Romans 8:26
[27] 1 Corinthians 10:1-12
[28] Daniel 3:16-28
[29] I Corinthians 6:19-20
[30] Ephesians 2:8-9
[31] Galatians 3:26
[32] 1 Thessalonians 2:13
[33] Romans 12:2
[34] Ephesians 6:18
[35] Romans 13:1

Chapter 3
What Can Prayer Do?

What Can Prayer Do? A Biblical Survey

Can prayer change things? Since our God can do anything, it would seem evident to me that it must, or why do we pray? Why does God call us, even command us, to pray? Some will argue against this truth - we will take that up a bit later in our discourse. Presently, let us look at the scriptures and see the plain, straightforward understanding of those who prayed to the mighty God of Heaven and Earth. Below is a sampling of passages and personages to examine. Open your Bible, read the passages presented, meditate on each of them, and you will see a consistent message concerning prayer. Those who prayed expected God to answer and do something in response to their prayer. I have made contextual comments or supplied quoted text of relevant passages, but reading the entirety of the passage would be helpful and insightful. In each Biblical account, God's people expected their mighty God to answer, and He did!

Moses   Exodus 8:30-31

Moses entreats (prays to) the Lord, and the Lord did according to the word of Moses. This is just one passage among many in Moses' conflict with Pharaoh. In each situation, Moses prays to God, and God responds.

> "And Moses went out from Pharaoh, and intreated the LORD. And the LORD did according to the word of Moses; and he removed the swarms of flies from Pharaoh, from his servants, and from his people; there remained not one." *Exodus 8:30-31*

Abraham's Servant Genesis 24:12-27; 42-48

The servant of Abraham prayed for God to reveal a wife for Isaac. Before he was done praying, Rebekah showed up, and he worshiped, seeing that God had answered his prayer.

> "And I bowed down my head, and worshipped the LORD, and blessed the LORD God of my master Abraham, which had led me in the right way to take my master's brother's daughter unto his son." *Genesis 24:48*

The entire chapter of Genesis 24 demonstrates God's answering of prayer and God's hand in His children's lives. Abraham's servant's faith response to what God is doing right before his eyes is a blessing to read. I encourage you to open your Bible to Genesis 24 and read and meditate upon God's Word.

Samson Judges 16:28-30

Samson is a fascinating judge for the Nation of Israel. He accomplished many incredible feats during his lifetime. When he is captured, blinded, and up against the wall, Samson prays that God will strengthen him one last time to avenge the Philistines for his two eyes. And the Lord answered his prayer. His strength returned, enabling him to collapse the entire building upon his captors.

Samuel 1 Samuel 12:6-25

Angry with the people of Israel, Samuel tells them that he will call upon the Lord for thunder and rain to validate that God sees what they have done in asking for a king, as great wickedness. Samuel fully believes that God will hear him and answer his prayer as he requested. Samuel expected God to answer his prayer in real time!

> "Now therefore stand and see this great thing, which the LORD will do before your eyes. Is it not wheat harvest to day? I will call unto the LORD, and he shall send thunder and rain; that ye may perceive and see that your wickedness is great, which ye have done in the sight of the LORD, in asking you a king. So Samuel called unto the LORD; and the LORD sent

> thunder and rain that day: and all the people greatly feared the LORD and Samuel. And all the people said unto Samuel, Pray for thy servants unto the LORD thy God, that we die not: for we have added unto all our sins this evil, to ask us a king."
> *1 Samuel 12:16-19*

Samuel then challenged the people not to turn aside from following the Lord but to serve Him with all their hearts. He also promised to pray for them and teach them how to live godly.

> "Moreover as for me, God forbid that I should sin against the LORD in ceasing to pray for you: but I will teach you the good and the right way:" *1 Samuel 12:23*

David, Absalom, and Ahithophel

2 Samuel 15:31-32, 37; 2 Samuel 16:20-23; 2 Samuel 17:1-15,23

This is a rather interesting account of David and his son, Absalom, who sought to overthrow his throne. David's most esteemed advisor, Ahithophel, had defected to be among the conspirators and was aiding Absalom. Absalom followed Ahithophel's advice, just as David had done. "And the counsel of Ahithophel, which he counseled in those days, was as if a man had enquired at the oracle of God: ...." David was very concerned about Ahithophel giving Absalom an undue advantage of counsel, so he prayed.

> "David said, O LORD, I pray thee, turn the counsel of Ahithophel into foolishness." *2 Samuel 16:23*

We find that God answers David's prayer:

> "And when Ahithophel saw that his counsel was not followed, he saddled his ass, and arose, and gat him home to his house, to his city, and put his household in order, and hanged himself." *2 Samuel 17:23*

Elisha   2 Kings 6:8-23

Elisha was a prophet of God for the Nation of Israel during a time when Syria was warring against Israel. Aram, the King of Syria, sent his armies multiple times to camp against Israel and try to take them by surprise. But Elisha would always spoil their plans through God's revelations to him. Elisha would inform the king of Israel of Aram's plans and thwart their campaign by taking appropriate defensive measures.

Aram was furious and thought he had a traitor in their midst. However, he was told by his counselors that Elisha, the prophet of Israel, was the one responsible for revealing his plans to the King of Israel. So, he chose to go after Elisha to eliminate him. The king sent spies to search for Elisha's location, and they found him at Dothan. Upon learning this, the king of Syria immediately sent an army of soldiers, horses, and chariots to surround the city and capture the prophet.

Elisha's servant awoke in the morning to see the entire city surrounded by the Syrian army. All seemed lost, but Elisha knew something that his servant did not. He knew that the armies of the Lord stood with him, even though they could not be seen with the human eye. He also knew that God answered prayer!

> "And Elisha prayed, and said, LORD, I pray thee, open his eyes, that he may see. And the LORD opened the eyes of the young man; and he saw: and, behold, the mountain was full of horses and chariots of fire round about Elisha. And when they came down to him, Elisha prayed unto the LORD, and said, Smite this people, I pray thee, with blindness. And he smote them with blindness according to the word of Elisha." *2 Kings 6:17-18*

Did you catch that? The Lord answered Elisha's prayer, and even as Elisha requested.

Solomon   2 Chronicles 6:12-42; 2 Chronicles 7:11-22

In 2 Chronicles 6 and 7, Solomon completes the Temple and dedicates it to the Lord with prayer and sacrifices. God confirms that He has heard Solomon's prayer and accepted his sacrifices by fire from heaven, and He appeared to him by night.

> "Now when Solomon had made an end of praying, the fire came down from heaven, and consumed the burnt offering and the sacrifices; and the glory of the LORD filled the house." *2 Chronicles 7:1*

> "Thus Solomon finished the house of the LORD, and the king's house: and all that came into Solomon's heart to make in the house of the LORD, and in his own house, he prosperously effected. And the LORD appeared to Solomon by night, and said unto him, I have heard thy prayer, and have chosen this place to myself for an house of sacrifice." *2 Chronicles 7:11-12*

Nehemiah   Nehemiah 1:4-11; Nehemiah 2:4

Nehemiah is burdened that the walls and gates of Jerusalem are broken down and in ruin. Nehemiah goes to God in prayer and seeks favor in the king's sight, since he was the king's cupbearer.

> "O Lord, I beseech thee, let now thine ear be attentive to the prayer of thy servant, and to the prayer of thy servants, who desire to fear thy name: and prosper, I pray thee, thy servant this day, and grant him mercy in the sight of this man. For I was the king's cupbearer." *Nehemiah 1:11*

> "Then the king said unto me, For what dost thou make request? So I prayed to the God of heaven." *Nehemiah 2:4*

It is fascinating to note that Nehemiah continues to pray to God during the entire wall rebuilding, and the Lord always answers his prayers. Nehemiah has no doubt when praying to God. God is there. God is listening. God is answering his prayers and requests. God is standing with them!

Apostle Paul

The Apostle Paul expected that the prayers of himself and others to God would deliver him from the unbelievers in Judea and prepare their hearts for the offering he was bringing to them from the Gentile churches. The Apostle Paul knew that God loved him and all His children. In Philemon 22, Apostle Paul is so confident in the effectual working of God through prayer that he asks Philemon to prepare a lodging for him.

> "Now I beseech you, brethren, for the Lord Jesus Christ's sake, and for the love of the Spirit, **that ye strive together with me in your prayers** to God for me; **That I** may be delivered from them that do not believe in Judaea; and that my service which I have for Jerusalem may be accepted of the saints;" *Romans 15:30-31*

> "Who delivered us from so great a death, and doth deliver: in whom we trust that he will yet deliver us; Ye also helping together by prayer for us, that for the gift bestowed upon us by the means of many persons thanks may be given by many on our behalf." *2 Corinthians 1:10-11*

> "But withal prepare me also a lodging: for I trust that through your prayers I shall be given unto you." *Philemon 22*

Ephesians 6:10-17 commands us to be strong in the Lord and the power of His might and to put on the whole armor of God. We are in a spiritual battle today. We are commanded to watch over others in prayer and supplication with all perseverance in this spiritual fight. Prayer is our weapon! Clearly, the Apostle Paul expected prayer to produce results in this spiritual battle. He expected prayer to aid in the protection and spiritual growth of the saints. He expected it to help him and others have the words to share with others. He expected prayer to enable him to gain boldness in sharing the gospel. He expected prayer to open doors and provide opportunities to witness. Apostle Paul fully expected prayer to be answered and produce results.

> "Praying always with all prayer and supplication in the Spirit, and watching thereunto with all perseverance and supplication for all saints; And for me, that utterance may be given unto me, that I may open my mouth boldly, to make known the mystery of the gospel, For which I am an ambassador in bonds: that therein I may speak boldly, as I ought to speak." *Ephesians 6:18- 20*

> "And this I pray, that your love may abound yet more and more in knowledge and in all judgment; That ye may approve things that are excellent; that ye may be sincere and without offence till the day of Christ; Being filled with the fruits of righteousness, which are by Jesus Christ, unto the glory and praise of God." *Philippians 1:9-11*

> "Continue in prayer, and watch in the same with thanksgiving; Withal praying also for us, that God would open unto us a door of utterance, to speak the mystery of Christ, for which I am also in bonds: That I may make it manifest, as I ought to speak." *Colossians 4:2-4*

> "For every creature of God is good, and nothing to be refused, if it be received with thanksgiving: For it is sanctified by the Word of God and prayer." *1 Timothy 4:4-5*

The Apostle Paul expected that his prayers would be effective in the lives of others. It is also true that individuals in their free will can deny God, but God does answer prayer. Apostle Paul fully expected God to answer his requests and enable him to have a prosperous journey to the Romans.

> "Brethren, pray for us." *1 Thessalonians 5:25*

> "For God is my witness, whom I serve with my spirit in the gospel of his Son, that without ceasing I make mention of you always in my prayers; Making request, if by any means now at length I might have a prosperous journey by the will of God to come unto you." *Romans 1:9-10*

> "Finally, brethren, pray for us, that the word of the Lord may have free course, and be glorified, even as it is with you: And that we may be delivered from unreasonable and wicked men…" *2 Thessalonians 3:1*

Jeremiah   Jeremiah 42:2-7

The people feared the King of Babylon and considered fleeing to Egypt. They asked Jeremiah to go to God for them and to find out what they should do. Jeremiah agrees to pray for them and give God's answer back to them. Note that Jeremiah expected God to answer his prayer.

> "Then Jeremiah the prophet said unto them, I have heard you; behold, I will pray unto the LORD your God according to your words; and it shall come to pass, that whatsoever thing the LORD shall answer you, I will declare it unto you; I will keep nothing back from you." *Jeremiah 42:4*

> "And it came to pass after ten days, that the word of the LORD came unto Jeremiah" *Jeremiah 42:7*

Jonah   Jonah 1:6-16

Jonah was fleeing from the presence of the Lord, running in the opposite direction from the city of Nineveh, where God had sent him. He got on a ship going to Tarshish. At sea, a great wind began to toss the ship violently upon the waves, and the ship was on the verge of destruction. All the mariners were afraid. Upon questioning, it was determined that the cause was Jonah and his disobedience to God. He told them what to do to save themselves. They needed to throw Jonah overboard. God immediately responds by quieting the sea and not holding them guilty for throwing Jonah overboard.

> "Wherefore they cried unto the LORD, and said, We beseech thee, O LORD, we beseech thee, let us not perish for this man's life, and lay not upon us innocent blood: for thou, O LORD, hast done as it pleased thee. So they took up Jonah, and cast him forth into the sea: and the sea ceased from her rage. Then the men feared the LORD exceedingly, and offered a sacrifice unto the LORD, and made vows." *Jonah 1:14-16*

Epaphras   Colossians 4:12-13

Epaphras was a servant of God, a friend of the Apostle Paul, and a fellow Colossian who understood the impact of prayer in the believer's life. The Word of God tells us he labored fervently for the Colossians in prayer. He was a prayer warrior for them, going to the throne of grace with great zeal and fervor. He prayed that they would stand perfect and complete in all the will of God (have maturity in their walk and do all the will of God). Epaphras labored in prayer because he believed that God answered prayer and that his prayers to God were effective.

> "Epaphras, who is one of you, a servant of Christ, saluteth you, always labouring fervently for you in prayers, that ye may stand perfect and complete in all the will of God. For I bear him record, that he hath a great zeal for you, and them that are in Laodicea, and them in Hierapolis." *Colossians 4:12-13*

James   James 5:16

James states clearly and without a doubt that prayer produces results. Effectual means that the prayer seeks an effect, a powerful change to the situation. Fervent encapsulates the heart and passion of the righteous individual seeking God in prayer. So, when the child of God goes to God in heartfelt, intentional prayer, making requests and supplications, it produces much!

> "...The effectual fervent prayer of a righteous man availeth much." *James 5:16*

Peter   Acts 10:3-4

An Angel appears to Cornelius and tells him that his prayers have come before God and that God has sent himself to him. Our God hears our prayers and answers them.

> "He saw in a vision evidently about the ninth hour of the day an angel of God coming in to him, and saying unto him, Cornelius. And when he looked on him, he was afraid, and said, What is it, Lord? And he said unto him, Thy prayers and thine alms are come up for a memorial before God." *Acts 10:3-4*

In summary, those who prayed in Scripture expected God to hear them. They expected God to answer them. They expected God to produce a real-time, right-now answer. They expected to see the power of God. They believed God could do what they prayed for. They expected their prayer to produce a result.

Expecting is not demanding. Expecting is a faith statement in the power of a loving God, knowing whom you are praying to, and the reality that He can do all things. And since you are His child, He is for you and will answer your prayer with good and do far more than you can possibly ask or think. Our God works all things together for good. Nothing is impossible for Him. Expect to see the mighty hand of God at work in your life.

Chapter 4
Prayer and Worship

Let us Worship

The Word of God proclaims that we are to worship our God, give praise, bring honor, and glorify Him with our words and actions. He is God and worthy of all we can give. There is no other God, and He can do all things! As Jeremiah 32 states, "Ah, Lord God! Behold, thou hast made the heaven and the earth by thy great power and stretched our arm, and there is nothing too hard for thee." Again, in the same chapter, the Word states, "Behold, I am the LORD, the God of all flesh: Is there anything too hard for me?" The answer is no! Thus, worship must pour from us to Him!

> "O come, **let us worship** and bow down: let us kneel before the LORD our maker." *Psalm 95:6*

> "**O worship the LORD** in the beauty of holiness: fear, all the earth, before him." *Psalm 96:9*

> "Give unto the LORD the glory due unto his name; **worship the LORD** in the beauty of holiness." *Psalm 29:2*

> "God is a Spirit: and **they that worship him must worship him in spirit and in truth.**" *John 4:24*

> "Saying with a loud voice, Fear God, and give glory to him; for the hour of his judgment is come: **and worship him** that made heaven, and earth, and the sea, and the fountains of waters."
> *Revelation 14:7*

The worship of God can take on many forms and paths. However, to be worship, acknowledging the one true God must be central and present in the believer's heart and mind. Worship is directed to God with purpose and intention. Many define worship as when we rise to our feet, music begins to play, and we sing. For many, this is a real time of worship, when the believer truly engages with the words of the music and lets them speak to them, thanking God and reflecting on what God has done.

Music and singing are excellent means of corporate worship, but the individual may or may not truly be worshipping God. Unfortunately, it is just that for far too many, singing and listening to some good music, but God is not on their mind or heart. The truth is that unless the individual engages with God in some fashion, it is not worship. Whether loud or soft, energetic, urgent, or somber, seated or standing, swaying or hands held high, worship is a product of the heart and mind directed to God, understanding who He is – God.

Prayer and the Word of God are two other paths that can engage the believer in worship. When a child of God reads the Bible or listens to a sermon (whether in church, on a podcast, YouTube, or Facebook) and is engaged with it, wanting to know what God wants in their life, then they are engaged in worshiping God. When one opens the Word of God and says in his heart, "Lord, speak to me, show me what you want to show me," then they are worshipping God.

However, if the believer is going through the motions, not considering who the Word's author is, there is no worship. As the child of God sits in the pew pondering today's lunch or dinner as the Word of God is preached, there is no worship. Or perhaps the believer is seated in the pews, Bible open, well, because that is what is expected. Well, there is no worship there, either. What about the saint listening to the Word being preached and judging others, thinking, "Wow, Barry over there needs to listen to this. He's got some problems!" Yes, you guessed it; no worship here either. Again, worship is purposeful, intentional, and directed to God.

So, what about prayer as a form of worship? Unless one is merely reading a passage of words or reciting a memorized script by rote, prayer is fundamentally a form of worship. To whom are you praying? It is God.

When you go to God in prayer, you are acknowledging who He is and that He can do all things. There is purpose in your prayer and intention, and it is directed to God. You are giving requests to the God of the universe, seeking His power and authority in your life. That is worship, powerful worship. It honors God; it glorifies God; it pleases God.[36] Prayer is the most straightforward form of worship because believers who bow their hearts humbly to God in prayer are coming to God in recognition of His Lordship and almighty power, and God receives worship.

Every time that we say, "Thank you, Lord," it is prayer, talking to God, and fundamentally worship. Worship occurs when we see a rainbow and remember God's promise. Worship happens when our children or grandchildren reach a milestone in their lives, and we think, "Wow, God, you are good!" or "Thank you, God." That is worship. When we pray to Him, we worship Him with our hearts and minds. When we come before His throne of grace seeking His intervention and power or thanking Him and praising Him, it is pure God-honoring worship. So, pray to the God who loves you more than you can ever comprehend. Pray to the God of the Bible, who works out the details of everything we pray about in less than a moment — perfectly for His glory and our good.

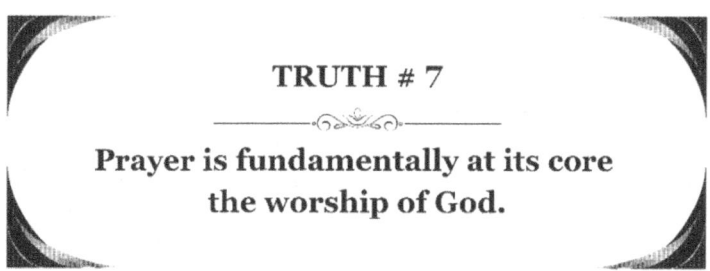

TRUTH # 7

Prayer is fundamentally at its core the worship of God.

What I will share now about the intimate connection between Prayer and Worship I find completely fascinating. God's Word often peels back the fabric of this physical world, allowing us to peer into the spiritual realm and see things we cannot know in any other way. Please read the following two verses and think about what they say.

> "And when he had taken the book, the four beasts and four and twenty elders fell down before the Lamb, having every one of them harps, and **golden vials full of odours, which are the prayers of saints.**" *Revelation 5:8*

> "And another angel came and stood at the altar, having a golden censer; and there was given unto him much incense, **that he**

Prayer and Worship

should offer it with the prayers of all saints upon the golden altar which was before the throne. And the smoke of the incense, which came with the prayers of the saints, ascended up before God out of the angel's hand."
Revelation 8:3-4

It will be a fantastic experience when we get to heaven and see God face-to-face and the majesty of His glory! But what is happening here? In God's throne room in heaven, our prayers become part of the continuous worship of our God. They become tangible, palpable, and even physical, and are mixed with sweet odors ascending from the golden altar before His throne. They are so intimately mixed with the sweet aroma of the incense rising from the angel's hand that they seem to be one and the same. Our prayers fill the throne room of God with a sweetness that the finite mind cannot understand but which tangibly honors and glorifies our God. Before we dismiss this as a metaphor or symbol, consider the Tabernacle in the wilderness that the Lord had Moses make and the ceremonial worship that took place.

God instructed Moses to make a golden altar and continually have sweet incense burned upon it. We read in **Exodus 30:1-10** about the details of this altar's attributes.

> "And thou shalt make an altar to burn incense upon: of shittim wood shalt thou make it…And thou shalt overlay it with pure gold, the top thereof, and the sides thereof round about, and the horns thereof; and thou shalt make unto it a crown of gold round about…And thou shalt put it before the vail that is by the ark of the testimony, before the mercy seat that is over the testimony, where I will meet with thee. And Aaron shall burn thereon sweet incense every morning…And when Aaron lighteth the lamps at even, he shall burn incense upon it, a perpetual incense before the LORD throughout your generations. Ye shall offer no strange incense thereon, nor burnt sacrifice, nor meat offering; neither shall ye pour drink offering thereon." *Exodus 30:1-10*

These selected quotes from Exodus 30:1-10 conclude with a solemn warning not to burn any strange incense, burnt sacrifice, meal offering, or drink offering on the altar of incense. This altar of incense is special. It is a place for the pure worship of Almighty God. Nothing must taint the pure, sweet incense God prescribes to burn on that altar before the mercy seat. According to Hebrews 8:1-5 and Hebrews 9:23-24, the Tabernacle in the wilderness is a pattern of the true sanctuary, the true Tabernacle that the Lord has pitched in the heavens. What we see in the Tabernacle in the wilderness is a shadow of what occurs in God's sanctuary and throne room. There are reasons for the exacting detail given to Moses for the ceremonial worship of God in that Tabernacle. It was to be a picture of the true Tabernacle and worship, which happens in heaven.

> "Now of the things which we have spoken this is the sum: We have such an high priest, who is set on the **right hand of the throne of the Majesty in the heavens; A minister of the sanctuary, and of the true tabernacle, which the Lord pitched, and not man.** Who serve unto the example and shadow of heavenly things, as Moses was admonished of God when he was about to make the tabernacle: for, See, saith he, that thou **make all things according to the pattern** shewed to thee in the mount." *Hebrew 8:1-2; 5*

> "It was therefore necessary that **the patterns of things in the heavens** should be purified with these; but the heavenly things themselves with better sacrifices than these. For Christ is not entered into the **holy places made with hands, which are the figures of the true; but into heaven itself**, now to appear in the presence of God for us:" *Hebrews 9:23-24*

Revelation 8:3-4 discloses that "the smoke of the incense, which came with the prayers of the saints, ascended up before God out of the angel's hand." On the day of atonement, the High Priest Aaron did the same thing on that golden altar of incense in the Tabernacle. He filled his hands with the sweet incense and put it on the burning coals of fire, which were on the altar of incense.

> "And he shall take a censer full of burning coals of fire from off the altar before the LORD, **and his hands full of sweet incense beaten small,** and bring it within the vail: **And he shall put the incense upon the fire before the LORD, that the cloud of the incense may cover the mercy seat** that is upon the testimony, that he die not:" *Leviticus 16:12-13*

The cloud, the incredibly sweet cloud and aroma, covered the mercy seat and allowed the High Priest to enter. It allowed him into the presence of a Holy God. That sweet cloud of incense that filled the Holy of Holies was a picture of what occurs in heaven when we pray. God's throne room fills with a beautiful, sweet odor from the prayers of the children of God.

In **Luke 1:8-10,** we have the account of Zacharias, John the Baptist's father, fulfilling his priestly duties.

> "And it came to pass, that while he executed the priest's office before God in the order of his course, according to the custom of the priest's office, **his lot was to burn incense** when he went into the temple of the Lord. And the **whole multitude of the people were praying without at the time of incense.**"

How remarkable it is that the Holy Spirit chose to share these details! The burning incense, which was part of the temple's worship ceremony, was also a type of what was occurring in the throne room of God. As the prayers of those outside the temple went up to God, they were mixed with sweet odors in the throne room, and God received worship. David puts it this way in Psalm 141:2: **"Let my prayer be set forth before thee as incense; and the lifting up of my hands as the evening sacrifice."** David understood that praying is the most authentic form of worship and that it glorifies God. Prayer is pure and holy to God, and God is richly pleased by it.

Chapter 4 Reference List

[36] Hebrew 11:6

Chapter 5
Prayer and Spiritual Warfare

The Days are Evil. Start PRAYING!

It is undeniable that the state of the world is far from perfect. A cursory examination of the news, media, and social platforms inundates us with the haunting reality that something is terribly wrong with the world and that it is not what it should be. We know that sin is everywhere because man is born a sinner, so sinful ways drive society and the hearts of men.

> "The heart is deceitful above all things, and desperately wicked: who can know it?" *Jeremiah 17:9*

We hear of the terrible atrocities that humanity does, and it makes us cry or cringe in horror, "How could anyone do such things?" The lost, those without Christ, have no hope and are driven by their sinful nature. However, there is a bigger picture of the evil that we see and know exists about us. Satan and his angels exist; they are not in Hell and are busy working against the cause of Christ and His children.

> "But if our gospel be hid, it is hid to them that are lost: In whom the **god of this world** hath blinded the minds of them which believe not, lest the light of the glorious gospel of Christ, who

is the image of God, should shine unto them." *2 Corinthians 4:3-4*

"And you hath he quickened, who were dead in trespasses and sins; Wherein in time **past ye walked according to the course of this world,** according to the **prince of the power of the air, the spirit that now worketh in the children of disobedience**: Among whom also we all had our conversation in times past in the lusts of our flesh, fulfilling the desires of the flesh and of the mind; and were by nature the children of wrath, even as others." *Ephesians 2:1-3*

Impactfully, we discover that according to 2 Corinthians 4:3-4, Satan, the Devil, is called "the god of this world" and is active, working to blind the minds of those who believe not. Ephesians 2:1-3 reveals that the Devil, also called "the prince of the power of the air," is the spirit that works in the children of disobedience. He has devised the course of this world in which we live. Satan is the driving influence of the lost. Our world system resonates with man's sinful nature like two tuning forks of the same frequency. This world system strikes a chord and resonates with the lust and desires of the flesh. You see it daily on commercials, billboards, and social media posts. Someone beautiful tries to sell you that shiny new car. You drink that unique soda, and you are promised real joy. The world system is all about getting whatever you can get, stepping on whomever to get to the top: money, prestige, power, and beauty. Many worship it instead of the true and living God.

The Apostle John in 1 John 2:16 says it this way: "For all that is in the world, the lust of the flesh, and the lust of the eyes, and the pride of life, is not of the Father, but is of the world." Even in the garden, we find Eve in Genesis 3:6 being tempted by the same three aspects of the world: "And when the woman saw that the tree was good for food, and that it was pleasant to the eyes, and a tree to be desired to make one wise..." The Devil had humanity figured out right at the start and scored the victory with one conversation with Eve.

The Devil's design of the world system is not an artificial construct of Satan's imagination but is directly from his experience. He is just using what drives him every day as well. Scripture reveals in Isaiah 14:12-15 the Devil's five "I wills," his lusts and wants. If we compare them to the description of who he is in Ezekiel 28:12-19, we discover that he corrupted his wisdom because of his beauty and was lifted up because of pride. This concisely summarizes the world system: corrupted wisdom, beauty, and pride. One of the Devil's "I wills" in Isaiah 14 is "I will be like the Most High." Like the other "I wills," this phrase has a very specific meaning. Notice this passage from Genesis 14, which discusses Abraham's encounter with Melchizedek, the king of Salem, who was the priest of the Most High God.

> "And Melchizedek king of Salem brought forth bread and wine: and he was the priest of the most high God. And he blessed him, and said, Blessed be Abram of the **most high God, possessor of heaven and earth:**" *Genesis 14:18-19*

Verse 19 defines what it means to be the Most High God. It means that He is the "possessor of heaven and earth." One of Satan's desires was to be the possessor of heaven and earth. To be sure, the Devil is not the possessor of the third heaven[37], paradise, where God the Father is. However, if scripture means what it says, he is presently the possessor of heaven and earth. How did that happen? Ezekiel 28:12-19 further pronounces that Satan sold his plan to many of the angels, and they followed him. Revelation 12 indicates that 1/3 of the angels followed Lucifer.[38] He effectively led a coup, took control of the universe's leadership structure (government), and became the possessor of heaven and earth. You see, the powers that be are ordained of God.[39] God ordered the Universe with a leadership structure made up of positions of authority to govern His creation. Colossians 1:16[40] instructs us to understand that some of these structures of power we can see and others are invisible. Some are on Earth, and others are in the Heavens. In God's sovereign will, He has ordained that His creation would be how He would govern the Universe. Knowing that God cannot lie, Satan took control of that authority structure with a coup.

We have already seen that he is "the prince of the power of the air," the "god of this world." And he has devised this world system in which we live. The Apostle Paul in Galatians states about Christ, "Who gave himself for our sins, **that he might deliver us from this present evil world**, according to the will of God and our Father:"[41] It is an evil world in which we live and Christ, by the cross, has redeemed us and "…**hath delivered us from the power of darkness**, and hath translated us into the kingdom of his dear Son:"[42] Praise God! If you need further convincing, after Christ was in the wilderness for 40 days and 40 nights[43], the Devil tempted Him and declared that he would give all the Earth's kingdoms to Christ if He would bow down and worship him. Christ does not correct him by saying, No, they are not yours, because the reality is that they were his.

The truth is that Satan is not in Hell. He is the guiding influencer of this world in which we live. One day, in the middle of the Tribulation, there will be a war in heaven; Michael and his angels will fight with the Devil and his angels.[44] Satan and his angels will lose that war, be cast out of heaven to the Earth, and lose their place in heaven. Things will get incredibly difficult on Earth at that time. Presently, the Devil and his angels are in the heavens, not where God the Father is, which is paradise, called the third heaven, but in our Universe.

So, was God caught off guard? Did the Devil fool Him? The answer is, "Of course not." God had already planned the redemption of humanity before He created the angels. "In hope of eternal life, which God, that cannot lie, promised before the world began,"[45] the scriptures declare. The Mystery, the truth for this age in which we live, the Dispensation of the Grace of God, is God's secret plan, which is now revealed, for taking back the heavenly places with the Body of Christ. God has not been caught off guard.

> "Even when we were dead in sins, hath quickened us together with Christ, (by grace ye are saved;) **And hath raised us up together, and made us sit together in heavenly places in Christ Jesus: That in the ages to come** he might shew the exceeding riches of his grace in his kindness toward us through Christ Jesus." *Ephesians 2:5-7*

> "**For our conversation is in heaven**; from whence also we look for the Saviour, the Lord Jesus Christ: Who shall change our vile body, that it may be fashioned like unto his glorious body, according to the working whereby he is able even to subdue all things unto himself." *Philippians 3:20-21*

Prophecy, or what God has spoken by the mouth of all His holy prophets, is about taking back the Earth. Note what God said to Adam:

> "And God blessed them, and God said unto them, Be fruitful, and multiply, and replenish the earth, **and subdue it**: and have dominion over the fish of the sea, and over the fowl of the air, and over every living thing that moveth upon the earth." *Genesis 1:27-28*

Subduing shows that things are out of control. The word, subdue, has the root idea of placing the "foot upon the head" to bring into subjection or bondage. The Earth needed to be brought into subjection because Satan had led a rebellion and was now the possessor of the leadership structure of the Universe.

Ephesians 1:9-11 states God's eternal purpose, that in the dispensation of the fullness of times (when everything is perfect – the new heaven and the new earth dispensation), God is going to gather everything in Christ, both which are in heaven and which are on earth. This is a future event. Therefore, it is not true now; that is, heaven and the earth are not presently gathered together in Christ.

The Whole Armor of God

Okay, so what does this have to do with prayer? Well, Ephesians 6:10-18, a familiar passage discussing the whole armor of God, states that we are to put on the whole armor of God that we may be able to stand against the wiles of the Devil and a full-on spiritual attack from angelic beings. Yes, that is what those principalities, powers, rulers of darkness, and spiritual wickedness are. As you read this passage, note that the believer is not wrestling with flesh and blood but is locked in a spiritual battle that cannot be fought with physical weapons of warfare. Prayer is our weapon.

> "Finally, my brethren, be strong in the Lord, and in the power of his might. Put on the whole armour of God, that ye may be able to stand against the wiles of the devil. For we wrestle not against flesh and blood, but against principalities, against powers, against the rulers of the darkness of this world, against spiritual wickedness in high places. **Wherefore take unto you the whole armour of God, that ye may be able to withstand in the evil day, and having done all, to stand... Praying always with all prayer and supplication in the Spirit, and watching thereunto with all perseverance and supplication for all saints:"** *Ephesians 6:10-13, 18*

Wow, this is like Star Wars stuff, but it is the Word of God! You may not see it with your eyes, but it is real. Ephesians clearly reveals that we are in a spiritual conflict and battle. We are to be strong in the Lord and the power of God's might and to put on the whole armor of God to stand against the wiles or tricks of the Devil. Our fight is against principalities, powers, the rulers of the darkness of this world, and spiritual wickedness in high places. We need to be prepared and equipped to fight this battle: traditional weapons of warfare will not work.

Angelic beings fill God's heavenly government defined by these positions of authority (principalities, powers, etc.). And Satan has effectively taken control of it, as previously shown, by convincing about one-third of the angels to follow him. The book of Colossians confirms that these principalities and powers are found both in heaven and on earth, and some are invisible, while others are visible. We can see examples of the visible ones on Earth, such as kings, governors, presidents, and mayors. These positions of authority also exist in the heavens.

> "For by him were all things created, that are in heaven, and that are in earth, visible and invisible, whether they be thrones, or dominions, or principalities, or powers: all things were created by him, and for him: And he is before all things, and by him all things consist. And he is the head of the body, the church: who is the beginning, the firstborn from the dead; that in all things he might have the preeminence." *Colossians 1:16-18*

We need to be spiritually equipped to withstand this evil day in which we live because the Devil and his cohorts are leveling spiritual attacks at each of us. Notice the analogy to wrestling and the posture of still standing. Satan cannot take away your salvation, but he can take you off your feet, wrestle you to the ground, and leave you ineffective for the cause of Christ. Your life can end up in confusion and chaos, almost indiscernible from someone who is not saved, who is not a child of God.

The Devil uses tricks and deception to trip you up and take you down. He cannot indwell you because you are sealed with the Holy Spirit, who indwells you, protects you, and has made you a part of God's family. You are His. But the Devil can wreak havoc if you are unprepared and unequipped for battle. Let us briefly review the whole armor of God so that we can be better prepared to wage spiritual warfare through prayer.

> "Stand therefore, having your **loins girt about with truth**, and having on the **breastplate of righteousness;** And your **feet shod with the preparation of the gospel of peace**; Above all, taking the **shield of faith**, wherewith ye shall be able to quench all the fiery darts of the wicked. And take the

helmet of salvation, and the sword of the Spirit, which is the Word of God:" *Ephesians 6:14-17*

Our Loins Girt about with the Truth: Jesus Christ is the way, **the truth,** and the life. We are to study to show ourselves approved unto God, a workman that needeth not to be ashamed, rightly dividing the Word of truth.[46] It is critical to know God's Word and which part of it is to you and for you. The implication is that not knowing the truth leaves you vulnerable to deception and can destroy your spiritual walk. Bad doctrine destroys lives all the time. For example, can you lose your salvation? Many preach and teach that you can. This error has taken out multitudes of individuals in this spiritual battle and has made them shipwrecked for the cause of Christ. However, salvation is a gift from God, received upon your faith in the finished work of Christ. Jesus Christ died for our sins, was buried, and rose again on the third day. He paid the wages of sin, which is death, and offers the gift of God, which is eternal life, to any and all that call upon His name in faith.[47] Whosoever shall call upon the name of the Lord shall be saved.[48] This offer is for anyone who calls upon the name of the Lord in faith. We are sealed by the Holy Spirit and secure in the love of Christ,[49] with nothing, not even our actions, being able to separate us from the love of God in Christ Jesus. So, you are secure and cannot lose your salvation, which was a gift from God anyway. You are secure because all you did was believe and trust in what Jesus Christ did for you, which was to die for your sin and rise again for your justification.[50] Another significant doctrinal error centers on the rapture, the blessed hope of Christ's coming for the Body of Christ at the end of this dispensation of Grace. Many are living halted spiritual lives, thinking they are in the Tribulation, that the rapture has happened already, or that the rapture and the second coming are the same. Doctrinal error can destroy lives and lead to ungodliness.[51]

The Breastplate of Righteousness: God's Word commands that we should live soberly, righteously, and godly in this present world.[52] Sin leaves holes in our armor for Satan to come after us and attack. He cannot indwell the believer since the Holy Spirit has sealed us. Still, if we have not dealt with our anger, jealousy, and pride, or we won't forgive others, we leave opportunities for the Devil to get hold of us - to knock us down and out of the battle.[53] It often begins with allowing our thoughts to dwell on and be consumed by earthly things, worrying about what we have or don't have. This can lead to being stuck in a sinful life of shame.[54] We are to flee youthful lusts and follow righteousness.[55] What we are called to do is to willfully choose to set our minds on heavenly things. In Colossians 3:1-4, we are instructed, "If ye then be risen with Christ, seek those things which are above, where Christ sitteth on the right hand of God. Set your affection on things above, not on things on the earth. For ye are dead, and your life is hid with Christ in God. When Christ, who is our life, shall appear, then shall ye also appear with him in glory."

> **NOTE:**
>
> **2 Timothy 2:26** in the context of verses 15-26 teaches us that doctrinal error and a sin filled life allows the Devil to take individual believers captive at his will. So, it is critical to put on the whole armor of God. He cannot indwell a believer, but he can capture him. Read it, it should shake you up and cause you to desire to understand the scriptures and to flee sin.

Feet Shod with the Preparation of the Gospel of Peace: Nothing makes a more significant gain for the cause of Christ than someone getting saved. A new believer has been rescued from the power of darkness and translated into His dear Son's kingdom. They were on the slippery downward spiral to Hell, but now they are on their way to Heaven. What a transformation! The believer should be ready to share their testimony with those God brings into their life. Notice it says with the preparation of the gospel. We are all called to be ambassadors for Christ and share the simple gospel of God's grace to all God brings our way.

The Shield of Faith: God says ABOVE ALL, take the shield of faith. This quenches all the fiery darts of the wicked. Nothing can get through the shield of faith to take you out and knock you down. Hebrews 11:1,3 says that faith is the substance of things hoped for; the evidence of things not seen. Faith is the means by which we come to know the works of God. Faith makes what God says real and palpable. Faith is the evidence of things you cannot see with your eyes.

> "If ye then be risen with Christ, seek those things which are above, where Christ sitteth on the right hand of God. **Set your affection on things above, not on things on the earth.**"
> *Colossians 3:1-2*

"For our light affliction, which is but for a moment, worketh for us a far more exceeding and eternal weight of glory; **While we look not at the things which are seen, but at the things which are not seen:** for the things which are seen are temporal; but the things which are not seen are eternal."
2 Corinthians 4:17-18

This is faith in action. Whatever Satan hurls at you in this life will not matter if heaven is real to you, God is real to you, and the rapture is real to you. Faith enables you to look past the difficulties and gaze steadfastly at the things that you cannot see with your eyes.[56] Faith gives you victory over the things in this life. Hebrews 11:6 states that faith is necessary to please God. Faith grows as we are in the Word of God and allow it to speak to us.[57] In Romans 5:2, we learn that we access the grace wherein we stand by faith. Faith defends us from the wicked one's attacks. Faith is the actuator of our lives and enables us to live for Jesus Christ. John H. Yates, in 1891, penned these words to the stately hymn, "Faith is the Victory:"

Faith is the Victory

Encamped along the hills of light, Ye Christian soldiers, rise,
And press the battle ere the night, Shall veil the glowing skies.
Against the foe in vales below, Let all our strength be hurled;
Faith is the victory, we know, That overcomes the world

Refrain:
Faith is the victory!
Faith is the victory!
Oh, glorious victory
That overcomes the world.

His banner over us is love, Our sword the Word of God;
We tread the road the saints above, With shouts of triumph trod.
By faith, they like a whirlwind's breath, Swept on o'er every field;
The faith by which they conquered death, Is still our shining shield

On every hand the foe we find, Drawn up in dread array;
Let tents of ease be left behind, And onward to the fray.
Salvation's helmet on each head, With truth all girt about,
The earth shall tremble 'neath our tread, And echo with our shout.

To him that overcomes the foe, White raiment shall be giv'n;
Before the angels he shall know, His name confessed in heav'n.
Then onward from the hills of light, Our hearts with love aflame,
We'll vanquish all the hosts of night, In Jesus' conqu'ring name.

The words of this hymn ring faithful to God's Word that we need to be equipped with the Shield of Faith to have victory!

The Helmet of Salvation: The helmet guards one's head; the idea here is our mind, our thinking. I have known multiple individuals who doubted that they were still saved. They felt that they had done something to lose their salvation. As I stated above in the section on "our loins girt about with the truth," such individuals have been wrestled to the ground and are effectively out of the battle, almost useless for the cause of Christ. How can they reach out to others in love if they are worried and fearful for themselves? The reality that all should see is that we are saved by grace through faith in the finished work of Jesus Christ for our sin. His blood has redeemed us from all iniquity. We are saved and secure in Christ through simple faith in what He has done. You cannot lose your salvation because you did not earn it. The Helmet of Salvation is the knowledge that we are secure in Jesus Christ and stand in His amazing Grace. (Romans 5:1-2) We did not earn our way to heaven; we trusted a Savior. He, who is the way, the truth, and the life, redeemed us with His blood. Salvation is a gift from God.

1 Corinthians 13:13 says, "and now abideth faith, hope, charity these three; but the greatest of these is charity." Charity is the greatest because it, being "agape" love, is selfless and reaches out to others despite self. God's love, "agape" love, chooses others first. When someone is consumed by worry and fear, it is nearly impossible for them to choose others first, to love others. Their faith needs to grow, which can then build into a hope that replaces their fear and worry. At that point, they can love. The Helmet of Salvation is the truth of God's love for you. You cannot be separated from Him. It supplies the ability to help guard your thinking amid all the hardships of life, knowing that you are secure in Christ, that you are His, a saint, a child of God, called by God to love and help others.

The Sword of the Spirit, which is the Word of God: Recall the account of the Lord Jesus Christ in Matthew 4 while in the wilderness. When the Devil tempted Him, Jesus Christ battled the Devil using scripture. The Word of God can defend you in every situation. The Psalmist said in 119:11, "Thy word have I hid in mine heart, that I might not sin against thee." Hebrews 4:12 says it this way:

> "For the Word of God is quick, and powerful, and sharper than any two-edged sword, piercing even to the dividing asunder of

soul and spirit, and of the joints and marrow, and is a discerner of the thoughts and intents of the heart." *Hebrews 4:12*

The Word of God is quick, meaning it is alive. It is a discerner. It reads you. It defends your weaknesses and is powerful. In 2 Timothy 3:16-17, we read these words:

"All scripture is given by inspiration of God, and is profitable for doctrine, for reproof, for correction, for instruction in righteousness: That the man of God may be perfect, throughly furnished unto all good works." *2 Timothy 3:16-17*

God's Word was given to enable the man and woman of God to be perfect (mature) and completely equipped to do what God calls them to do. And as Ephesians 6 says, our God wants us to engage in the spiritual battle around us and, having done all, remain standing. This implies being victorious, as the adversary cannot take you down. Since you are standing, the adversary has fled, and the victory is ours and God's.

> **NOTE:**
>
> **We need to memorize scripture to be prepared in the day of battle, because the days are evil. We need to redeem the time.**

Praying Always with All Prayer and Supplication in the Spirit: When you get to Ephesians 6:18, God's Word calls the believer to arms, to action for the cause of Christ. The armor that God calls us to put on protects us from spiritual attack and enables us to remain standing for the cause of Christ. The passage of Ephesians 6:13-17 is the believer effectively getting dressed and prepared for a spiritual battle. We are told to put on the whole armor of God and to be strong in the Lord and the power of His might.

Each of us is to prepare to go into a spiritual battle, which is the reality of the world in which we live. We put on each piece of armor to cover our vulnerabilities and protect us (the belt of Truth, the breastplate of righteousness, and the feet shod with the gospel of peace). We defend ourselves from attacks with the shield, helmet, and sword, and are now ready to go into the world to battle.

And how we do that is by "praying." Praying is the means to carry out both spiritual defense and offense. The Word of God and prayer, we know, go hand in hand. As we have discussed, everything is sanctified to God by the Word of God and prayer. We are, without a doubt, prayer warriors: "Praying always with all prayer and supplication in the Spirit, and watching thereunto with all perseverance and supplication for all saints." We are to be watching over other believers, protecting them, defending them, and fighting for them in prayer. We are not to falter, hesitate, or cease but to be continuous and perseverant in our prayers for others. That is what a soldier does. They are on the battlefield for others. In love, we watch over each other and fight a spiritual battle with spiritual weapons, prayer, and the Word of God. In this way, we redeem the time. We help one another on the battlefield of life. With the whole armor of God, we can withstand the evil days and, having done all, remain standing.

Again, in Ephesians, we read:

> "Wherefore he saith, Awake thou that sleepest, and arise from the dead, and Christ shall give thee light. **See then that ye walk circumspectly, not as fools, but as wise, Redeeming the time, because the days are evil.** Wherefore be ye not unwise, but understanding what the will of the Lord is. And be not drunk with wine, wherein is excess; but be filled with the Spirit;" *Ephesians 5:14-18*

We must wake up and realize that we are in a spiritual conflict. We need to be wise, redeem the time, and understand the will of the Lord. We need to be filled with His Spirit, fully equipped for the day of battle.

> "Thou **therefore endure hardness, as a good soldier of Jesus Christ**. No man that warreth entangleth himself with the affairs of this life; that he may please him who hath chosen him to be a soldier." *2 Timothy 2:3-4*

And having done all, pray…pray…pray to the God of the Universe who can do all things, even exceedingly abundantly, above all that we can ask or think. Tomorrow awaits. Pray. And God receives the glory.

TRUTH # 8

Our response to a wicked and evil world in this spiritual battle is to Pray! Put on God's armor and pray!

Chapter 5 Reference List

[37] II Corinthians 12:2-4 Third heaven = paradise
[38] Revelation 12:4
[39] Romans 13:1
[40] Colossians 1:16 For by him were all things created, that are in heaven, and that are in earth, visible and invisible, whether they be thrones, or dominions, or principalities, or powers: all things were created by him, and for him:
[41] Galatians 1:4
[42] Colossians 1:13
[43] Matthew 4:8-9
[44] Revelation 12:7-8
[45] Titus 1:2
[46] 2 Timothy 2:15
[47] Ephesians 2:8-9; Romans 6:19
[48] Romans 10:13
[49] Ephesians 1:13-14; Romans 8:38-39
[50] Romans 4:24-25
[51] II Timothy 2:16-18
[52] Titus 2:12
[53] Ephesians 4:26-27; 2 Corinthians 2:10-11; 1 Timothy 3:6
[54] Philippians 3: 18-19
[55] 2 Timothy 2:22
[56] 2 Corinthians 4:17,18
[57] Romans 10:17

Chapter 6
What, When, and Whom Should We Pray For?

Be careful for nothing!

Before getting into the specifics of the "what, when, and whom we should pray for," we should be clear that whatever is on your heart should lead your prayer life. Philippians 4:6 states,

> "**Be careful for nothing; but in everything** by prayer and supplication with thanksgiving let your requests be made known unto God."

Our God wants us to share our concerns, feelings, worries, needs, and requests. You do not have to force it, use big words, or make it sound special. It is your personal conversation with the Lord, who loves you deeply and is on your side. So, pray to Him about everything.

However, in this life, we find ourselves in a spiritual battle, and there are things we should also add to our prayer life. We must broaden our focus and grow our hearts to pray for the spiritual needs of ourselves and others. The following sections help focus the expansion of our prayer life to make it more impactful in our daily walk and for the cause of Christ.

For We Know Not What We Should Pray for as We Ought.

> "Likewise **the Spirit also helpeth our infirmities**: for **we know not what we should pray for as we ought: but the Spirit itself maketh intercession for us with groanings** which cannot be uttered. And he **that searcheth the hearts knoweth** what is the mind of the Spirit, because **he maketh intercession for the saints according to the will of God.**"
> *Romans 8:26-27*

I once heard someone say that praying was a waste of time, since we are not God and cannot know the best things for which to pray. Thus, prayer does not matter because we are flawed humans, by nature selfish and foolish. We are just blindly praying without any real idea of what to pray about. They referred to this passage as evidence. Well, there is nothing further from the truth! The verse does not say that we do not know what to pray for, but it says we do not know what to pray for as we ought, meaning we do not know what the best solution should be for the situation. The scriptures are clear on what to pray about; literally, everything on your heart, and then some.[58]

We will delve into some prayer areas in a moment, but let us first further address this topic and analyze the two verses presented above. **"Likewise, the Spirit also helpeth our infirmities:"** "Likewise" goes back to the previous verses of the chapter in which we find that all of creation is in the bondage of corruption, **groaning** and travailing in pain, as "even we ourselves **groan** within ourselves, waiting for the adoption, to wit, the redemption of our body."[59] Because of Adam's sin, all creation was plunged into the bondage of corruption. Everything in this Universe decays and falls apart. But one day, we will be gloriously delivered from this bondage of corruption on the day of redemption, when we will receive our glorified bodies. We call this the rapture.

The "likewise" refers to the reality that we, and all creation, are groaning within ourselves, waiting for the day when the pain, suffering, and death all go away. That **groaning** is a yearning, a longing, a deep, heartfelt desire for the day that the Lord comes back to catch us away in the air.

Likewise, the Holy Spirit helps our infirmities. These are not physical weaknesses and problems, but the infirmity of our knowledge in that we do not know the best answer to our prayer. You see, we are limited; we are creatures of time. James says our lives are a vapor, and Paul says we are frail earthen vessels. We do not know the future and cannot see things from God's clear, infinite perspective. We have infirmities regarding wisdom and knowing what the outcome of any situation should be. However, the Holy Spirit steps in and intercedes for our infirmities, **since we do not know what we should pray for as we ought.**

The Holy Spirit does not just step in to make intercession for us without emotion; instead, Scripture says that He makes that intercession with groanings that cannot be uttered. Those groanings are a deep, heartfelt yearning and compassion resulting from a depth of love for us that cannot be expressed in words. These groanings envelop the intercessory work of the Spirit as He intercedes in our prayers to God the Father. God the Father searches each of our hearts and knows the mind of the Spirit because the Holy Spirit is making intercession for the saints according to God's will.

The Spirit does something amazing. He transforms our prayer into what it "ought" to be, aligning it with God's Word and His will without losing the purpose, requests, intention, and heart of the believer who prayed. Wow, as the song says…our God is a great God and worthy to be praised! He knows us to the very core and intercedes for us in love. Close your eyes and think about that for a bit. Thank you, Lord.

> "And he that searcheth the hearts knoweth what is the mind of the Spirit, because he maketh intercession for the saints according to the will of God." *Romans 8:27*

No wonder God further shares these added truths in Romans 8.

> "What shall we then say to these things? If God be for us, who can be against us? He that spared not his own Son, but delivered him up for us all, how shall he not with him also freely give us all things? Who shall lay any thing to the charge of God's elect? It is God that justifieth. Who is he that condemneth? **It is Christ that died, yea rather, that is risen again, who is even at the right hand of God, who also maketh intercession for us.** Who shall separate us from the love of Christ? shall tribulation, or distress, or persecution, or famine, or nakedness, or peril, or sword? As it is written, For thy sake we are killed all the day long; we are accounted as sheep for the slaughter. Nay, in all these things we are more than conquerors through him that loved us. For I am persuaded, that neither death, nor life, nor angels, nor principalities, nor powers, nor things present, nor things to come, Nor height, nor depth, nor any other

What, When, and Whom Should We Pray For?

creature, shall be able to separate us from the love of God, which is in Christ Jesus our Lord." *Romans 8:31-39*

It just gets better and better. The one who knows tomorrow as if it were yesterday knows me and intercedes for me when I pray. No wonder the Apostle Paul exclaimed the following:

> "That I may know him, and the power of his resurrection, and the fellowship of his sufferings, being made conformable unto his death; If by any means I might attain unto the resurrection of the dead. Not as though I had already attained, either were already perfect: but I follow after, if that I may apprehend that for which also I am apprehended of Christ Jesus. Brethren, I count not myself to have apprehended: but this one thing I do, forgetting those things which are behind, and reaching forth unto those things which are before, I press toward the mark for the prize of the high calling of God in Christ Jesus." *Philippians 3:10-14*

Paul wanted to know the Lord Jesus Christ in a fuller and more profound way. He wanted to experience the life-giving resurrection power of Jesus Christ over the dead things in his life and live a life of humility and obedience to His Savior. He knew he was not perfect or exactly what God wanted him to be, but he sought it; he focused on being who God said he was. He pressed forward, forgetting about past failures and victories, and striving for the prize —the goal of finishing his course, running his race, and being who God said he was: a saint, a child of God, a holy one, loved. We, too, ought to do the same as the Apostle Paul. Let us press towards the mark for the prize of God's high calling in Jesus Christ for our lives. Let us **be careful for nothing; but in everything** by prayer and supplication with thanksgiving, let our requests be made known unto God. The Spirit is our intercessory advocate for our requests, intercessions, prayers, praises, and thanksgivings to God and aligns our prayers with God's will. There is no downside to praying, so pray.

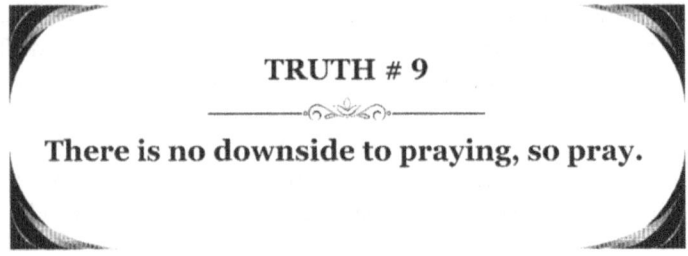

TRUTH # 9

There is no downside to praying, so pray.

Pray for Those in Authority

In this evil day, the spiritual battle is real, and we are in the thick of it. To redeem the time, we need to be "Praying always with all prayer and supplication in the Spirit, and watching thereunto with all perseverance and supplication for all saints:"[60] Prayer is our offensive weapon in this conflict, the means by which we fight a spiritual battle. Remember, when we pray, what we pray for is sanctified to God, and it becomes His personal possession. He is at work on it immediately, powerfully shaping our tomorrow.

A walk through the scriptures provides details on what, when, and for whom to pray.

> "I exhort therefore, that, first of all, **supplications, prayers, intercessions, and giving of thanks, be made for all men; For kings, and for all that are in authority;** that we may lead a **quiet and peaceable life in all godliness and honesty**." *1 Timothy 2:1-2*

> "I thank my **God, making mention of thee always in my prayers,**" *Philemon 1:4*

> "Always in **every prayer** of mine for you all **making request with joy,** For your fellowship in the gospel from the first day until now;" *Philippians 1:4-5*

> "**We give thanks to God** always for you all, **making mention of you in our prayers**; Remembering without ceasing your work of faith, and labour of love, and patience of hope in our Lord Jesus Christ, in the sight of God and our Father;" *1 Thessalonians 1:2-3*

"**First of all,**" we are exhorted to pray for all men[61] and all those in authority. Not only to pray but to make supplications, intercessions, and giving of thanks for them as well. It is so easy to attack and tear down others, to be displeased, bitter, and dissatisfied with those in authority over us. The "all men" referred to in 1 Timothy include God's children and those who are not - the lost. These are the individuals in your life: family, friends, children, your church family, neighbors, colleagues, the waiter/waitress at the restaurant, the person who cut you off on the highway, etc. "All in authority" means all, not just those you or I consider good or godly leaders.

In the apostles' day, Rome was the authority of the day and was utterly corrupt and vile. However, our God called the believers of that day to pray FOR them, and that instruction still holds true today. We are to seek good for those in authority, that they will do God's will, that God will convict them, that God will raise up good advisors, and so on. Remember, our God is for us,[62] which means He does all that is possible for us. He is on our side. He wants what is best for us. He supports us and looks out for our best. To be sure, we are not told to obey sinful directions. We are not told to condone or blindly allow the decimation of all that is holy and good. We need to stand for decency and godly causes. And there are times we must say "No more," and as David cried, "Is there not a cause?"[63] And for sure, we are not to do as they do. However, we are to be "examples of the believers!"[64] Through it all, we need to pray for those in authority and those who are lost so that we might lead a **quiet and peaceable life in all godliness and honesty**. We are to manifest the love of Christ to those about us. We are commissioned to be ambassadors for Christ; everyone should see Christ in us!

Paul considered the time of this Grace age to be short, and thus, our focus, our efforts, and our time should be entirely for the cause of Christ, to carry out His will. 1 Timothy 2:3-4 reveals that God's will for all men is for them to be saved and come to the knowledge of the truth. So, until He comes, we are to pray for ALL those in leadership and all men. It is the only way to undertake a spiritual battle and WIN. The "arm of flesh"[65] will fail you. We need to be and are called to be in prayer for those in authority.

Perhaps this bothers you, especially in our politically charged climate that we seem to find ourselves in more and more. Our ability to insulate ourselves with like-minded opinions and like-minded zealots is easy in our social media-driven culture and a la carte media selection. But let God's Word speak to us and lead us in our response to evil authority in our society. Consider God's attitude toward authority and our response. In Jude 1:8, we read, "Likewise also these filthy dreamers defile the flesh, **despise dominion**, and **speak evil of dignities**." Despising those in authority and speaking evil of them is wrong and sinful, as described in this passage. Jude links these characteristics to a group of filthy dreamers, unbelievers who defile the flesh.

In 2 Peter 2:1-3, we have a description of evil men who have found their way amongst the believers of the early Kingdom church. Take note of God's Word for His children found in 2 Peter 2:9-10; "The Lord knoweth how to deliver the godly out of temptations, and to reserve the unjust unto the day of judgment to be punished: But chiefly them that walk after the flesh in the lust of uncleanness, **and despise government. Presumptuous are they, self-willed, they are not afraid to speak evil of dignities."** This seems to be a recurring theme in every conversation we hear today, when individuals speak of those in authority. But it does not honor our God. Now, it is true that these passages are specific about a particular group of individuals during the tribulation that has infiltrated the believers of this future day. However, God is identifying their specific sinful behavior, which is their conduct and actions related to those in authority. Consider what the Holy Spirit says in the below-excerpted passage concerning our relationship with those in authority.

> "Let every soul be subject unto the higher powers. For there is no power but of God: **the powers that be are ordained of God. Whosoever therefore resisteth the power, resisteth the ordinance of God:** and they that resist shall receive to themselves damnation…" *Romans 13:1-2*

> **"For he is the minister of God to thee for good.** But if thou do that which is evil, be afraid; for he beareth not the sword in vain: **for he is the minister of God**, a revenger to execute wrath upon him that doeth evil. **Wherefore ye must needs be subject, not only for wrath, but also for conscience sake**. For for this cause pay ye tribute also: **for they are God's ministers**, attending continually upon this very thing. **Render therefore to all their dues: tribute to whom tribute is due; custom to whom custom; fear to whom fear; honour to whom honour.**" *Romans 13:4-7*

The takeaway that we must remember is that there is no power but of God, and the powers that be are ordained of God. In the book of Titus, God says this:

> Put them in mind to be **subject to principalities and powers**, to **obey magistrates**, to be ready to every good work, To speak evil of no man, to be no brawlers, but gentle, shewing all meekness unto all men. For we ourselves also were sometimes foolish, disobedient, deceived, serving divers lusts and pleasures, living in malice and envy, hateful, and hating one another. *Titus 3:1-3*

Before we came to Christ and were saved, this is who we were. But it should not be who we are now. Instead of speaking evil of men and dignitaries and despising those in authority, we should pray for them. The

Apostle Paul exhorts that "...first of all, supplications, prayers, intercessions, and giving of thanks, be made for all men; For kings, and for all that are in authority."[66] If we are not praying for them, we are out of the will of God in this aspect of our lives. We are to be examples of believers in this case by praying for all people and those in authority. This creates the spiritual environment necessary for a quiet and peaceable life that we can experience in all godliness and honesty. The world in which we live and are impacted daily can be changed as we go to the throne of grace. This is God's way, and in truth, the best way – so pray.

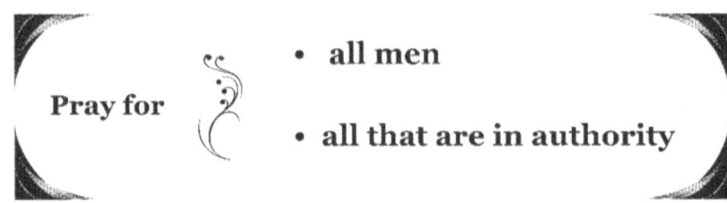

Pray for the Brethren and Yourself

A brief reading of the prayers of the Apostle Paul to the churches of his day can offer us valuable insight into spiritually driven directions for our own time in prayer. Below are several of the apostle's prayers showing his heart's path when he came before the throne of grace. They provide us with solid guidance for our prayers, supplications, intercessions, and requests that we should lift up to God, for ourselves and others, including family, friends, neighbors, and colleagues.

> "And this **I pray, that your love may abound yet more and more in knowledge and in all judgment**; That ye may **approve things that are excellent;** that ye **may be sincere and without offence** till the day of Christ; Being **filled with the fruits of righteousness,** which are by Jesus Christ, unto the glory and praise of God." *Philippians 1:9-11*

> "For this cause we also, since the day we heard it, **do not cease to pray for you,** and to desire that ye might be **filled with the knowledge of his will in all wisdom and spiritual understanding**; That ye might **walk worthy of the Lord** unto all pleasing, **being fruitful in every good work**, and increasing in the knowledge of God; Strengthened with all might, according to his glorious power, **unto all patience and longsuffering with joyfulness**; Giving thanks unto the Father,

which hath made us meet to be partakers of the inheritance of the saints in light:" *Colossians 1:9-12*

"Cease not to give thanks for you, making mention of you in my prayers; That the God of our Lord Jesus Christ, the Father of glory, may give unto you **the spirit of wisdom and revelation in the knowledge of him**: The **eyes of your understanding being enlightened**; that ye may **know what is the hope of his calling,** and what **the riches of the glory of his inheritance in the saints,** And what is the **exceeding greatness of his power to us-ward who believe**, according to the working of his mighty power," *Ephesians 1:16-19*

"For this cause **I bow my knees** unto the Father of our Lord Jesus Christ, Of whom the whole family in heaven and earth is named, That he would grant you, according to the riches of his glory, **to be strengthened with might by his Spirit in the inner man;** That **Christ may dwell in your hearts by faith;** that ye, being rooted and grounded in love, **May be able to comprehend with all saints what is the breadth, and length, and depth, and height;** And to **know the love of Christ,** which passeth knowledge, **that ye might be filled with all the fulness of God.** Now unto him that is able to do exceeding abundantly above all that we ask or think, according to the power that worketh in us," *Ephesians 3:14-20*

We can only share a glimpse of what is found in these four prayers in this exposition. However, what we can easily see is powerful. From the above passages from Philippians, Ephesians, and Colossians, Paul shares his sincere prayers for his spiritual children. We find a general pattern of spiritual concern that he had for them, covering four primary areas, which we will examine.

- Knowledge and Wisdom
- Understanding and Judgment
- A Worthy Walk that Bears Fruit
- Strength and Power for Living

Knowledge and Wisdom

We all need to grow in the knowledge and wisdom of God and His Word. It is foundational to the believer's life. "The fear of the LORD is the beginning of knowledge..."[67] According to the book of Romans, faith cometh by hearing, and hearing by the Word of God. We need to know

God's Word and make it a part of our daily bread so that our faith grows and our subsequent walk becomes godly.

> "All scripture is given by inspiration of God, and is profitable for doctrine, for reproof, for correction, for instruction in righteousness: That the man of God may be perfect, throughly furnished unto all good works." *2 Timothy 3:16-17*

God gave His Word so that we could become who He wants us to be and carry out His will in our lives. God, the Holy Spirit, takes the Word as we read it and meditate on it, and transforms us by renewing our minds. This enables us to see the world the way God the Father does. Being transformed keeps us from conforming to this world and falling into its sinful traps and disarray.[68] Solomon, the wisest of the wise, wrote this:

> "Wisdom is the principal thing; therefore get wisdom: and with all thy getting get understanding." *Proverbs 4:7*

That wisdom, that knowledge of God, is the foundation upon which our life is built.

Understanding and Judgment

On top of the foundation of wisdom and knowledge, we need understanding, that is, knowing how to do what God says. Understanding is the exercise of the knowledge that we have. In the Apostle Paul's prayers, he calls upon God to help believers make sound judgments and decisions, and to be filled with the knowledge of His will in all wisdom and spiritual understanding. The result is a walk that is sound and godly. In Philippians 3:10, Paul shared his heartfelt desire to know Christ in a fuller and richer way. He wanted to know the power of Christ's resurrection in his daily walk and the fellowship of His sufferings as he lived for Christ day by day. Paul was seeking to know his Savior in an honest and experiential way. As he stated in Philippians 1:21, "For to me to live is Christ, and to die is gain." What a powerful testimony of faith. Seeking God's hand in helping us grow in understanding and judgment is a powerful request to our God.

Furthermore, in Philippians 1:9-11, it is clear that we should approve things that are excellent, that is, to choose the best of the good things that God brings into our lives. This requires spiritual discernment and understanding. Our God knows tomorrow, so seeking His aid in our path of life should be a priority. Proverbs 3:5-6 states, "Trust in the LORD with all thine heart; and lean not unto thine own understanding. In all thy ways acknowledge him, and he shall direct thy paths." Prayer is acknowledging Him, leaning on Him instead of self, and trusting Him. Wow, this is a powerful direction our prayers should take as we approach the throne of grace for others and ourselves.

A Worthy Walk that Bears Fruit

A third area vital in Paul's prayers is **our walk before the Lord and how we live each day**. It sits upon the foundation of knowledge and understanding spoken of above. Do others see Christ in us? Are we walking by faith? Are we prepared for every good work our Savior calls us to do? Are we vessels of honor, sanctified, and meet for the master's use?[69] Or, on the contrary, are we vessels unto dishonor? Our walk, experiences, and actions in this life should be a critical part of our prayer time, both for ourselves and for others. Paul prayed that we would be sincere, faithful, and pure in our lives for the cause of Christ, and that we do so without offense, hurting, or causing others to stumble in their walk with God.

Additionally, we should be fruitful in our lives for Christ, allowing the Holy Spirit to work in us, producing the fruits of righteousness.[70] It is monumentally true that we need to solicit God's aid in helping us along these paths in our lives and the lives of others. Paul shares his struggle with the flesh in Romans 7, and if he found the fight difficult, it is at least as true for each of us as well. Galatians 6:1-4 speaks to helping a brother or sister who has fallen into a fault and guarding ourselves from the same temptations. We must fervently pray about our daily walk, seeking God's strength and ever-watchful care as we face the challenges of living in this present evil world.

Strength and Power for Living

The fourth general area of Paul's prayers **is experiencing God's strength and power.** In Philippians 4:13, we read the familiar verse, "I can do all things through Christ which strengtheneth me." Paul learned this truth through the many trials of life. It did not just immediately happen.[71] He found that Jesus Christ never forsook him and was with him through every trial and tribulation. And every time, he had the peace, the comfort, and the presence of God in his life. And we can all experience that if we are "…careful for nothing; but in everything by prayer and supplication with thanksgiving let your requests be made known unto God. And the peace of God, which passeth all understanding, shall keep your hearts and minds through Christ Jesus." [72] In Ephesians 6:10, we are told to be strong in the Lord and in the power of His might. God strengthens our inner man; it is renewed day by day.

Paul, in his prayers presented at the beginning of this section, made request to God that we:

- might be filled with all the fullness of God.
- would know what is the exceeding greatness of his power to us-ward who believe
- might be strengthened with all might,
- would be strengthened with might by his Spirit in the inner man;

As the Apostle Paul prayed, so ought we to pray as well. We all face life's challenges. Clearly, we are part of a sin-cursed creation engaged in a spiritual battle. We need to pray, and as God challenged Joshua[73], we must remain strong and courageous. We need to be filled with the fullness of God, facing the world knowing who we are: children of the creator of the Universe. If God be for us, who can be against us?[74] Is there anything too hard for God?[75] He is all-powerful, bringing that power to bear in, on, and through our lives. We need to go to Him for our every need and every concern. There is nothing too small and nothing too large for our God. He wants you to bring everything to Him, seeking His grace in times of need and plenty. Your prayer in the hands of our mighty, loving God leads to changed lives.

Pray for:
- **Knowledge and Wisdom**
- **Understanding and Judgment**
- **A Worthy Walk that Bears Fruit**
- **Strength and Power for Living**

One final note on these specific prayers of Paul. These prayers that we have examined are addressed to the local churches of the Apostle Paul's day: Ephesus, Philippi, and Colossae. They have a broad, general, and global feel because all local church members have the same overall spiritual needs and concerns: Knowledge and Wisdom; Understanding and Judgment; A Worthy Walk that Bears Fruit; and Strength and Power for Living. For each church member of those congregations, the specifics of God's answer would be unique. Each child of God is at a particular maturity level and has unique needs and concerns. The Lord knows each

76 Praying to a Mighty God

individual intimately, and His answers to those prayers would be specific to each person. It is likely that Paul did not know everyone individually, as the local churches were growing quickly. However, he did know many personally, and for those, he would also have prayed to God for them with specific requests.

Pray for Physical Protection, Deliverance, and Safe Journeys.

Even though we are in a spiritual battle, and we wrestle NOT against flesh and blood, the reality is that this spiritual warfare discussed earlier spills over into the physical reality of our lives. **There are real flesh-and-blood adversaries in life.** Satan works in the children of disobedience, and some become unreasonable, wicked people who can enter our lives and create havoc, stress, intimidation, heartache, pain, and persecution. Paul tells Timothy, "Alexander the coppersmith did me much evil: the Lord reward him according to his works: Of whom be thou ware also; for he hath greatly withstood our words."[76] Satan can sway the children of disobedience to be envious of you, despise you, and even attack you. The days are evil is an evident truth. We need to pray for protection from wicked men in this evil day. And not only for ourselves but for our families, our grandkids, our church family, our friends, and our coworkers. A brutal truth but an absolute reality are these words in 2 Timothy 3:12, "Yea, and all that will live godly in Christ Jesus shall suffer persecution." When we stand up and shine the light of Christ about us, wicked and evil men will try to shut us down. Our posture should be head down in prayer and our eyes up in watching over the saints! No wonder we are commanded to be constantly praying. **"Continue in prayer, and watch in the same with thanksgiving;"**[77]

In Ephesians 5, we are commanded to awake from our spiritual slumber, rise to a living stance, and get busy with the cause of Christ. But as we seek to carry out the cause of Christ, we are cautioned further to "walk circumspectly, not as fools, but as wise, redeeming the time, because the days are evil."[78] The child of God needs to walk circumspectly, paying attention in all directions for attacks because the days are evil. All believers need to pray for God's protective and guarding hand in their lives. God's Word also tells us to be engaged in prayer, watching over all the saints.[79] Prayer is the primary method of waging spiritual warfare. Prayer engages God in helping defend us from the physical attacks from wicked men. So, we, just like the Apostle Paul, should pray for protection from evil and unreasonable people. Further, we should pray for protection from their motivator, the spirit that works in them, the Devil.

Caution and wariness are necessary for the believer. A quick perusal of the following scriptures will immediately alert you to be watchful, careful, and aware of your surroundings. We must be vigilant in prayer, focused on protecting others and ourselves.

Pray for others in ministry, that God's Word will reach everyone, and for protection and deliverance from wicked men.

> "Finally, brethren, **pray for us, that the Word of the Lord may have free course**, and be glorified, even as it is with you: And that we may **be delivered from unreasonable and wicked men:** for all men have not faith." *2 Thessalonians 3:1-2*

Pray that you faithfully carry out your calling.

> "But **watch thou in all things, endure afflictions**, do the work of an evangelist, make full proof of thy ministry," *2 Timothy 4:5*

Pray for an ability to see what is really happening.

> "Therefore **let us not sleep**, as do others; **but let us watch and be sober.**" *1 Thessalonians 5:6*

Pray for protection and acceptance.

> "Now I beseech you, brethren, for the Lord Jesus Christ's sake, and for the love of the Spirit, that ye **strive together with me in your prayers to God for me; That I may be delivered from them that do not believe** in Judaea; and **that my service which I have** for Jerusalem **may be accepted of the saints**;" *Romans 15:30-31*

Pray to stay in the battle.

> "**Watch ye**, stand fast in the faith, quit you like men, **be strong.**" *1 Corinthians 16:13*

Pray for travel.

> "For God is my witness, whom I serve with my spirit in the gospel of his Son, that without ceasing I make mention of you always in my prayers; **Making request, if by any means now**

> at length I might have a prosperous journey by the will of God to come unto you." *Romans 1:9-10*

Pray for open doors and deliverance from people who hinder the cause of Christ, who attack us, and who harm us.

> "Continue in prayer, and watch in the same with thanksgiving; Withal praying also for us, that **God would open unto us a door of utterance,** to speak the mystery of Christ, for which I am also in bonds: **That I may make it manifest, as I ought to speak.**" *Colossians 4:2-4*

We need to watch over the individuals in our lives, guarding them in prayer, calling on God to protect them, and bringing to naught the works of the Devil and his coworkers of evil. This truth continually challenged me to be in fervent prayer for my children when they were young. When they left home for school or went to a friend's house or a sporting event, I could no longer physically watch over and protect them from the world's evils. So, I prayed. My God was with them, watching over them, guarding them. When they got married and left home, I continued to pray. And today, I am still praying for them, and not only for them but also for my grandchildren. The world has not become a better place. Evil lies everywhere. We need to watch in prayer. We need to strive together in prayer. We need to be strong in prayer! The Apostle Paul, as he examines his life in Philippians 4, states this powerful conclusion:

> "Not that I speak in respect of want: **for I have learned**, in whatsoever state I am, therewith to be content. I know both how to be abased, and I know how to abound: every where and in all things I am instructed both to be full and to be hungry, both to abound and to suffer need. **I can do all things through Christ which strengtheneth me.**" *Philippians 4:11-13*

The Apostle Paul learned this through experience. Through praying[80] and a spiritual walk close to the Lord, he experienced a life filled with Christ. He found that a living relationship with his Savior filled his life with power and grace. The Apostle Paul found real joy, comfort in tribulation, and strength to continue despite adversity. He proved in his life that Christ's grace was sufficient. He experienced the reality of a prayer-filled life, a closeness to Christ that was palpable. The Apostle Paul experienced the God who answers all prayers and never forsakes or fails. He had personally experienced the hand of the Lord, who works all things together for good to them that love God, to those who are called according to His purpose. He saw the hand of God in his own life and in the lives of those he ministered to. The God of peace was with him, and he experienced it. He lived the truth that the more he prayed, the more he experienced God's hand in his life. So, he can conclude nothing else but what he declares, "I can do all things through Christ which strengtheneth me."

Listen to the words of the Apostle Paul as he shares his trials and tribulations in sharing the gospel.

> "Are they ministers of Christ? (I speak as a fool) I am more; in labours more abundant, in stripes above measure, in prisons more frequent, in deaths oft. Of the Jews five times received I forty stripes save one. Thrice was I beaten with rods, once was I stoned, thrice I suffered shipwreck, a night and a day I have been in the deep; In journeyings often, in perils of waters, in perils of robbers, in perils by mine own countrymen, in perils by the heathen, in perils in the city, in perils in the wilderness, in perils in the sea, in perils among false brethren; In weariness and painfulness, in watchings often, in hunger and thirst, in fastings often, in cold and nakedness." *2 Corinthians 11:23-27*

> "In Damascus the governor under Aretas the king kept the city of the Damascenes with a garrison, desirous to apprehend me: And through a window in a basket was I let down by the wall, and escaped his hands." *2 Corinthians 11:32-33*

But note just a few verses later, the Apostle Paul's attitude concerning the physical reality of those spiritual attacks. He penned these words: "And He" (Christ) "said unto me, My grace is sufficient for thee: for my strength is made perfect in weakness. Most gladly therefore will I rather glory in my infirmities, that the power of Christ may rest upon me. Therefore, I take pleasure in infirmities, in reproaches, in necessities, in persecutions, in distresses for Christ's sake: for when I am weak, then am I strong."[81]

The adversary and his children, fitted for wrath, are real and daunting. Paul knew he needed help in preaching the Word and facing the tricky situations and people that would confront him. He requested the Colossians pray for him with these words: "Continue in prayer, and watch in the same with thanksgiving; Withal praying also for us, that God would open unto us a door of utterance, to speak the mystery of Christ, for which I am also in bonds: That I may make it manifest, as I ought to speak."[82] Paul needed boldness and open doors to preach the gospel. I suspect we need the same.

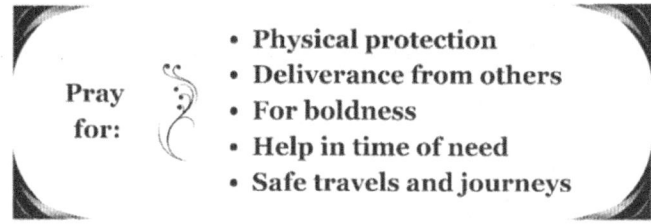

Pray for:
- Physical protection
- Deliverance from others
- For boldness
- Help in time of need
- Safe travels and journeys

Pray Without Ceasing and with Thankful Expectation.

God's Word challenges the believer to be in continuous prayer, a realization of His presence with us at all times. We are called to have an effortless and natural conversation with Him, as one would with someone they know pretty well. The Word of God clearly commands each of us:

to pray without ceasing	– 1 Thessalonians 5:17
to continue in prayer	– Colossians 4:2
to pray always	– 2 Thessalonians 1:11
to be instant in prayer	– Romans 12:12
to be careful for nothing	– Philippians 4:6
in everything by prayer	– Philippians 4:6
in everything give thanks	– 1 Thessalonians 5:18
to pray everywhere	– 1 Timothy 2:8

Our God wants us to "first of all" come to Him, to lean on Him, to call on Him, because He loves us, and we are His dear children. It is His very nature to give and to give bountifully. Ephesians 3:20 explodes with this truth: "Now unto him that is able to do exceeding abundantly above all that we ask or think, according to the power that worketh in us." It is His nature to give because He is love. When we come to Him in prayer, He can show His love to us in a powerful way. He is for us and chooses to answer us each time we call on Him. He is a mighty God.

Additionally, God desires that we come to Him expectantly, knowing that He can do all things. He wants us to go to Him in faith. Hebrews 11:6 says, "But without faith it is impossible to please him: for he that cometh to God must believe that he is, and that he is a rewarder of them that diligently seek him." God wants you to have faith when you pray, knowing He can do whatever you ask. You can be assured that God "works all things together for good to them that love God, to them that are called according to His purpose." So, we can pray expectantly, waiting and watching for what God will do. We can rest in the hope that we have in Him. And we each can have a heart of gratitude and thanksgiving because God answers our prayers and requests immediately upon our feeble formation and utterance of the words from our hearts to Him. So, we can always be thankful knowing that He has answered our prayers perfectly.

Furthermore, in the Book of Hebrews, God the Holy Spirit says, "Come boldly unto the throne of grace." Not because we have some upper hand on God or He owes us something, but because He has given us access through His Son, the Lord Jesus Christ. As His children, we can come to Him with anything on our hearts. "Boldly" implies that the entrance is without fear, rejection, or harm. "Boldly" further indicates expectation. You can confidently expect that God will answer you. And that answer is always good. What a privilege to have such access to the creator of the Universe and all flesh.

Pray
- **Continuously and without ceasing**
- **With thanksgiving**
- **Expectantly**
- **Boldly by faith**

How Long Do We Pray for a Specific Situation or Request? Is it Wrong to Keep Praying for the Same Thing Repeatedly?

Since our God hears all our prayers and works on them right at the start, is it wrong to continue praying for a situation you have already prayed about? Is it a lack of faith or trust to do so? Shouldn't I give my requests to God, let go of them, and pray about other things now? I have had individuals over the years present me with similar thoughts, wondering if they were wrong to keep praying about the same things over and over again. God's Word gives us a clear picture of how long we should pray about specific things. Let's see what it has to say.

Personal Requests:

First, let us look at our requests to God. We will examine three examples from Scripture where individuals went to God for a particular request.

82 **Praying to a Mighty God**

In 2 Samuel 12:15-23, we have the heartbreaking account of the prophet Nathan coming to David with God's judgment for his sin. David had taken another man's wife to bed, and she became pregnant. To cover up his sin, he had the man killed in battle. Nathan informs David that his son born in this union would die because of his sin.

> "And Nathan departed unto his house. And the LORD struck the child that Uriah's wife bare unto David, and it was very sick. David therefore besought God for the child; and David fasted, and went in, and lay all night upon the earth. And the elders of his house arose, and went to him, to raise him up from the earth: but he would not, neither did he eat bread with them. And it came to pass on the seventh day, that the child died. And the servants of David feared to tell him that the child was dead: for they said, Behold, while the child was yet alive, we spake unto him, and he would not hearken unto our voice: how will he then vex himself, if we tell him that the child is dead? But when David saw that his servants whispered, David perceived that the child was dead: therefore David said unto his servants, Is the child dead? And they said, He is dead. Then David arose from the earth, and washed, and anointed himself, and changed his apparel, and came into the house of the LORD, and worshipped: then he came to his own house; and when he required, they set bread before him, and he did eat. Then said his servants unto him, What thing is this that thou hast done? thou didst fast and weep for the child, while it was alive; but when the child was dead, thou didst rise and eat bread. And he said, While the child was yet alive, I fasted and wept: for I said, Who can tell whether GOD will be gracious to me, that the child may live? But now he is dead, wherefore should I fast? can I bring him back again? I shall go to him, but he shall not return to me." *2 Samuel 12:15-23*

David, a man after God's own heart, had sinned greatly and paid a harsh penalty - the death of his son. But while his son was alive, David prayed continuously for seven days and nights. And then, when his son died, he stopped praying and then worshipped God.

So, how long did David pray? He prayed until he had an answer. When his son died, it was clear what God's answer was. So, he stopped praying about it, and he worshipped God. He had sinned against God, and even though the judgment was harsh, he knew he was wrong and now worshipped God.

In 2 Corinthians 12, the Apostle Paul prays to have a thorn in the flesh removed from his life. He prayed three times. Why didn't he pray more times? The reason is that God gave Paul a clear answer after three. In this case, God told Paul directly that His grace was sufficient and that the thorn in the flesh was needful for him. So, Paul chose to glory in the difficult things, knowing that they were there for him, for when he was weak, then he was truly strong.

> "And lest I should be exalted above measure through the abundance of the revelations, there was given to me a thorn in the flesh, the messenger of Satan to buffet me, lest I should be exalted above measure. For this thing I besought the Lord thrice, that it might depart from me. And he said unto me, My grace is sufficient for thee: for my strength is made perfect in weakness. Most gladly therefore will I rather glory in my infirmities, that the power of Christ may rest upon me. Therefore I take pleasure in infirmities, in reproaches, in necessities, in persecutions, in distresses for Christ's sake: for when I am weak, then am I strong." *2 Corinthians 12:7-10*

In Daniel 10, the prophet Daniel is wondering about the hard things that will happen to Israel, his nation, so he prays to God. For 21 days, Daniel prayed. An angel appears to him and explains that his words were heard at the very beginning of his prayer and that he (the angel) was sent to speak with Daniel, but he was delayed. If you read on, you will see that Daniel stopped praying. Why? He received a clear answer from God concerning what he was praying about by a visit from an angel.

> "In those days Daniel was mourning three full weeks. I ate no pleasant bread, neither came flesh nor wine in my mouth, neither did I anoint myself at all, till three whole weeks were fulfilled." *Daniel 10:2-3*

> "And he said unto me, O Daniel, a man greatly beloved, understand the words that I speak unto thee, and stand upright: for unto thee am I now sent. And when he had spoken this word unto me, I stood trembling. Then said he unto me, Fear not, Daniel: for from the first day that thou didst set thine heart to understand, and to chasten thyself before thy God, thy words were heard, and I am come for thy words." *Daniel 10:11-12*

From these three passages, we can conclude that you pray until you receive a clear answer. That makes sense. That is precisely what each of these men of God did. Notice that God did not reprimand them for continuing to pray, but Scripture honors them by sharing their faithfulness to continue in prayer until an answer was received. They stopped praying at that point. It is evident as to why, as they had their answer. It is like the expression that many say, "I found it in the last place I looked." The reasoning is apparent: why would you keep looking for something after you found it?

Another truth we find here is that they worshipped and glorified God after receiving their answer—an answer different from what they had wanted. David's son died, Paul's thorn remained, and Daniel's people would still experience extremely tough times ahead. They knew that our God is good even when the answer was hard. They understood who God is and honored Him regardless of the response they received. I think of Job in Job 1:20-22; after receiving wave upon wave of grief-laden news, he fell down and worshipped God.

> "Then Job arose, and rent his mantle, and shaved his head, and fell down upon the ground, and worshipped, And said, Naked came I out of my mother's womb, and naked shall I return thither: the LORD gave, and the LORD hath taken away; blessed be the name of the LORD. In all this Job sinned not, nor charged God foolishly." *Job 1:20-22*

No Clear Answer:

Okay, what if you do not receive a clear answer from God? Today, we do not receive spoken responses from the Lord, nor do we experience visions, dreams, or angel visits. Such things were in operation until the Word of God was completed.[83] We have God's Holy Word to study and read, which the Holy Spirit uses to build us up. And we have prayer to talk to God. So, with no clear answer, how long do you pray?

Have you ever experienced a situation in your life where there was a burden that you prayed about all the time, and then one day, you noticed that you were no longer praying about it? It fell off your 'care' list of things to pray about. What happened to it? You did not get an answer, but it no longer burdens you. Somehow, you have peace concerning what once burdened you. In Philippians 4, we find this familiar passage,

> "Be careful for nothing; but in everything by prayer and supplication with thanksgiving let your requests be made known unto God. And the peace of God, which passeth all

understanding, shall keep your hearts and minds through Christ Jesus." *Philippians 4:6-7*

God promises the peace of God to all who bring everything to Him. God has answered what you prayed about, has taken possession of it, and it has become sanctified to Him. You cannot see the answer, but He has given you peace. Peace shows us that He has it under control, and it is no longer our concern. This is the peace of God that guards and protects our hearts and minds.

Years ago, I was praying about a complex and demanding situation with a friend, which seemed to consume my prayer life. Whenever I went to the throne of grace, this situation dominated my prayer time. I know that I prayed for months concerning it. And then, one day, I noticed that I was no longer praying or concerned about it. The Lord had given me peace! I remember praying to the Lord and saying Thank you, Lord. I know that you have it. Thank you for taking it. Your way is best. I had my clear answer, and I thanked Him, praised Him, and worshipped. The burden was gone, and the Lord had answered my prayer. It was in His control, in His timing.

Thus, we pray until we have peace, until what we prayed about is no longer a concern. Peace determines how long we should pray about something. God says to be careful for nothing, but in everything, pray. When you have peace, you are no longer full of care for those things. God has it; it is His. It is sanctified unto Him, and what you had prayed about is now His personal possession, and He is working on it. You can be sure that the Lord has answered your prayer, even if you cannot see the answer, because you have peace. He has taken ownership of the burden. So, we can be content in knowing that our mighty God has it, and there is nothing more to do but say thank you, Lord.

Thanksgiving, Praise, Worship, and Watchings:

As you know, prayer is not just making personal requests to God for our needs and concerns. It is about praising and worshipping our God and bringing thanksgiving to Him. Prayer is also about watching over those in your life for their protection and good.

> "Continue in prayer, and watch in the same with thanksgiving; Withal praying also for us, that God would open unto us a door

of utterance, to speak the mystery of Christ, for which I am also in bonds:" *Colossians 4:2-3*

"Praying always with all prayer and supplication in the Spirit, and watching thereunto with all perseverance and supplication for all saints;" *Ephesians 6:18*

"Giving thanks always for all things unto God and the Father in the name of our Lord Jesus Christ;" *Ephesians 5:20*

"And whatsoever ye do in word or deed, do all in the name of the Lord Jesus, giving thanks to God and the Father by him." *Colossians 3:17*

How long should we praise, worship, and give thanks to the Lord our God? Well, that is easy: forever. We should continually be thankful to our God, and our prayer to God should express that thanksgiving. Our giving of thanks gives Him praise and worships Him. He is worthy, and He is answering all our prayers. He is God. And when we go to Him, we need to recognize that is who He is.

The Scriptures call us to also continue in prayer and to watch in prayer for others. How long should we watch over others the Lord has brought into our lives? Again, the answer is quite simple. We pray for them as long as they are in your life. We are to watch with all perseverance and supplication for all saints. Therefore, when watching over others in prayer, we should do so continually. We are praying for their safety, spiritual growth, God's blessing and peace, and for God's hand to be in their lives, as well as for specific requests.

The Bible states that Job faithfully watched over his family's spiritual life and continually interceded on their behalf to God.[84] It is just as true today that we should constantly watch in prayer over our families, friends, coworkers, neighbors, church family, and others who enter our lives.

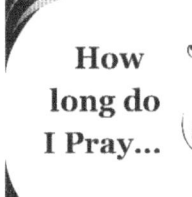

How long do I Pray...
- for requests? - Until you get a clear answer or have peace
- with thanksgiving, praise, and worship to God? - Forever
- for others? - As long as they are in your life

What, When, and Whom Should We Pray For?

Chapter 6 Reference List

[58] Philippians 4:6,7
[59] Romans 8:23
[60] Ephesians 6:18
[61] Everyone, all mankind
[62] Romans 8:31
[63] I Samuel 17:29
[64] I Timothy 4:12
[65] II Chronicles 32:8
[66] 1 Timothy 2:1-2
[67] Proverbs 1:7
[68] Romans 12:2
[69] 2 Timothy 2:21 If a man therefore purge himself from these, he shall be a vessel unto honour, sanctified, and meet for the master's use, and prepared unto every good work.
[70] Galatians 5:22-23
[71] Philippians 4:11-12
[72] Philippians 4:6-7
[73] Joshua 1:1-9
[74] Romans 8:31
[75] Jeremiah 32:27
[76] 2 Timothy 4:14-15
[77] Colossians 4:2
[78] Ephesians 5:14-16
[79] Ephesians 6:18
[80] Philippians 4:7-10
[81] 2 Corinthians 12:9-10
[82] Colossians 4:2-4
[83] Colossians 1:24-27; I Corinthians 13:8-13
[84] Job 1:5

Chapter 7
How Do I Pray?

Prayer: No Magical Set of Words

There is no magical set of words or prescription for prayer in order to have God listen to your prayer. If you are a believer, you have access, you have God's ear, and you have His heart. In Scripture, we find the thrilling account of Elijah contesting with the 450 prophets of Baal and the 400 prophets of the grove, as described in 1 Kings 18:17-40. Scripture highlights that God answers His children's prayers because of our relationship with Him. It further highlights that we do not "have to get God's attention" - He is always listening and responding. No amount of intricate works, incantations, yelling, crying, or wild antics impresses God. **God answers our call because of a relationship.** Elijah had a relationship with the one true God; the 850 false prophets did not and had little hope, and Elijah knew that.

> "So Ahab sent unto all the children of Israel, and gathered the prophets together unto mount Carmel. And Elijah came unto all the people, and said, How long halt ye between two opinions? if the LORD be God, follow him: but if Baal, then follow him." *1 Kings 18:20-21*

In the extended passage, 1 Kings 18:17-40, a contest is set up where Elijah will pray to his God, and the false prophets will pray to their gods for an answer of fire to come down from heaven and burn up the sacrifice on the altar. The result of the contest will decide who is God for the people. The prophets of Baal cry unto their gods from morning until noon, crying out for Baal to hear them. But there is no answer. Elijah mocks them (it is pretty interesting), and they get even more animated, leaping upon the altar, crying aloud, and cutting themselves with knives and lancets until the blood gushes out. This they did until the evening. And still no response from their gods.

> "And they cried aloud, and cut themselves after their manner with knives and lancets, till the blood gushed out upon them. And it came to pass, when midday was past, and they prophesied until the time of the offering of the evening sacrifice, that there was neither voice, nor any to answer, nor any that regarded." *1 Kings 18:28-29*

It is now Elijah's turn. Elijah instructs the people to drench the sacrifice in water three times until it is saturated and lying in the water.

> "And it came to pass at the time of the offering of the evening sacrifice, that Elijah the prophet came near, and said, LORD God of Abraham, Isaac, and of Israel, let it be known this day that thou art God in Israel, and that I am thy servant, and that I have done all these things at thy word. Hear me, O LORD, hear me, that this people may know that thou art the LORD God, and that thou hast turned their heart back again. Then the fire of the LORD fell, and consumed the burnt sacrifice, and the wood, and the stones, and the dust, and licked up the water that was in the trench. And when all the people saw it, they fell on their faces: and they said, The LORD, he is the God; the LORD, he is the God." *1 Kings 18:36-38*

Elijah did not have to do anything spectacular, but just spoke to God, and the fire came down. He had a relationship with God, and God heard and responded. The prophets of Baal…well, they met their demise without a whimper from their gods.

Prayer: It is Not a Repetition of Words

It has never been true that praying some set of words like a prescription or incantation gets a set result or even honors God. The Lord Jesus Christ clearly says that vain repetition is what the heathen do and is not honoring to God.

> "But when ye pray, use not vain repetitions, as the heathen do: for they think that they shall be heard for their much speaking."
> *Matthew 6:7*

Repeating the same mantra, prayer, or chant without the heart and purposeful intention of the praying individual does not impress God. Prayer is a heartfelt pouring out of yourself to God for His intervention or to glorify Him. Once, about 20 years ago, while attending an academic dinner function, I was asked to pray for the meal. When I finished praying, the person beside me, whom I knew well, said quietly, "John, you prayed just like you were talking to God." I smiled and said to her, "Well, yes, I did, didn't I? So, who do you talk to when you pray, then?" What she heard from me was far different than her own experience. This person had grown up where prayers were formalized, repeated, sometimes written and read, but seldom a personal conversation with a personal God.

Caution: This May Trouble You

This next section could be a touchy subject for some, so bear with me for a moment. If what I am about to share troubles you, take a moment to pray, let the scriptures speak, and see whether what is being shared here is true. Sometimes, things that we have always assumed were true, in reality, are not. The Earth was once believed to be flat by some of the most renowned thinkers of the past. The Sun was thought to rotate around the Earth. For nearly two thousand years, it was thought that heavier objects would hit the ground sooner than lighter objects if dropped simultaneously from the same height. The reality is that both will hit the ground simultaneously. Who knew? Try it for yourself. Drop a book or a brick alongside a pen or a golf ball from the same height. They will hit the ground at the same time. Maybe this is a new truth for you. There are always things to learn or discover, even in scripture. Some false understandings about the world were passed on without question for many generations. They were absolute facts until, eventually, the truth won out. With that preamble, consider what the scriptures say about the following.

Let us consider the instructions given by the Lord Jesus Christ concerning the Lord's Prayer. Interestingly, many individuals recite the

Lord's Prayer from memory, as found in Matthew, shown below, or in Luke. For many, no thoughtful understanding of what is being prayed seems evident as it is repeated week after week, again and again. Of course, this prayer is a perfect prayer model since the Lord said to pray after this manner. But it is a model! Not to be repeated verbatim and ad infinitum throughout the centuries, but to guide individuals of the Nation of Israel in their specific prayer needs during the Tribulation, a time of great calamity that they, as a nation, will face.[85][86][87]

>"But thou, when thou prayest, enter into thy closet, and when thou hast **shut thy door, pray to thy Father which is in secret**; and thy Father which seeth in secret shall reward thee openly. **But when ye pray, use not vain repetitions, as the heathen do**: for they think that they shall be heard for their much speaking. Be not ye therefore like unto them: for your Father knoweth what things ye have need of, before ye ask him. **After this manner therefore pray ye**: Our Father which art in heaven, Hallowed be thy name. Thy kingdom come. Thy will be done in earth, as it is in heaven. Give us this day our daily bread. And forgive us our debts, as we forgive our debtors. And lead us not into temptation, but deliver us from evil: For thine is the kingdom, and the power, and the glory, forever. Amen."
>*Matthew 6:6-13*

It is interesting that the Lord Jesus Christ, just two verses earlier in Matthew 6:7, commands, "But when ye pray, use not vain repetitions, as the heathen do:" The reason is that prayer is personal and part of a relationship with the Creator of everything, and repetition removes that engagement. Yet, countless individuals are inconsistent with the handling of God's Word here, reciting this prayer with little thought. As Matthew 6:6 reveals, prayer is personal and much like a conversation with the Father. It is not a public demonstration or an act or play. Vain repetitions do not honor our God. Yet the vast majority who speak this prayer are doing just that, repetition without any personal interaction with God. Also, the Lord did not say to recite this prayer as is, but He said, "after this manner." This means that those to whom this is written should pray in the same style and with a similar range of concerns. Leaning on the Lord is critical to every believer, and the Lord Jesus Christ is instructing the Jewish Christian believers on how to survive in tough times, the Tribulation.

If I have stepped on anyone's toes, I apologize; however, consider what the Word of God says in this context. This is not a set of words that the

Lord intended to be repeated endlessly throughout time. Instead, it is a model or roadmap for the requests to God made by His children, Israel, in the difficult days ahead, during the tribulation. This is the next tick on Israel's prophetic clock of events. An overview is given by the Lord in some detail in Matthew 24 and 25.

The Prayer of Jabez

In the book of 1 Chronicles, we find the "prayer of Jabez," which some have taken as a unique set of words that you can or should pray, and God will answer you with a resounding "Yes," since God granted the request of Jabez. This is an improper handling of the Word of God, which leads to error and disappointment. Those who teach a "prosperity gospel" tend to espouse this thinking. Ignoring the context and failing to recognize the dispensational nature of God's Word can lead to ruined lives and a stunted Christian walk. Read the passage closely.

> "And Jabez was more honourable than his brethren: and his mother called his name Jabez, saying, Because I bare him with sorrow. And Jabez called on the God of Israel, saying, Oh that thou wouldest bless me indeed, and enlarge my coast, and that thine
>
> hand might be with me, and that thou wouldest keep me from evil, that it may not grieve me! And God granted him that which he requested." *1 Chronicles 4:9-10*

So why did God grant Jabez his request? Well, it clearly says that he was more honorable than his brethren. Jabez was a vessel of honor who had a relationship with his God. It is always about the relationship and not some mystical incantation or repetition of words. God loves His children. As for why God granted Jabez's request, it is because He could. Now, that may seem to be a strange answer, but it is a correct one. Jabez was where he needed to be in his relationship with God, and God was able to say yes to his requests. We discussed earlier that God answers every prayer, just not always with a yes. We will discuss the mechanics of how God answers every prayer and how He chooses the answer to our prayer in a later chapter. Suffice it now to understand that God said yes to Jabez's prayer because He could.

I do not believe, as some, that Jabez was focused solely on personal physical gain when he prayed. God accounted Jabez as honorable, so his prayer had to go beyond himself with the intention of helping others.

Otherwise, it was a selfish prayer. Throughout God's Word, God has blessed individuals so that they might be a blessing to others. He has given to individuals so that they might give to others, and He has comforted individuals so that they might be of comfort to others, and so on. As members of the Body of Christ today, we all have unique gifts and callings, yet they are all for the benefit of the Body, for the sake of others.[88]

An Application of Jabez's Prayer

I think it is necessary to mention that Jabez's prayer covers four areas of life that we all should be praying about, even today in the dispensation of the Grace of God. Jabez prayed for the following:

- That thou wouldest bless me indeed
- Enlarge my coast
- That thine hand might be with me
- That thou wouldest keep me from evil, that it may not grieve me

That thou wouldest bless me indeed:

To bless means to show favor or to wish well, and Jabez went to God seeking blessings, which are good things and favor. Today, in the Dispensation of Grace, we are positionally in Christ and have all spiritual blessings in heavenly places.[89] We stand in grace, literally in God's blessings and favor. All members of the Body are equally blessed in our standing before God. We are so blessed. However, experientially, we can pray for good things and blessings to be part of our daily life. We can also pray to be a blessing to others.

Our prayer life should be balanced, praying for our spiritual situation and the spiritual situation of others, as well as our experiential relationship with God. We are not promised physical blessings in this life, but God does bless us in physical ways. The air we breathe and the food we eat are all from our God, so we say thanks and bless His name for all He has given us. So, feel free to ask God to bless you indeed. Our God is a giver. "He that spared not his own Son, but delivered him up for us all, how shall he not with him also freely give us all things?"[90] There is nothing good that our God will hold back from His children. God is good. This is not the wishes and whims of whiny children, but this good has lasting and eternal value for each of us.

> "Every man according as he purposeth in his heart, so let him give; not grudgingly, or of necessity: for God loveth a cheerful

giver. And God is able to make all grace abound toward you; that ye, always having all sufficiency in all things, may abound to every good work:" *2 Corinthians 9:7-8*

"By whom also we have access by faith into this grace wherein we stand, and rejoice in hope of the glory of God." *Romans 5:2*

"And we know that all things work together for good to them that love God, to them who are the called according to his purpose." *Romans 8:28*

"Now thanks be unto God, which always causeth us to triumph in Christ, and maketh manifest the savour of his knowledge by us in every place." *2 Corinthians 2:14*

Enlarge my coast:

Jabez prayed to enlarge his coast. This is a prayer to increase what Jabez had or a request for more of his reach and impact. The question of "Is it okay to pray for more?" is examined in more detail in the next section, so we will discuss this there.

That thine hand might be with me:

Jabez prayed that God's hand would be with him. This means that God would be for him and not against him. He was praying that good things from God would come his way, not hard things. Jabez was an honorable man and understood that being under the Mosaic Law, God's hand would be with him if he did things God's way as required by the Law. So Jabez was, in essence, praying, Lord, keep me faithful to you. This is very much like what God told Joshua in the first chapter of the book of Joshua. God said He would be with Joshua, but Joshua had to allow God's Word to direct his life. Then he would have good success.[91] As God's children, we know today that we are in Christ and that nothing can separate us from Him and His love. This is our standing. Nothing can change that. Our Lord is for us and working in us to do His will. We can experience God's hand in our lives just as Paul did when all others forsook him.

> "Notwithstanding the Lord stood with me, and strengthened me; that by me the preaching might be fully known, and that all the Gentiles might hear: and I was delivered out of the mouth of the lion. And the Lord shall deliver me from every evil work, and will preserve me unto his heavenly kingdom: to whom be glory for ever and ever. Amen." *2 Timothy 4:17-18*

In Philippians, we learn that we can experience God's peace when we are careful for nothing but in everything pray.

> "Be careful for nothing; but in every thing by prayer and supplication with thanksgiving let your requests be made known unto God. **And the peace of God, which passeth all understanding, shall keep your hearts and minds through Christ Jesus."** *Philippians 4:6-7*

But also notice this fantastic truth: we can experience the God of peace. The one who brings peace.

> "Finally, brethren, whatsoever things are true, whatsoever things are honest, whatsoever things are just, whatsoever things are pure, whatsoever things are lovely, whatsoever things are of good report; if there be any virtue, and if there be any praise, think on these things. Those things, which ye have both learned, and received, and heard, and seen in me, do: **and the God of peace shall be with you."** *Philippians 4:8-9*

It is already true that God is with us. The entire triune God has taken up residence in us. We are the temple of God today. That is positional truth. What Philippians 4:8-9 teaches is similar to what God told Joshua. God said He would be with Joshua, but he needed to follow God's leading through His Word. Colossians 3:16 says to let the Word of Christ dwell in you richly. That is what is being said here. Think about these things, meditate and ponder all of these godly things, and then choose to do them. Do not turn to the left or turn to the right. Refrain from doing things your way. Choose the best way, God's way.

The result will be a knowledge that is real and palpable; the God of peace shall be with you. You will see Him at work in you and know He is with you every step of your day. Like the Apostle Paul, you can be assured that the Lord stands with you and strengthens you, even during difficult times. Additionally, others can tell that the Lord is with you. You do not have an aura around you or something strange, but the things you do as you serve the Lord seem to be blessed. They bear good fruit. You see, God is with you. The life of Joseph can provide further insight into this if you wish to explore these references.[92]

Thus, pray that you stay faithful to God and walk in His ways, not your flesh. Pray that others remain true to God. Let us pray that we each take God's Word into our hearts and then do it and live it. Then God's hand will be with you. The God of peace shall be with you. You will know that

God is with you. "Faith is the substance of things hoped for, the evidence of things not seen."[93]

That thou wouldest keep me from evil, that it may not grieve me:

Jabez prayed that God would keep[94] him from evil and that it might not grieve him. Three principal evils or adversaries are working against the child of God, seeking to destroy you. The Devil, the world, and our flesh. This was also true in Jabez's day. Jabez was praying for protection from all of them. Prayer is that spiritual weapon that can enable victory in battles with the Devil and the world system he devised. The Word of God defends us and protects us. But when we pray, we can gain victories for the cause of Christ, redeeming the time because the days are evil.

The remaining aspect of evil would be his sinful flesh. In this case, he was praying to God to help him have victory over his flesh so that he would not have to suffer the consequences of sin. Jabez was living under the Mosaic Law, which was a rigid schoolmaster. If individuals under the Law sinned, they suffered physical effects, a byproduct of the curses of the Law. Jabez was praying that God would keep him pure so that he would not suffer the consequences of the law.

As for us today, there are no curses to contend with, but our old nature —the flesh—is no less real. Even though our old man was crucified with Christ that we henceforth should not serve sin,[95] the old man remains and works against our new man, our new life in Christ.[96] We need the Lord to help us stay strong through the temptations that come our way, which allure the flesh. But we, as members of the body of Christ, have been given the Holy Spirit, who convicts us, strengthens us, and empowers us when our flesh rises up. "Walk in the Spirit, and ye shall not fulfill the lust of the flesh." We have an advantage that Jabez never had: the Holy Spirit. We also have an advocate in the Holy Spirit, and we can pray and find victory over our flesh. We should pray for protection from the flesh, the world, and the Devil for ourselves and others so that we can finish our courses with joy and be those vessels of honor that we each should be for our God.

Is it okay to pray for MORE as Jabez did?

Most of us seem to share the sentiment that we should be satisfied with what is. God's Word also declares that godliness with contentment is great gain.[97] Isn't God's will for my life the situation I am in? Well, that depends. Your situation could be the result of God's hand, but it could also be the result of your flesh, the actions of others, or the Devil. You could be in God's will and exactly where God wants you, a life filled with a godly walk. You could also be out of God's will and living a sinful life. We all have this old sin nature, which was crucified with Christ so that we would not have to serve sin anymore.

> "Knowing this, that our old man is crucified with him, that the body of sin might be destroyed, that henceforth we should not serve sin." *Romans 6:6*

We have a new life in Christ created in true holiness and righteousness. We are not to yield to the flesh, but to the Spirit; as Apostle Paul shares in Romans 7, it is a war, an intense battle. We find victory over the flesh, our sinful nature, when we walk after the Spirit.

> "But I see another law in my members, warring against the law of my mind, and bringing me into captivity to the law of sin which is in my members. O wretched man that I am! who shall deliver me from the body of this death?" *Romans 7:23-24*

> "This I say then, Walk in the Spirit, and ye shall not fulfill the lust of the flesh. For the flesh lusteth against the Spirit, and the Spirit against the flesh: and these are contrary the one to the other: so that ye cannot do the things that ye would." *Galatians 5:16-17*

If your life is on the wrong path, you need a change. Things need to be different. You are not where God wants you to be. You need more of God in your life and less of your flesh. Pray about it and seek the Spirit's leading to a God-honoring life with peace and joy as a regular outpouring of His presence.

So, what if you are on the right path, God is central to your life, and you want to serve and honor God with your days? We all battle with our flesh, but you have found victory on most days. Amen. So, is it okay to pray for more like Jabez?

> "And Jabez called on the God of Israel, saying, Oh that thou wouldest bless me indeed, and enlarge my coast, and that thine hand might be with me, and that thou wouldest keep me from evil, that it may not grieve me! And God granted him that which he requested." *1 Chronicles 4:10*

Jabez had prayed that his coast or boundary would be enlarged. Perhaps to have more resources or riches, but remember, he was more honorable. His less honorable brethren may have had less honorable intentions. Being honorable, Jabez prayed this not for selfish reasons, or God would not have answered his prayer with a yes, so his intentions had to align with God's will. We are not told what his intentions were, but since the Lord granted the request, it fits God's will, heart, intention, and plan. You cannot fool God and hide false intentions from Him.

The question remains: is praying for changes and more in contradiction to "godliness with contentment is great gain?"

> "But godliness with contentment is great gain. For we brought nothing into this world, and it is certain we can carry nothing out. And having food and raiment let us be therewith content."
> *1 Timothy 6:6-8*

Contentment is being satisfied with where God has you and what God is doing in your life. That is, contentment is NOT disputing, complaining, and murmuring against God and what He is doing in your life. God is at work in your life to create a will and ability to serve. We need to trust Him and that He knows what He is doing.

> "For it is God which worketh in you both to will and to do of his good pleasure. Do all things without murmurings and disputings:" *Philippians 2:13-14*

> "Being confident of this very thing, that he which hath begun a good work in you will perform it until the day of Jesus Christ:" *Philippians 1:6*

The "murmurings and disputings" refer to Israel in the wilderness repeatedly complaining to God about their situation. They were where God wanted them then, and He cared for them providentially. Yet, they wanted more because of selfishness, unbelief, and self-desire. They were discontent with where God had them.

However, this does not mean you cannot or should not pray for something different or desire more. Not seeking change, more, or an increase is potentially fatalistic. God's Word commands us to pray without ceasing, to continue instant in prayer, and to be careful for nothing but in everything by prayer and supplication with thanksgiving to make our requests known unto God. These requests and supplications are, by their nature, a desire for changes to the status quo, whether they be spiritual or physical issues. We pray for health issues, for financial stability to pay the bills, for problems at work, for weather changes, for salvation for a loved one, for open doors to preach the gospel, for strength to meet challenges, for deliverance from wicked and evil men, and on and on. These are all changes to what is; we are praying for a change to our present situation.

None of this is wrong or improper in and of itself, and it is even encouraged by our God. Paul repeatedly prayed for increases and gains in the believers' lives. Most were spiritual things, but not all. So, pray for more understanding, more wisdom, greater strength, improved health, increased impact, more open doors, greater opportunities for service, increased boldness, additional resources, and even more financial resources. God knows the intents of your heart. Is it honorable, or is it purely selfish and of the flesh? You cannot fool God and slip one by.

Spiritual growth produces change in our physical walk.

As we mature in our relationship with God, what we pray for will also change. When we were children, our prayers were often driven by immediate needs (or, more likely, wants) that we had. A young boy may have prayed, "Lord, I need that red wagon I saw at the store. Please get me that wagon." This may appear to be a fleshly, selfish prayer, but perhaps it is not. God knows the heart and its intentions. Maybe the young boy wanted the wagon to help his family by allowing him to carry more apples to more homes or markets and sell them to help support his financially struggling family. He loves his family. The request went from physical and fleshly to spiritual and godly just by intention.

Remember, God did not reprimand Paul for praying three times to remove the thorn in the flesh. He was praying for a physical situation in his life. Was Paul being selfish? I am sure that in the Apostle's mind, he thought that if he could get rid of this thorn in the flesh, he could do more for the Lord. But God, in this case, told Paul no, not because it was wrong to pray about it, but because for Paul, it was more needful for him to have that thorn to keep his heart focused on the Lord. So, Paul was content with what God was doing in his life. He gloried in it. Paul knew it was what was best. God's grace is sufficient for all things.[98]

Note the Apostle Paul's practice of praying for more in the following verses. His requests include "abounding" and "the receiving of more." These verses primarily focus on spiritual things that need to be increased, such as abounding in hope, love, and grace. However, there is a significant impact on our lives from the increase of spiritual things; they affect our physical walk in this world.

> "Now the God of hope fill you with all joy and peace in believing, that ye may abound in hope, through the power of the Holy Ghost." *Romans 15:13*

> "And this I pray, that your love may abound yet more and more in knowledge and in all judgment;" *Philippians 1:9*

> "And the Lord make you to increase and abound in love one toward another, and toward all men, even as we do toward you:" *1 Thessalonians 3:12*

> "And God is able to make all grace abound toward you; that ye, always having all sufficiency in all things, may abound to every good work:" *2 Corinthians 9:8*

The reality is that the outworking of the increase and abounding of these spiritual attributes translates into a physical walk that is worthy of the Lord. Hope causes the believer to look to the horizon, heaven, and where our Lord Jesus Christ is seated. The believer is less inclined to physically sin as they focus on the prize of the high calling of God. That is a physical result of a spiritual walk. Furthermore, as the believer abounds in more knowledge, judgment, and love towards others, they make decisions and choices on where to go, how to live, what to buy, and whom to talk to, etc., in more loving ways. These, too, are ultimately physical results.

Our spiritual walk impacts our physical walk in this world. What we wear, where we go, how we live, and the choices we make day by day are physical actions influenced by our spiritual maturity and growth. Notice that as the grace of God abounds in us, we can abound in every good work. Those good works are physical actions manifested in our everyday experience, our walk before God. So, pray for the increase and abounding in these things. However, it is also worth noting that, even though Paul prayed for increases in the spiritual attributes of love, hope, and grace in these verses, he was clear that God could also cause physical things to abound in the believer's life. In Philippians 4:18-19, he shares his love for the Philippian saints.

> "But I have all, and abound: I am full, having received of Epaphroditus the things which were sent from you, an odour of a sweet smell, a sacrifice acceptable, well pleasing to God. But my God shall supply all your need according to his riches in glory by Christ Jesus." *Philippians 4:18-19*

The things sent from the Philippian believers to Paul were physical items. The "all your need" that God supplies, thus, must also include physical needs in addition to the spiritual needs that God meets. God is able to supply all your needs![99]

> "Likewise the Spirit also helpeth our infirmities: for we know not what we should pray for as we ought: but the Spirit itself maketh intercession for us with groanings which cannot be uttered. And he that searcheth the hearts knoweth what is the mind of the Spirit, because he maketh intercession for the saints according to the will of God." *Romans 8:26-27*

A final point concerning praying for physical or spiritual things, which many overlook, is that our prayer life matures over time, at least it should. As we spend time in the Word, we grow in our walk, and our prayer life should also mature. But at every stage in our life, when we pray, as Romans 8:26-27 reveals, God the Holy Spirit intercedes for us with a deep, heartfelt love. We do not know what we should pray for as we ought, but we know we should pray for whatever is on our hearts. The Holy Spirit intercedes according to the will of God and makes our prayer what it ought to be. Therefore, all our prayers reach the throne room of God, perfectly aligned with God's will. So, pray for whatever is on your heart. God is waiting for you to come to Him in prayer. He is a mighty God who can do anything and all things.

Chapter 7 Reference List

[85] Daniel 9:24-27 The 70th week of Daniel is next on Israel's clock.
[86] Matthew 24:3-31; 25:31-46 The Lord describes the Tribulation and Second Coming and the setting up of the Kingdom on Earth.
[87] The Lord's intent here is to instruct individuals in the Nation of Israel on the key issues needing prayer that they will face as the Tribulation approaches. This is still in the future and will occur after the Rapture of the Body of Christ.
[88] I Corinthians 12:12-27
[89] Ephesians 1:3
[90] Romans 8:32
[91] Joshua 1: 3-9
[92] Genesis 39:3; 39:21; 39:23; 41:38; Joshua 1:5-9; I Samuel 3:19; 18:12-14; I Chronicles 11:9
[93] Hebrews 11:1
[94] Guard or protect.

[95] Romans 6:6
[96] Galatians 5:17
[97] I Timothy 6:6
[98] 2 Corinthians 12:7 - 10
[99] Remember, there is a vast difference between our needs and our wants.

Chapter 8
Prayer is a Dispensational Subject

The Dispensational Character of the Word of God

The prayer of Jabez serves as a jumping-off point for discussing the dispensational character of the Word of God and prayer. Those who preach that we should pray this prayer, the prayer of Jabez, "expectantly," are doctrinally in error and decidedly wrong. Taking scripture out of context is a mistake that many make. The prayer of Jabez is **not** a prayer that we are told to recite today expecting that God will answer it as He did Jabez. Nowhere is it even implied to us that we should even think that. It describes a man praying to God and God's response to him. That is it. Perhaps you have never heard of the term dispensation. It is a Biblical word and appears several times in the Apostle Paul's epistles, specifically in the books of Romans through Philemon.

> "If ye have heard of the **dispensation of the grace of God** which is given me to you-ward: How that by revelation he made known unto me the mystery; (as I wrote afore in few words,"
> *Ephesians 3:2-3*

> "For if I do this thing willingly, I have a reward: but if against my will, a **dispensation of the gospel** is committed unto me."
> *1 Corinthians 9:17*

105

> "That in the **dispensation of the fulness of times** he might gather together in one all things in Christ, both which are in heaven, and which are on earth; even in him:" *Ephesians 1:10*

> "Whereof I am made a minister, according to **the dispensation of God which is given to me for you,** to fulfil the Word of God;" *Colossians 1:25*

A dispensation can be thought of as a period of time (although not precisely accurate) in which God has a defined way of interacting with humanity and humanity with God. For instance, God's interaction with mankind before and after Adam sinned vastly differs. Before Adam sinned, there was communion with God. After he sinned, he and Eve were driven from the garden. Further, as we examine the Scriptures, we see how God has interacted with man and how it has changed through the ages. These are the dispensations in scripture.

Today, we live in the dispensation of the Grace of God,[100] sometimes called the age of Grace. All believers today are part of the Body of Christ, and the Lord Jesus Christ is the Head of the Body. The Body is made up of Jews and Gentiles, and God says there is no difference today between them. There is no favored nation. In effect, all are Gentiles today, as there is no national distinction in the Body. Anyone, anywhere, and at any time, can call on the name of the Lord to be saved. We are no longer under the law but under grace. The law has been nailed to the cross, and Grace reigns today. Everywhere and in every direction that we look, we are standing in God's grace. We are saved by grace through faith, and it is grace that motivates us to action.[101] Today, when we pray, because of the work of Jesus Christ on the cross, we can come boldly before the throne of grace with our prayers and supplications. We have full access to the throne of grace and God.

This is a vast change from the previous dispensation, the law. From its beginning in Exodus 24, when God gave Israel the law and its 613 commandments, Israel was God's people, and Gentiles had no hope apart from coming to God through Israel. But things have changed today. It is a new dispensation. Today, we are the Body of Christ! Ephesians says it this way:

> "Wherefore remember, that ye being in time past Gentiles in the flesh, who are called Uncircumcision by that which is called the Circumcision in the flesh made by hands; That at that time ye were without Christ, being aliens from the commonwealth of Israel, and strangers from the covenants of promise, having

no hope, and without God in the world: But now in Christ Jesus ye who sometimes were far off are made nigh by the blood of Christ. For he is our peace, who hath made both one, and hath broken down the middle wall of partition between us; Having abolished in his flesh the enmity, even the law of commandments contained in ordinances; for to make in himself of twain one new man, so making peace; And that he might reconcile both unto God in one body by the cross, having slain the enmity thereby:" *Ephesians 2:11-16*

The law of commandments, the Mosaic Law, has been abolished. Today, God is working in and through the Body of Christ. This change affects how you approach the Bible. Even though the entire Word of God is for us, not all of it is directly to you or me. For example, you are not called to build an ark, a Tabernacle in the wilderness, or sacrifice a lamb for atonement. God's dealings with humanity have changed. This speaks to the dispensational character of God's Word, the Bible. The Scriptures command us today to study God's Word, and that to correctly understand it requires it to be rightly divided.

> "Study to shew thyself approved unto God, a workman that needeth not to be ashamed, rightly dividing the Word of truth."
> *2 Timothy 2:15*

Rightly Dividing is understanding that all of God's Word is for us and is valuable, but only part of it is written directly to us. If this discussion is new to you, take a moment to pray, seeking God's light on this matter. Take your time and examine each point to see whether it is true. No one should take anything on blind faith. Open the Bible and see whether the Scriptures bear out what is being shared here.

The Apostle Paul contends that he is the Apostle of the Gentiles,[102] different from the twelve in calling and message.[103] To him was directly revealed the truth for today, the Dispensation of the Grace of God and, at its core, the Body of Christ.[104] The Apostle Paul is the one who reveals that salvation is a free gift of God through grace, that Christ died for your sins, and that redemption is through the blood of Christ.[105] All individuals saved today are in Christ, part of the Body of Christ, and have a heavenly home.[106] He was also tasked with completing[107] the Word of God we still have today.

The following chart shows a simplified outline of the Dispensational nature of the Word of God. A full description would cause us to lose focus on the purpose of this book, but this should suffice. This simple breakdown of the dispensations will give us the framework to understand why some aspects of prayer we see in the Bible are not for us today. A dispensation is marked by a difference in how God and man interact together. The nature of God never changes: "Jesus Christ is the same

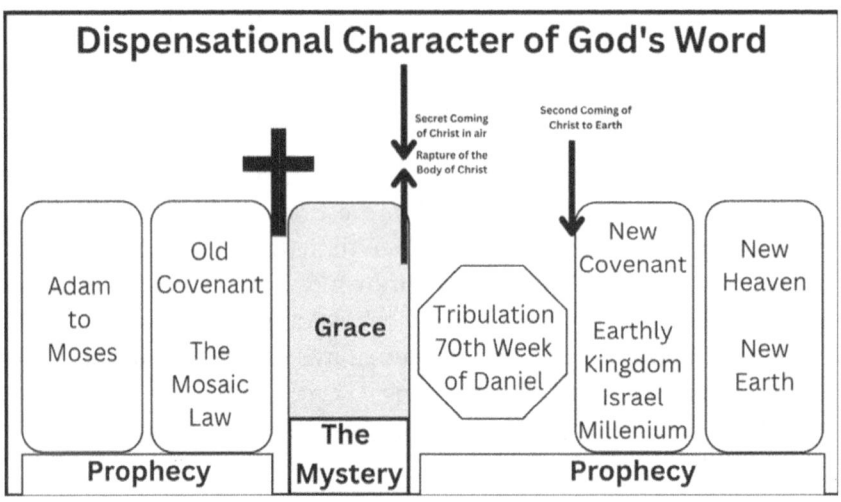

yesterday, today, and forever."[108] However, how God interacts with man has and will change.

I have already described some of the characteristics of this age of Grace we are presently in. It is vastly different than being under the Law. The Apostle Paul in Galatians describes the law as a schoolmaster. When those living in that time got out of line, the schoolmaster would bring the paddle. The Law, which is the Old Covenant, was given to Moses and the Nation of Israel. If Israel kept the whole Law, which included 613 commandments (moral, ceremonial, and social), God promised them blessings upon blessings. However, if they disobeyed the Law and did not keep it, God promised them curses upon curses,[109] the schoolmaster at work. Here is a sampling from Deuteronomy 28.

> "And it shall come to pass, if thou shalt hearken diligently unto the voice of the LORD thy God, to observe and to do all his commandments which I command thee this day, that the LORD thy God will set thee on high above all nations of the earth: **And all these blessings shall come on thee, and overtake thee,** if thou shalt hearken unto the voice of the LORD thy God. Blessed shalt thou be in the city, and blessed shalt thou be in the field. Blessed shall be the fruit of thy body, and the fruit of thy ground, and the fruit of thy cattle, the

increase of thy kine, and the flocks of thy sheep. Blessed shall be thy basket and thy store. Blessed shalt thou be when thou comest in, and blessed shalt thou be when thou goest out." *Deuteronomy 28:1-6*

"But it shall come to pass, if thou wilt not hearken unto the voice of the LORD thy God, to observe to do all his commandments and his statutes which I command thee this day; **that all these curses shall come upon thee, and overtake thee:** Cursed shalt thou be in the city, and cursed shalt thou be in the field. Cursed shall be thy basket and thy store. Cursed shall be the fruit of thy body, and the fruit of thy land, the increase of thy kine, and the flocks of thy sheep. Cursed shalt thou be when thou comest in, and cursed shalt thou be when thou goest out." *Deuteronomy 28:15-19*

Today, we are not under the schoolmaster in the Dispensation of the Grace of God. We are the Body of Christ, and grace reigns today. The Law has been nailed to the cross[110] with its physical blessings and curses. We are told in Galatians that we have received the adoption,[111] meaning we are now treated as adult sons, having liberty and responsibility to live as children of God.[112]

Many believe that God is finished with Israel. However, scripture says otherwise. The book of Romans tells us that Israel (as a nation) is blinded today, for a season, until the fullness of the Gentiles has come in.[113] This is after both the Rapture and the Tribulation.

" For I would not, brethren, that ye should be ignorant of this mystery, lest ye should be wise in your own conceits; **that blindness in part is happened to Israel, until the fulness of the Gentiles be come in**. And so all Israel shall be saved: as it is written, **There shall come out of Sion the Deliverer, and shall turn away ungodliness from Jacob: For this is my covenant unto them, when I shall take away their sins.**" *Romans 11:25-27*

The end of the Age of Grace is marked with a secret coming[114] of the Lord Jesus Christ for the Body of Christ, the Rapture. The Body of Christ is not appointed to wrath[115] and thus will be caught up to heaven before the Tribulation. Israel, however, will not escape the Tribulation. It is the prophesied 70th week of Daniel, which they as a nation must still go through, as all 70 weeks are determined upon Israel and their holy city, Jerusalem. The Tribulation is a time of incredible hardship, misery, and difficulty for all on Earth. Zechariah 13 describes it as a refiner's fire for

Israel. The tribulation ends with Christ's second coming, described in Revelation 19:11-21. He is called Faithful and True, "and in righteousness he doth judge and make war."

After the second coming of Jesus Christ, Israel will be a nation of priests in Christ's earthly kingdom.[116] The prophets of old and the Lord Jesus Christ Himself spoke much about the Kingdom, with Christ telling the 12 to go forth and preach that the Kingdom of Heaven[117] is at hand. The Apostles even asked the Lord Jesus Christ moments before His ascension if He was going to restore the Kingdom to Israel now. "When they therefore were come together, they asked of him, saying, Lord, wilt thou at this time restore again the kingdom to Israel?"[118] God's inability to lie is a fundamental truth of His nature. God's Word promises a coming Kingdom on Earth with Christ as King and with Israel as God's people. Isaiah 9:6-7 is clear: "The **zeal** of the Lord of Hosts will perform this." It is also clearly revealed that this Kingdom is promised to Israel, not the Body of Christ. We, the Body of Christ, are promised the heavenly places with Jesus Christ as our Head.[119] We also have an inheritance, a heavenly inheritance, [120] and we will reign with Christ.

Why does this even matter?

Well, it is essential because each dispensation is like an economy that works under different rules, expectations, and relationships between God and mankind. Let us examine the chart on the Dispensational Character of God's Word more closely by analyzing the dealings and interactions between God and mankind in each of the divisions noted in the chart. To see how God's dealings with man have changed dramatically over time, we will look at two ordinary scenarios or actions that you might have done if you lived during each period or dispensation in the chart.

The two scenarios are: 1) You sinned, 2) You are sick. The following tables, entitled **"What Happens if...,"** provide a brief explanation for each scenario of what is required by God for that dispensation to deal with the situation. I have focused on sharing God's requirements for a child of God in that age, one whom God has made righteous —a saved person who has come to God by faith, like Abraham.[121] Take time to examine each situation, comparing the various rules or expectations in each dispensation.

Please understand that God is not changing; however, because the "rules" in each dispensation have changed, mainly due to the failure of mankind, God is dispensing and dealing out actions and expectations differently. God's dealings with mankind have clearly changed in the past and will again in the future. Spend some time contemplating what you find in these tables.

What Happens If ... A Dispensational Comparison

Dispensation Period	You sinned
Adam to Moses ~2000 years	Even though this was before the Mosaic Law, the Father or Elder of each household acted as a priest for his family and offered the blood of a sinless animal sacrifice to God.
The Law, Old Covenant ~2000 years	Very prescribed in the Law, Old Covenant. You would bring the proper animal sacrifice to the Levite priests, who would prepare it according to the law and offer it according to the Law for your sin. Once a year, the High Priest would enter into the Holy of Holies to offer sacrifices for himself and the people of Israel on the day of Atonement.
Grace -Today- (Romans thru Philemon)	Your sin has already been forgiven and paid for by the blood of Christ and His sinless sacrifice. Sin creates a relational separation between you and God. He is there, with and in you, but because of sin, you struggle to 'experience' Him. Pray, let the Lord know you are sorry. Remember, He died to pay for that sin.
Tribulation Seven years	For Israel, this is a transitional period in which the Old Covenant is ready to vanish away and be replaced by the New Covenant. The curses of the Law are no longer being applied. The spiritual aspects of the New Covenant had begun for Israel, but the physical blessings await the second coming of Christ. The relationship between God and mankind is similar to the Early Acts period, chapters 1 - 8. Sin is forgiven when individuals believe on the Lord Jesus Christ. He is the Messiah, He is alive, and He is the Judge. The Body of Christ is already in Heaven, and do not sin.
New Covenant, Earthly Kingdom, Israel 1000 years	All believers will not sin. They are all righteous—the New Covenant to Israel is fully operational. Christ is reigning as King on Earth and Head of the Body in Heaven. Satan cannot tempt or deceive anyone, as he is in the bottomless pit. His angels are in Hell. Unbelievers can sin; if they do, they are immediately judged and cast into Hell. Death only occurs if a person sins outwardly.
New Heaven, New Earth	All sin has been dealt with, so no one sins. All are righteous. It is perfect.

What Happens If ... A Dispensational Comparison

Dispensation Period	You get sick
Adam to Moses ~2000 years	The Universe is under the bondage of corruption as judgment for Adam's sin. Getting sick is a natural result of a sin-cursed creation. It is appointed unto man once to die. We all fall apart and will return to dust.
The Law, Old Covenant ~2000 years	Under the Law, if a person sinned, there were physical repercussions. God cursed people with sickness, as well as other calamities. The Law was a schoolmaster that spanked you if you disobeyed it. The opposite is also true. If people kept the Law and did not sin, God gave them health, well-being, and other blessings. Read Deuteronomy 28 for details. So, under the law, if you got sick, it meant something was not right in your walk before God, so bring a sacrifice to God for the priests to offer to get you back into right standing with God and get your health back.
Grace -Today- (Romans thru Philemon)	The Law has been nailed to the cross. If you are sick, it is because you are part of a sin-cursed creation. We all have frail natural bodies and are under the bondage of corruption that grips all creation due to Adam's sin. God is for you and loves you. Sickness is a natural result of our bodies wearing out. Physical death follows us all. But we have hope! I Thessalonians 4:16-17; Titus 2:13; I Corinthians 15:51-57
Tribulation Seven years	The Tribulation is unique. Every individual on Earth will have the gospel of the Kingdom shared with them within the first 3 ½ years. Antichrist then sets up the mark of the Beast. Those who take the mark are damned to Hell forever. Just like the period of early Acts, there will be those with spiritual gifts of tongues, healing, knowledge, etc., who will help believers during this time. Since everyone on Earth will hear the gospel of the Kingdom in such a short time, those who spread that truth will have the gift of tongues. No one can buy or sell once the mark is set, so even visiting a hospital cannot be done. There will be some with gifts of healing to help those who are sick, and God will answer the prayers of the elders in a local assembly to heal the sick. God is not judging His Children with curses but with positive chastisement to guide them. Being sick could be a natural result of a sin-cursed creation or God chastening His children to better actions. We, the Body of Christ, are in Heaven with new bodies that do not get sick.
New Covenant, Earthly Kingdom, Israel 1000 years	The curse is lifted. Individuals on Earth only die if they sin outwardly, and that death results from swift and immediate judgment. They will be cast into a lake of fire, Hell. The Body of Christ is in Heaven. There is no sickness or death. We have new bodies.
New Heaven, New Earth	No more death, no more dying, no sickness. It is perfect.

It seems clear that there are profound operational differences between each of these time periods or dispensations. Knowing that God's dealings with mankind are different in each dispensation should help us understand how God responds to prayer might also be different in each dispensation. How God responds to prayer in Grace differs from how He responded when mankind was under the Law. During the Tribulation, there will be incredible pressures upon God's people; as such, God's dealings with man related to prayer will also be different.

It is important to note that there is at least one constant in all dispensations concerning prayer. God answers every prayer for His children and with an answer that is best. The fundamental truths about prayer discussed earlier are valid in every dispensation because they are directly related to the fundamental nature of God. He is love, and He loves His children.

However, God's dealings with man have changed significantly over time, and they will change again in the future. We will see that specific prayer promises are dispensational in nature, being addressed to particular people at a specific time for a specific purpose. Failure to examine them in this light causes confusion and hurt. Don't close your mind if this seems foreign to you. You owe it to yourself to examine what is presented and compare it to God's Word. Let God speak and see whether it be so.

Dispensational Explanation of "Why my Prayers are Not Answered?"

Why are my prayers not answered? Don't I have enough faith? The two of us got together and earnestly prayed, but they were not healed. Doesn't God love me? Doesn't God care? These and other questions have been asked of me through the years. Many have approached me with concerns about their spiritual life, believing that something must be terribly wrong. They were nearly defeated, as some had told them they were living in unbelief. Some were told that God was angry with them. Some even doubted their salvation. Still, others had lost their confidence in the Word of God; their faith was shattered. In almost every case, they were trusting in "prayer promises" from the Word of God. However, their prayer resulted in silence, followed by internal questioning and disbelief that gutted their heart and souls. Let us examine these "prayer promises" from the Word of God and see what is happening here. Are these Christians suffering needlessly in self-doubt and disbelief? Is there another explanation? I have grouped the "prayer promises" in Scripture by type to examine them more easily.

Type 1: Prayer Promises that pledge that if you have Faith, two are gathered together and agree, or whatever you pray for, you shall receive.

> "Jesus answered and said unto them, Verily I say unto you, **If ye have faith, and doubt not,** ye shall not only do this which is done to the fig tree, but also if ye shall say unto this mountain, Be thou removed, and be thou cast into the sea; it shall be done. **And all things, whatsoever ye shall ask in prayer, believing, ye shall receive."** *Matthew 21:21-22*

> "Verily I say unto you, Whatsoever ye shall bind on earth shall be bound in heaven: and whatsoever ye shall loose on earth shall be loosed in heaven. **Again I say unto you, That if two of you shall agree on earth as touching any thing that they shall ask, it shall be done for them of my Father which is in heaven.** For where two or three are gathered together in my name, there am I in the midst of them." *Matthew 18:18-20*

> "For verily I say unto you, **That whosoever shall say unto this mountain, Be thou removed, and be thou cast into the sea; and shall not doubt in his heart, but shall believe that those things which he saith shall come to pass; he shall have whatsoever he saith.** Therefore I say unto you, **What things soever ye desire, when ye pray, believe that ye receive them, and ye shall have them.** And **when ye stand praying, forgive, if ye have ought against any: that your Father also which is in heaven may forgive you your trespasses. But if ye do not forgive, neither will your Father which is in heaven forgive your trespasses."** *Mark 11:23-26*

A summary of the promises found in these verses includes:
- If you have faith and doubt not, you can say, Mountain, be thou removed, and it shall be done. (Matthew 21:21; Mark 11:23)
- All things whatsoever ye shall ask in prayer, believing, ye shall receive. (Matthew 21:22)
- What things soever ye desire, when ye pray, believe that ye receive them, and ye shall have them. (Mark 11:24)

- That if two of you shall agree on earth as touching anything that they shall ask, it shall be done for them of my Father which is in heaven. (Matthew 18:19)

Have you ever claimed these promises? Many have and have come up empty. So why is that the case? Is it a lack of faith or unbelief? The short answer is that it has nothing to do with a lack of faith or unbelief, but rather that these promises do not apply to us today. As has already been shown, all of God's Word is for us, but only part of it is to us.[122] These verses and promises are to another group of individuals, not to us, the Body of Christ. The Lord Jesus Christ was giving specific instructions to the Nation of Israel, who will go through the Tribulation, the next tick on Israel's prophetic clock. Just as at Pentecost, believers will be filled with the Spirit and know God's will. They will be able to pray completely in the will of God, supernaturally empowered by the Spirit. So that whatever they pray for, they will receive because it will absolutely be God's will. It is not so that they can have all their whims, wishes, and wants. The Tribulation will be a time of incredible difficulty and strife, and these promises will enable them to navigate the harshness of the time. The Lord has not given us these promises today, but instead has made a different promise to us. The Lord Jesus Christ is coming back to deliver us, the Body of Christ, from this wrath to come.[123] We are not going through the Tribulation. "For God hath not appointed us to wrath, but to obtain salvation by our Lord Jesus Christ."[124] This is our Blessed Hope!

To further solidify that these promises are not intended for you, consider the promises in the last part of Mark 11:23-26, concerning forgiveness.

> "And when ye stand praying, **forgive,** if ye have ought against any: **that your Father** also which is in **heaven may forgive you your trespasses.** But **if ye do not forgive, neither will your Father** which is in heaven **forgive your trespasses."** *Mark 11:23-26*

These promises say that you must forgive in order for the Father to forgive you, and if you do not forgive, God will not forgive you. Let that sink in. God will NOT forgive you if you do not forgive those in your life. That is a PROMISE, but not a promise to you because this is not true today in the Dispensation of the Grace of God and for the Body of Christ. The truth about forgiveness today is found in verses like these in Apostle Paul's writings, Romans to Philemon.

> "And be ye kind one to another, tenderhearted, **forgiving one another, even as God for Christ's sake hath forgiven you.**"
> *Ephesians 4:32*

> "And you, being dead in your sins and the uncircumcision of your flesh, hath he quickened together with him**, having forgiven you all trespasses;**" *Colossians 2:13*

What is true in Grace today is that we should forgive others because **God has already forgiven us.** This is not conditional, but what we ought to do because of what God has already done for us. This is grace. This is entirely different from what is found in the Gospel of Mark and the other three Gospel letters. The promises and instructions in these epistles are written to someone else, the Nation of Israel. They are not written to the Body of Christ. We can absolutely learn from them, and they are for us in that way, but they are not to us.

It is like they are someone else's mail. If you opened someone else's mail and read it, and that letter stated that you had received a prize or a fine, is it your prize or fine? Of course not. The promised prize or fine was to someone else. These prayer promises and other instructions in the four Gospels are not for the Body of Christ, but for individuals in the tribulation who will need supernatural deliverance and help. Therefore, it is not a matter of how much faith or unbelief someone has; these promises are simply not intended for us, the Body of Christ.

Type 2: Prayer Promises concerning Healing of the Sick; Praying over the sick and anointing them for healing?

The mishandling of Biblical passages concerning healing the sick, or praying over the sick, and anointing them for healing is rampant. The Word of God is often taken out of context, with those doing so failing to rightly divide the Word of truth.[125] Frankly, there are also those who are entirely deceptive and lying in wait to take advantage of desperate individuals with these teachings.

Bear with me as we show a few truths. First, we understand in scripture that the Lord Jesus Christ healed people. From messages taught to us or things we have seen on television or other media, the perception is that Christ healed a blind man, a leper, a mute person, a lame person, raised Lazarus from the dead, cast out some demons, and performed some other miracles. Yet, the facts shared in Scripture state that He miraculously healed many thousands of people. He healed everyone who came to Him. Here are a few verses from the four gospels attesting to this truth:

> "And his fame went throughout all Syria: and **they brought unto him all sick people that were taken with divers diseases and torments, and those which were possessed with devils, and those which were lunatick, and those that had the palsy; and he healed them.**" *Matthew 4:24*

> "And Jesus went about all the cities and villages, teaching in their synagogues, and **preaching the gospel of the kingdom, and healing every sickness and every disease among the people.**" *Matthew 9:35*

> "But when Jesus knew it, he withdrew himself from thence: and **great multitudes followed him, and he healed them all;**" *Matthew 12:15*

> "Now when the sun was setting, **all they that had any sick with divers diseases brought them unto him; and he laid his hands on every one of them, and healed them.**" *Luke 4:40*

Also Matthew 8:16, 14:35-36, Luke 6:17-19. The Lord Jesus Christ healed everyone who came to Him. The Apostle John makes this statement concerning all the miracles that Jesus did, "And there are also many other things which Jesus did, the which, if they should be written every one, I suppose that even the world itself could not contain the books that should be written. Amen."[126] He further states, "And many other signs truly did Jesus in the presence of his disciples, which are not written in this book:"[127].

So why was Christ healing everyone who came to Him? Many had no faith or even an opportunity to share their faith. None of the healed people magically became believers in God. Let us examine Mark 2:1-12 to see some interesting truths. This is the account of the man who was sick, brought to Jesus by his four friends. The crowds were so thick that they cut a hole in the roof and let him down to where Jesus was.

> "And when they could not come nigh unto him for the press, they uncovered the roof where he was: and when they had broken it up, they let down the bed wherein the sick of the palsy lay." *Mark 2:4*

Now, read closely the reaction of Jesus and what He says.

> "When Jesus saw their faith, he said unto the sick of the palsy, Son, thy sins be forgiven thee." *Mark 2:5*

Note: **He saw the faith of the four friends, not the faith of the sick person,** and then He says something interesting, if not strange. He says to the sick man, "Thy sins be forgiven thee." But the man was sick of the palsy, and the Lord said, "Thy sins are forgiven?" That seems strange, doesn't it? Now, there were scribes in the crowd, and they reasoned within themselves that Jesus was speaking blasphemies. "Who can forgive sins but God only?" (Mark 2:6-7) The Lord, knowing their thoughts, responds to the scribes, saying,

> "...Why reason ye these things in your hearts? Whether is it easier to say to the sick of the palsy, Thy sins be forgiven thee; or to say, Arise, and take up thy bed, and walk?" *Mark 2:8-9*

Okay, now, it is essential that you understand what the Lord Jesus Christ is saying here. He is speaking to the scribes that "thy sins be forgiven" is the same as saying "arise, and take up thy bed, and walk." Jesus equates forgiveness of sins to healing. It is precisely what it says. He confirms this in the following two verses of the passage.

> "But that ye may know that the Son of man hath power on earth to forgive sins, (he saith to the sick of the palsy,) I say unto thee, Arise, and take up thy bed, and go thy way into thine house." *Mark 2:10-11*

This is not the same forgiveness of sins that we know of in the Dispensation of the Grace of God, which we live in today. The forgiveness of sins in Grace is about your soul and your eternal destiny. Is it Heaven, or is it Hell? We have redemption through His blood. Salvation is a gift of God by grace through faith, in believing in Christ and what He did for us on the cross.

> "And you, being dead in your sins and the uncircumcision of your flesh, hath he quickened together with him, having forgiven you all trespasses;" *Colossians 2:13*

> "Being justified freely by his grace through the redemption that is in Christ Jesus:" *Romans 3:24*

> "And be ye kind one to another, tenderhearted, forgiving one another, even as God for Christ's sake hath forgiven you." *Ephesians 4:32*

> "In whom we have redemption through his blood, the forgiveness of sins, according to the riches of his grace;" *Ephesians 1:7*

So, what is this forgiveness that the Lord Jesus was sharing with the scribes, which He equates with physical healing? The reality is that Israel, as a nation, was under the curse of the Law as described in Deuteronomy 28. Because they were under the curse of the Law, God had brought sickness and disarray upon them because of their sin. It is the promise God made to them under the Law that if they did not obey, He would bring difficulties upon difficulties. They were under Roman rule, and sickness was everywhere. And when Christ comes on the scene, He begins to heal everyone who comes to Him. He is lifting the curse, forgiving their sin against God and the Old Covenant. The scribes stumbled over the truth, "Who can forgive sins but God?" they asked Jesus Christ, that very God. His healing of everyone shouted that He was the Messiah, Immanuel, God Himself, standing amongst them. Only He could lift the curse since He brought it upon them because of their disobedience and disbelief. His message was that the Kingdom of Heaven is at hand. Christ's Kingdom on Earth with Israel as a Nation of Priests was within reach. They, as a nation, will be righteous, their sins forgiven.

This healing was a physical forgiveness of sins. The penalty of the curse of Deuteronomy 28 was being lifted. Now, elsewhere in the gospels, soul issues of forgiveness are also addressed. For instance, in John 3, the Lord Jesus Christ states that ye must be born again. However, the healings were entirely tied to the curse that the nation was under due to their disobedience. The Earthly Kingdom of Christ is a promise to Israel and the subject of the New Covenant. I encourage you to read Ezekiel 36:22-38, Jeremiah 31:27-34, and Isaiah 9:6-7 to see how God actively judged Israel for disobedience. Because God chooses to redeem His name, He will unconditionally purify Israel, bring them back to the land, and establish His Kingdom.

As Christ carried out His ministry while on the earth, He also gave His disciples the power to heal and lift the curse of the Law. He told them not to go into the way of the Gentiles or Samaritans but to go to the lost sheep of the House of Israel. Israel had strayed, and they were under the curse. To them was promised the Kingdom. So, Jesus Christ sent them to Israel, healing all and lifting the curse on all.

> "And when he had called unto him his twelve disciples, he gave them power against unclean spirits, to cast them out, and to heal all manner of sickness and all manner of disease." *Matthew 10:1*

> "These twelve Jesus sent forth, and commanded them, saying, **Go not into the way of the Gentiles, and into any city of the Samaritans enter ye not**: But go rather to the lost sheep of the house of Israel. And as ye go, preach, saying, **The kingdom of heaven is at hand. Heal the sick, cleanse the lepers, raise the dead, cast out devils: freely ye have received, freely give.**" *Matthew 10:5-8*

After Christ's resurrection, the next event on the prophetic clock was the 70th week of Daniel, the Tribulation. The Lord Jesus Christ, in Matthew 24 and 25, provided detailed information concerning this period, culminating in His return at the Second Coming and establishing His Kingdom.

Before the Lord ascended to Heaven, He commissioned His apostles.

> "And Jesus came and spake unto them, saying, All power is given unto me in heaven and in earth. **Go ye therefore, and teach all nations, baptizing them in the name of the Father, and of the Son, and of the Holy Ghost:** Teaching them to observe all things whatsoever I have commanded you: and, lo, I am with you alway, even unto the end of the world. Amen." *Matthew 28:18-20*

> "And said unto them, Thus it is written, and thus it behoved Christ to suffer, and to rise from the dead the third day: **And that repentance and remission of sins should be preached in his name among all nations, beginning at Jerusalem.** And ye are witnesses of these things. And, behold, I send the promise of my Father upon you: but tarry ye in the city of Jerusalem, until ye be endued with power from on high." *Luke 24:46-49*

> "And he said unto them, Go ye into all the world, and preach the gospel to every creature. **He that believeth and is baptized shall be saved**; but he that believeth not shall be damned. And these signs shall follow them that believe; **In my name shall they cast out devils; they shall speak with new tongues; They shall take up serpents; and if they drink any deadly thing, it shall not hurt them; they shall lay hands on the sick, and they shall recover.** So then after the Lord had spoken unto them, he was received up into heaven, and sat on the right hand of God." *Mark 16:15-19*

The pertinent passages above have some confusing parts bolded. So, what does this mean? Again, the answer is that these are NOT commissions to the Body of Christ to carry out. They are the commission to the twelve and their followers. Israel must go through the Tribulation to get into the Kingdom. It is what Christ was teaching them throughout His earthly ministry. He explicitly told them what would happen to them in Matthew 24 and 25, as well as in Luke 21:7-28. He was preparing them to go through the Tribulation.

Notice what the Apostles asked Him minutes before He ascended into heaven.

> "When they therefore were come together, they asked of him, saying, **Lord, wilt thou at this time restore again the kingdom to Israel?** And he said unto them, It is not for you to know the times or the seasons, which the Father hath put in his own power. **But ye shall receive power, after that the Holy Ghost is come upon you:** and ye shall be witnesses unto me both in Jerusalem, and in all Judaea, and in Samaria, and unto the uttermost part of the earth. And when he had spoken these things, while they beheld, he was taken up; and a cloud received him out of their sight." *Acts 1:6-9*

The Spirit came at Pentecost, and they were given power from on high. From Mark's commission, the signs that would follow those who believed actually happened. The believers in the early part of Acts showed powers. These powers will be needed during the prophetically predicted Tribulation. Believers cannot buy or sell[128] during the last three and a half years of the Tribulation. They will not be able to go to hospitals. Every person on the earth will have the gospel shared with them, people of all languages. Therefore, spiritual gifts such as the gift of tongues, healings, and knowledge will be necessary to fulfill the commission to reach the whole world. As the Lord said, the Apostles manifested great signs and wonders, as seen in Acts 5:12-16.

> "And by the hands of the apostles were many signs and wonders wrought among the people; (and they were all with one accord in Solomon's porch. And of the rest durst no man join himself to them: but the people magnified them. And believers were the more added to the Lord, multitudes both of men and women.) Insomuch that they brought forth the sick into the streets, and laid them on beds and couches, that at the least the shadow of Peter passing by might overshadow some of them. There came also a multitude out of the cities round

about unto Jerusalem, bringing sick folks, and them which were vexed with unclean spirits: and they were healed every one."
Acts 5:12-16

But instead of the Tribulation occurring, God had a secret plan that interrupted what prophecy said was next. The Mystery, the truth for today, the core of which is the Body of Christ, interrupted the prophetic revealed plan.[129] Christ saved Saul, whose name was changed to Paul, and he became an apostle with a new message for the Body of Christ—believers with a new heavenly purpose. We are not Israel. Those spiritual gifts endowed from on high are not necessary for us. We are not going through the tribulation. Christ is going to rapture us out before that time.[130] It is our blessed hope, the glorious appearing of our great God and Savior, Jesus Christ. Those gifts of healing, tongues, knowledge, and others quickly faded away in the early church as they were no longer needed.[131] God is doing something different now.

With this groundwork, we can now address the questions about the Prayer Promises related to healing the sick, praying over them, and anointing them for healing. We find these "promises" in the book of James.

> "Is any among you afflicted? let him pray. Is any merry? let him sing psalms. Is any sick among you? let him call for the elders of the church; and let them pray over him, anointing him with oil in the name of the Lord: And the prayer of faith shall save the sick, and the Lord shall raise him up; and if he have committed sins, they shall be forgiven him. Confess your faults one to another, and pray one for another, that ye may be healed. The effectual fervent prayer of a righteous man availeth much."
> *James 5:13-16*

Upon examination, you will see that the truths in this passage align with those shared concerning the Lord Jesus Christ's healing of the man with palsy. To let the cat out of the bag, these promises are not for us today, but are for the Kingdom saints —believers who will go through the Tribulation and reign with Christ on Earth. We are the Body of Christ; thus, this is not written to us. Let's examine the passage in detail.

> "Is any among you afflicted? let him pray." *James 5:13a*

This is true in any dispensation and dealings between God and mankind through the ages. Our God wants us to always come to Him with our difficulties, afflictions, joys, and rejoicing.

> "Is any sick among you? let him call for the elders of the church; and let them pray over him, anointing him with oil in the name of the Lord:" *James 5:14*

During the Tribulation, especially the second half of the Tribulation, believers will not be able to buy or sell. That also means they cannot go to hospitals. There will be incredible hardships, disease, war, and famine around the world - even in the first half of the tribulation. God will endue some believers with gifts of healing (Mark 16, Acts 5:12-16) or answer prayer with healing when two or more are gathered together. We see here the calling of the elders to pray over the sick person, anointing them with oil in the name of the Lord. (Read Mark 6:13) What is the result?

> "And the prayer of faith shall save the sick, and the Lord shall raise him up;" *James 5:15a*

The prayer of faith shall save the sick. Take note that it is not the ill person praying. It is the elders praying. There are churches today that profess this prayer promise as truth for the present day. However, when a sick person comes to their elders and is prayed over, but there is no healing, they blame it on the ill person's lack of faith or sin in their life. The verse is clear: the elders' faith should be what is in question. However, that is not the reason the healing does not happen. This is for the nation of Israel. It is not for us today but for those going through the Tribulation. Also, the saving part here is a physical saving, and the prayer of faith shall, not might, save the sick person, that is, heal them. During the Tribulation, there will be a 100% recovery rate when elders pray over a sick person and anoint them with oil. The prayer of faith shall save the sick person, and the Lord will raise him up. How many have had their faith destroyed by taking this promise today and being told that God has not healed them because they do not have enough faith? Injury upon injury, crushed lives, and spirits litter the path.

> "...and if he have committed sins, they shall be forgiven him." *James 5:15b*

This is not talking about issues of the soul and whether someone goes to heaven or not. The passage talks about sins and forgiveness in a physical way, just like the passage about the man with palsy. The forgiveness of sins is healing. It is the lifting of the curse that Israel is under. This, too, shows us that this passage is not for us today. It is for Israel and their needs during the Tribulation.

Prayer is a Dispensational Subject

> "Confess your faults one to another, and pray one for another, that ye may be healed." *James 5:16*

This should seem familiar, as it is the same truth found in Mark 11:23-25. They must confess their faults one to another. This is the process they must follow to forgive one another. When they have forgiven one another, they will pray for each other. They need to, or the Lord will not heal them, or, as Mark 11 says, He will not forgive their trespasses. This healing results from the physical forgiveness of sins. The Lord will not heal them if they do not forgive one another.

> "And when ye stand praying, forgive, if ye have ought against any: that your Father also which is in heaven may forgive you your trespasses. But if ye do not forgive, neither will your Father which is in heaven forgive your trespasses." *Mark 11:25-26*

This, as with the book of James, is for Kingdom saints entering and going through the Tribulation. These instructions are not for the Body of Christ.

An Important Truth

Before going on to other questions, I would be remiss not to state emphatically that God can and does heal. He can do anything He chooses. But it is not on demand or in response to the prayer promise of James 5 or other promises found in the four gospels. These are for another time, the Tribulation. In Philippians 2, we read the account of Epaphroditus, who was sick and very close to death.

> "For he longed after you all, and was full of heaviness, because that ye had heard that he had been sick. **For indeed he was sick nigh unto death: but God had mercy on him;** and not on him only, but on me also, lest I should have sorrow upon sorrow. I sent him therefore the more carefully, that, when ye see him again, ye may rejoice, and that I may be the less sorrowful. Receive him therefore in the Lord with all gladness; and hold such in reputation: **Because for the work of Christ he was nigh unto death, not regarding his life**, to supply your lack of service toward me." *Philippians 2:26-30*

Why was he sick if such promises were for us today? Why didn't the believers and Paul pray over him? The reason is that today, in Grace, we do not have such promises as found in James 5. Instead, we see that God had mercy on him and healed him, but not in response to people or elders praying over him, or to two or three gathered together. I am sure that the believers and the Apostle Paul prayed for him, just like you and I pray for a sick friend or loved one. Epaphroditus and his sickness became sanctified unto God, and the request became God's. And He worked all things together for good; in this case, Epaphroditus was healed and able to return to serving and ministry. God's answer to prayer is His will.

The Body of Christ is not promised any physical blessings today. We do have all spiritual blessings in heavenly places.[132] We stand in God's grace, which is sufficient for us. We are promised the fruit of the Spirit as we live for Him.[133] We also share in the sufferings of Christ[134] as we live for Him. Even though we are not promised physical blessings, our Lord does bless physically all the time, but not according to these promises, which are for others in another dispensation. So, pray for healing, for health, for good things. You don't have to call for the elders or wait and find another to pray with. God loves you, hears you, and answers every prayer. You can boldly enter the throne of grace at any time and wherever you are. You have His ear. If it is on your heart, pray for it. God has called us to pray for everything on our hearts.[135] He will work everything together for good to those who love God and are called according to His purpose.[136]

Type 3: A Misunderstanding: What is the Lord's Prayer About?

We have already discussed the Lord's Prayer and how it is sometimes handled. Many repeat it without thinking, a rote prayer with little thought, even in the context of the Lord saying that vain repetition does not honor God. We also know that this is to be a model prayer, with the Lord's intent to instruct the individual on the key issues they will face, which will need prayer. At this point, I hope that you have come to understand that since this prayer is found in the four gospels, it is not for the Body of Christ, whose instructions are located in the books of Romans to Philemon. The two verses right after the Lord's prayer, Matthew 6:14-15, should solidify this truth since they speak of the requirement of forgiving others in order to be forgiven, dealing with physical forgiveness and healing.

The Lord's prayer is a model prayer for those going through the Tribulation, seeking God's Kingdom on Earth. It outlines how they should come before God's throne in prayer and the things for which they should pray. The prayer speaks explicitly to the needs that they will face due to the awful challenges during this time. The Lord warned, "For then shall be great tribulation, such as was not since the beginning of the world to this time, no, nor ever shall be. And except those days should be shortened, no flesh should be saved: but for the elect's sake those days shall be shortened."[137]

Since they cannot buy or sell,[138] they will need God to provide for them and give them their daily bread. They will ask God to forgive them, as they forgive those who have sinned or hurt them. The 'as' implies forgiveness is only to the same level that they forgive others. Recall that this is physical forgiveness, healing from disease and sickness. They cannot go to hospitals or the regional urgent care facility because they are unable to buy or sell. Additionally, they will pray to be protected from evil, including the evil one, Satan. The Tribulation is a dark and terrible time. There will be many antichrists and deceivers. The love of many will wax cold. Iniquity and sin will abound. Great trials and difficulties await believers during the Tribulation. Delivering from evil can also be the evil one, the Devil, or Antichrist. They will pray that God will guard them and lead them away from temptation and testing. They will pray to be delivered from the evil actions of others and the evil one.

If you need to take some time to digest this, do so. See what the Scriptures say. Let them speak. Pray and ask the Lord to help. If this conflicts you, come back to this later. Go to the next chapter and see what God says about "praying without ceasing."

Chapter 8 Reference List

[100] Ephesians 3:1-12
[101] Titus 2:8-14
[102] Romans 11:13
[103] Galatians 1:11-2:10
[104] Ephesians 3:1-6
[105] Ephesians 2:8-9; Romans 3:21-28; 4:23-25; I Corinthians 15:1-4
[106] Ephesians 2:6-7; Philippians 3:20-21
[107] Colossians 1:25-27
[108] Hebrews 13:8
[109] Deuteronomy 28
[110] Colossians 2:13-14
[111] Galatians 4:1-7
[112] Galatians 5:1,13
[113] Romans 11:25-29
[114] The Rapture is a secret coming. Apostle Paul calls this event a Mystery, kept secret but now revealed. I Thessalonians 4:13-18; I Corinthians 15:51-53
[115] I Thessalonians 5: 9-11
[116] I Peter 2:9-10

[117] The Kingdom of Heaven. When Christ returns from heaven, He will set up His Kingdom on the Earth and reign as King of the Earth. The Kingdom is from heaven to Earth.
[118] Acts 1:6
[119] Ephesians 2:6, 7; Philippians 3:20-21; I Thessalonians 4:13-18
[120] Ephesians 1:9-11 verse 11   also
[121] Genesis 15:6; Romans 4:1-5
[122] 2 Timothy 2:15; 2 Timothy 3:16-17
[123] 1 Thessalonians 1:10
[124] 1 Thessalonians 5:9
[125] 2 Timothy 2:15
[126] John 21:25
[127] John 20:30
[128] Revelation 13:17
[129] Romans 11:25-29; Ephesians 3:1-6; Galatians 1:11-2:10
[130] 1 Thessalonians 4:13-18, 5:9-11; Titus 2:13; 1 Corinthians 15:51-53
[131] I Corinthians 13:8-13
[132] Ephesians 1:3
[133] Galatians 5:22-23
[134] Philippians 3:10; II Corinthians 12:9-10; Philippians 1:29
[135] Philippians 4:6-7
[136] Romans 8:28
[137] Matthew 24:21-22
[138] Revelation 13:17

Chapter 9
Pray Without Ceasing

What Does "Pray Without Ceasing" Look Like?

Daniel prayed three times a day, most agreeing that he prayed morning, noon, and night. This was Daniel's routine; however, it was not the only time he prayed. As we examine the scriptures, we will find that Daniel was a man of faith who always went to God in prayer.

> "Now when Daniel knew that the writing was signed, he went into his house; and his windows being open in his chamber toward Jerusalem, **he kneeled upon his knees three times a day, and prayed, and gave thanks before his God, as he did aforetime.** Then these men assembled, and found Daniel praying and making supplication before his God." *Daniel 6:10-11*

In Daniel 2, we find that Daniel and his companions (Hananiah, Mishael, and Azariah) are in danger as the King has decreed to kill all the wise men because none could tell his dream. Daniel calls his friends together and requests they pray to God, seeking His mercies concerning the secret that only God could reveal.

> "Then Daniel went to his house, and made the thing known to Hananiah, Mishael, and Azariah, his companions: That they would desire mercies of the God of heaven concerning this secret; that Daniel and his fellows should not perish with the rest of the wise men of Babylon. **Then was the secret revealed unto Daniel in a night vision.**" *Daniel 2:17-19*

And upon receiving the answer, Daniel thanked and praised God for making known what they wanted of Him. This, too, is prayer. And this was in the middle of the night.

> "**Then Daniel blessed the God of heaven.** Daniel answered and said, Blessed be the name of God forever and ever: for wisdom and might are his: And he changeth the times and the seasons: he removeth kings, and setteth up kings: he giveth wisdom unto the wise, and knowledge to them that know understanding: He revealeth the deep and secret things: he knoweth what is in the darkness, and the light dwelleth with him. I thank thee, and praise thee, O thou God of my fathers, who hast given me wisdom and might, and hast made known unto me now what we desired of thee: for thou hast now made known unto us the king's matter." *Daniel 2:20-23*

Daniel went to God anytime he had need. He had a regular daily routine of prayer, and then he also sought God and thanked God throughout the day. Other examples of Daniel's prayers are found in Daniel 8:15-16. From these passages, we begin to understand what it means to "pray without ceasing."

One interesting observation from the book of Daniel is that our God is instantly aware of our praying and without hesitation, has begun responding with an answer. Notice in Daniel 9 that there is no delay in God's answering our prayer.

> "**And whiles I was speaking, and praying,** ... **and presenting my supplication before the LORD my God** for the holy mountain of my God; Yea, whiles I was speaking in prayer, even the man Gabriel, whom I had seen in the vision at the beginning, being caused to fly swiftly, touched me about the time of the evening oblation. And he informed me, and talked with me, and said, O Daniel, I am now come forth to give thee skill and understanding. **At the beginning of thy supplications the commandment came forth, and I am**

come to shew thee; *for thou art greatly beloved: therefore understand the matter, and consider the vision." Daniel 9:20-23*

What a fantastic realization and truth. When we pray, God does not put our prayer on the back burner and muse about it for a while. He takes ownership of our requests and immediately takes action to answer our prayer.

The book of Nehemiah sheds further light on the topic of "praying without ceasing." In this book, we see Nehemiah, a man seeking to do God's will, going to God in all life circumstances and with all kinds of prayers. We also see that God answers all his prayers. An examination of his prayers reveals much. Nehemiah prayed with conviction, but first prepared his mind and body for prayer. He sat down, wept, mourned, and fasted, then he prayed.

> **"And it came to pass, when I heard these words, that I sat down and wept, and mourned certain days, and fasted, and prayed before the God of heaven,** And said, I beseech thee, O LORD God of heaven, the great and terrible God, that keepeth covenant and mercy for them that love him and observe his commandments: Let thine ear now be attentive, and thine eyes open, that thou mayest hear the prayer of thy servant, which I pray before thee now, day and night, for the children of Israel thy servants, and confess the sins of the children of Israel, which we have sinned against thee: both I and my father's house have sinned. We have dealt very corruptly against thee, and have not kept the commandments, nor the statutes, nor the judgments, which thou commandedst thy servant Moses. Remember, I beseech thee, the word that thou commandedst thy servant Moses, saying, If ye transgress, I will scatter you abroad among the nations: But if ye turn unto me, and keep my commandments, and do them; though there were of you cast out unto the uttermost part of the heaven, yet will I gather them from thence, and will bring them unto the place that I have chosen to set my name there. Now these are thy servants and thy people, whom thou hast redeemed by thy great power, and by thy strong hand. **O Lord, I beseech thee, let now thine ear be attentive to the prayer of thy servant, and to the prayer of thy servants, who desire to fear thy name: and prosper, I pray thee, thy servant this day, and grant him mercy in the sight of this man."** *Nehemiah 1:1-11*

This prayer was a prayer of intercession for his nation, people, and friends. He also prayed that God would work on the king's heart so that he, Nehemiah, could share his people's plight with the king and find help for them. It is interesting how God's answer to this prayer is twofold. First, Nehemiah's heaviness of heart is not lifted by his going to God; instead, it is intensified, causing the King to ask him why he is so sad. He had never been sad in the King's presence before, as he was the King's cupbearer. When the King asks Nehemiah what is wrong, he becomes incredibly scared but boldly proclaims the plight of his people.

> "…Then I was very sore afraid, And said unto the king, Let the king live forever: why should not my countenance be sad, when the city, the place of my fathers' sepulchres, lieth waste, and the gates thereof are consumed with fire?" *Nehemiah 2:2-3*

Second, the King could have responded in many ways, most of which would have spelled grave difficulty for Nehemiah (beatings, prison, death) in forgetting his position while in the King's presence. But instead, the King shows mercy and asks Nehemiah what his request is.

> "Then the king said unto me, For what dost thou make request? **So I prayed to the God of heaven.** And I said unto the king, If it please the king, and if thy servant have found favour in thy sight, that thou wouldest send me unto Judah, unto the city of my fathers' sepulchres, that I may build it." *Nehemiah 2:4-5*

Here we see Nehemiah go to God in prayer in a heartbeat. The King asks him a question, and he must respond. Unlike the earlier example, this prayer had zero preparation and was uttered instantly, like a reflex. We do not know the actual words of Nehemiah's prayer, but considering the context, it was short, a momentary calling on God for help. He could not bow his knees, speak aloud, or even close his eyes; in the blink of an eye, he silently called out to God in his mind for help. This is what it means to pray without ceasing. Nehemiah's first reaction was to go to God, lean on Him, and seek His hand.

Have you ever done this? Under your breath, in a challenging situation, said, "Lord, help me," or "Lord, I need You now!" Or, perhaps on the other extreme, when there is joy, beauty, or something amazing, and your heart cries out to God with "Thank you, Lord" or "Amen." These are all types of prayer - talking to God. And they all demonstrate what it means to pray without ceasing, being instant in prayer, and continuing in prayer.

You, too, can find yourself in a continuous open conversation with the Lord. A conversation that is natural and responsive to what is happening in your life. Just like Nehemiah, your first response can be, "So I prayed to the God of heaven." As we experience our day, we ought to be in conversation with our God naturally and regularly with thanksgiving, with needs, with amazement, with praise, with yearnings, with hurts, and with joys. How real is God to you? If you are praying without ceasing, He is real in a very tangible way.

Nehemiah's relationship with God was real. Nehemiah says it this way, "And the king granted me, **according to the good hand of my God upon me."**[139] We see from these other verses that Nehemiah had unwavering conviction based upon his relationship with God, which he readily shared with others.

> "Then answered I them, and said unto them, **The God of heaven, he will prosper us;** therefore we his servants will arise and build: but ye have no portion, nor right, nor memorial, in Jerusalem." *Nehemiah 2:20*

> "And it came to pass, when our enemies heard that it was known unto us, **and God had brought their counsel to nought,** that we returned all of us to the wall, every one unto his work." *Nehemiah 4:15*

> "In what place therefore ye hear the sound of the trumpet, resort ye thither unto us: **our God shall fight for us."** *Nehemiah 4:20*

> "For they all made us afraid, saying, Their hands shall be weakened from the work, that it be not done. **Now therefore, O God, strengthen my hands."** *Nehemiah 6:9*

Corporate Prayer – Praying Together

To round out what it means to pray without ceasing, God's Word reveals that Nehemiah also prayed corporately with other believers. In Nehemiah 5:13, he says, "Also I shook my lap, and said, So God shake out every man from his house, and from his labour, that performeth not this promise, even thus be he shaken out, and emptied. And all the congregation said, Amen, and praised the LORD. And the people did according to this promise." The congregation prayed together in response to the grave danger and demands placed upon them as they built the walls and gates. We should not forget the importance of the saints praying and worshipping together in this way. This shared testimony binds us together as brothers and sisters in the Lord, encouraging one another and helping one another.

"And at midnight Paul and Silas prayed, and sang praises unto God: and the prisoners heard them." *Acts 16:25*

"And from Miletus he sent to Ephesus, and called the elders of the church…And when he had thus spoken, he kneeled down, and prayed with them all." *Acts 20:17, 36*

"And when we had accomplished those days, we departed and went our way; and they all brought us on our way, with wives and children, till we were out of the city: and we kneeled down on the shore, and prayed." *Acts 21:5*

"And say ye, Save us, O God of our salvation, and gather us together, and deliver us from the heathen, that we may give thanks to thy holy name, and glory in thy praise. Blessed be the LORD God of Israel forever and ever. And all the people said, Amen, and praised the LORD." *1 Chronicles 16:35-36*

"And Ezra opened the book in the sight of all the people; (for he was above all the people;) and when he opened it, all the people stood up: And Ezra blessed the LORD, the great God. And all the people answered, Amen, Amen, with lifting up their hands: and they bowed their heads, and worshipped the LORD with their faces to the ground." *Nehemiah 8:5-6*

In Hebrews 10:24-25, we encounter a disheartening reality: some believers see no value in gathering together to worship. "And let us consider one another to provoke unto love and to good works: **Not forsaking the assembling of ourselves together, as the manner of some is…**" Life is challenging, make no mistake, but even more so if one tries to go it alone. With today's ubiquitous ways to access 'church' online, virtually or on demand, it is becoming increasingly common for some to stay at home and not enter the doors of the local church. Much is lost to the child of God who separates himself from other believers. You can learn new truths and even grow in faith, but you cannot fully exercise your gifts or be ministered to by others without personal interaction. This may not seem important at this moment, as everything is fine now, but when things go south, the bottom falls out, or pain comes wave upon wave, it will become very important. This is the reality of life: there are ups and downs, and sometimes, the downs are almost more than one can bear. But God has an answer: other believers, members of the Body of Christ, who can comfort, help, and pray for you because they have gone through similar difficulties themselves.

> "Blessed be God, even the Father of our Lord Jesus Christ, the Father of mercies, and the God of all comfort; Who comforteth us in all our tribulation, **that we may be able to comfort them which are in any trouble, by the comfort wherewith we ourselves are comforted of God.**" *2 Corinthians 1:3-4*

God calls us to be others-centered. Philippians 2:5-8 shows this truth as Christ chose us first. He left the throne of heaven to enter this world to go to the cross because of love. He exercised His love for us. He is the perfect example. The local church is the place, the proving ground, for exercising your gifts. God's Word calls us to gather together, encourage one another, edify one another, love one another, pray for one another, and so on. The believer who stays away, forsaking assembling with others, is hindered, even stunted, in developing their God-given gifts. We are to be channels of blessing, not reservoirs of blessing. Let us gather as God desires, to minister to one another and to be ministered to. When prayer is lifted up, we should join in that prayer, participating in the prayerful worship of God alongside like-minded saints. When we gather, we see one another and realize that others are hurting or rejoicing; we talk, share, and grow together as a family. We are brothers and sisters in the Lord, are we not? And now prayer takes on more meaning; we can pray more effectively because we know more about the local family of God, and we can use our gifts for others and be thankful.

Thus, "pray without ceasing" encompasses a regular daily routine of prayer, as well as corporate and shared prayer times where believers labor together in prayer for a specific purpose. Finally, the moment-to-moment conversational prayer with our God (sharing our cares, needs, joys, and praises as they happen) completes what a mature prayer life should be.

In the book of Nehemiah, the first six chapters are filled with conflict, adversity, and challenging problems for Nehemiah and his people. Nehemiah engages in prayer as a first response in each situation, and God directly answers every prayer in bringing to fruition the rebuilding of the wall and gates of the city. Nehemiah challenges us to see things differently than perhaps we do. Instead of worrying, our first reaction should be to pray and trust in the God of heaven. God knows tomorrow and is good and on the side of the right. God hears us at our first call and does answer prayer. And we, too, can have a faith-filled experience if we open our hearts to God, see Him in the details of our days, and talk to Him about all the matters of life. Tomorrow is brighter for the praying child of God.

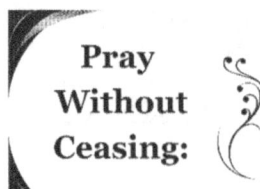

Pray Without Ceasing:
- **Regular routine prayer**
- **Corporate prayer**
- **Moment-by-moment conversational prayer**

Chapter 9 Reference List

[139] Nehemiah 2:8

Chapter 10
God Is for Us… So Pray!

God is on our side

God is for us! What a life-altering truth! Romans 8:31 declares, "What shall we then say to these things? If God be for us, who can be against us?" Our God, the Creator of the universe and all living things, is on our side, working all things together for our good. He is for us and desires us to come before Him in prayer. We must never allow our communication with our God to languish. We should come before the throne of grace often—when we are thankful, when we are afraid, when we hurt, when things are well, and in every other circumstance. Every action of God in our lives is to our benefit. He never works against us or tries to hurt us. He loves us and cherishes us.

> "Therefore being justified by faith, we have peace with God through our Lord Jesus Christ: **By whom also we have access by faith into this grace wherein we stand**, and rejoice in hope of the glory of God." *Romans 5:1-2*

We have complete access to God's grace, His favor, as we exercise faith. We literally stand in grace. Prayer is our "faith line" to the God who loves us, who gave His Son for us, and who intercedes for us. There are manifold ways God is for us, and they call us to pray, trusting in His love, grace, and power.

Furthermore, our heavenly Father is heavily invested in us. "For ye are bought with a price, therefore glorify God in your body, and your spirit, which are God's!"[140] The precious blood of Jesus Christ was shed for each of us to redeem us out of sin and from the power of darkness. Apostle Paul in Romans 8:32 states it this way, "He that spared not his own Son, but delivered him up for us all, how shall he not with him also freely give us all things?" Our God wants us to grow, mature, and be spiritually fruitful. He has already given us His Best, His Son, so why wouldn't He continue to be on our side and seek to provide us with good things?

Life in this World

Life in this sin-cursed world brings affliction and hardship, but God is for us in our trials. Many people blame God when things fall apart in their lives, but they are mistaken. In truth, our flesh often leads us down poor decision-making paths, bringing difficulties upon ourselves. At other times, the hardships are brought on by others who cross our paths or are part of our lives. Of course, the Devil is busy as well, since we wrestle not against flesh and blood, but against the wiles of the devil.

> "For our light affliction, which is but for a moment, worketh for us a far more exceeding and eternal weight of glory; While we look not at the things which are seen, but at the things which are not seen: for the things which are seen are temporal; but the things which are not seen are eternal." *2 Corinthians 4:17-18*

Our troubles, when examined through the lens of eternal things, are temporary, and God reveals that they have value and produce eternal glory. When Paul faced his thorn in the flesh, God told him, "My grace is sufficient for thee: for my strength is made perfect in weakness."[141] Paul rejoiced, saying, "Most gladly therefore will I rather glory in my infirmities, that the power of Christ may rest upon me." God's grace is enough, and His strength can shine in our weakness.

When I reflect on this life and its many joys and sorrows, I think of Job and his response when his life was turned completely upside down in a matter of moments. He lost everything. Consider God's servant Job and his response:

> "Then Job arose, and rent his mantle, and shaved his head, and fell down upon the ground, and worshipped, And said, Naked came I out of my mother's womb, and naked shall I return thither: the LORD gave, and the LORD hath taken away; **blessed be the name of the LORD**." *Job 1:20-21*

Job's faithfulness challenges us to worship our God regardless of life's circumstances, because our God is good and He is for us. God is for us in every trial.

Eternity

God is for us not just in this life, but for eternity. Colossians 1:5 speaks of "the hope which is laid up for you in heaven, whereof ye heard before in the word of the truth of the gospel." Because God is for us, we have a sure hope of eternal life. 1 Thessalonians 5:10 assures us, "Who died for us, that, whether we wake or sleep, we should live together with him." Christ's death guarantees our eternal future with Him, whether we live or die. This hope isn't wishful thinking; it's a certainty. We have been secured by Christ's sacrifice and sealed by the Holy Spirit of promise unto the day of redemption.

> "Even when we were dead in sins, hath quickened us together with Christ, (by grace ye are saved;) And hath raised *us* up together, and made *us* sit together in heavenly *places* in Christ Jesus: That in the ages to come he might shew the exceeding riches of his grace in *his* kindness toward us through Christ Jesus." *Ephesians 2:5-7*

In addition, our Lord has seated us in the heavenly places in Christ. His sovereign will is to show the exceeding riches of his grace towards us throughout all the ages to come. What a fantastic future awaits the child of God. Hence, God's word calls us to seek those things above and to set our affections on them.

> "If ye then be risen with Christ, seek those things which are above, where Christ sitteth on the right hand of God. Set your affection on things above, not on things on the earth. For ye are dead, and your life is hid with Christ in God. When Christ,

God Is for Us....So Pray!

who is our life, shall appear, then shall ye also appear with him in glory." *Colossians 3:1-4*

So let us each turn our eyes upon Jesus and look full into His wonderful face. Amen.

God's love for us

Romans 5:8 proclaims, "But God commendeth his love toward us, in that, while we were yet sinners, Christ died for us." Before we ever thought to seek Him, while we were lost in sin, God loved us. He didn't wait for us to clean up our act or become worthy. No, His love moved Him to send His only begotten Son to die for us. Think about that for a moment—while we were rebellious, enemies of God, He gave His Son to pay our sin debt. That's how much He is for us! Ephesians 5:2 adds, "And walk in love, as Christ also hath loved us, and hath given himself for us an offering and a sacrifice to God for a sweetsmelling savour." Christ's death was a sweet offering to God, not just to save us, but to show us the depth of God's love. God cannot lie, and He promised eternal life before the world began.[142] What a deep love He has for us!

This love should compel us to pray, to be thankful. We can come boldly to the throne of grace, knowing that the God who loved us enough to give His Son is listening and answering every prayer. Galatians 1:4 tells us, "Who gave himself for our sins, that he might deliver us from this present evil world, according to the will of God and our Father." Jesus didn't just die to save us so that we could go to heaven; He died to deliver us from the grip of this sinful world, and to enable us to have fruitful lives with a secure eternal destiny in His presence. God is for you, and His sacrificial love is a rudder to our lives.

Intercession

Our Lord Jesus Christ is presently seated at the right hand of the Father. This has tremendous implications for the child of God. Romans 8:34 asks, "Who is he that condemneth? It is Christ that died, yea rather, that is risen again, who is even at the right hand of God, who also maketh intercession for us." Amen and amen, Jesus Christ is alive, seated in glory, and ever interceding! He's our advocate before the Father. At the moment of salvation, we are baptized by the Holy Spirit into Christ, being totally identified with Him. We are as righteous as God in Jesus Christ because of this standing.

> "For he hath made him to be sin for us, who knew no sin; that we might be made the righteousness of God in him." *2 Corinthians 5:21*

Jesus took our sin and gave us His righteousness. We stand before God not as condemned sinners, but as saints, holy ones, clothed in Christ's holy righteousness. We are in the Son, and nothing can separate us from the Father's love.

> "For I am persuaded, that neither death, nor life, nor angels, nor principalities, nor powers, nor things present, nor things to come, Nor height, nor depth, nor any other creature, shall be able to separate us from the love of God, which is in Christ Jesus our Lord." *Romans 8:38-39*

This truth should encourage us to seek the Father in prayer. When the enemy whispers that you're a failure, remember that Christ is for you, interceding for you, and has made you righteous. Titus 2:14 adds, "Who gave himself for us, that he might redeem us from all iniquity, and purify unto himself a peculiar people, zealous of good works." God is for us, shaping us into the image of His Son for His glory. So, pray! Thank Him for His righteousness. Ask Him to make you zealous for good works. Come to Him when you're weak, knowing He's for you and on your side.

Furthermore, we are frail, earthen vessels who do not know what tomorrow holds. We are stumbling about in the darkness of not knowing. But our God is all-knowing! Romans 8:26 says, "Likewise the Spirit also helpeth our infirmities: for we know not what we should pray for as we ought: but the Spirit itself maketh intercession for us with groanings which cannot be uttered." We don't always know the right words or the best solution, but the Holy Spirit steps in with deep, heartfelt intercession. The Spirit takes our feeble prayers and aligns them with God's perfect will. He's for us, working in us, even when we don't know how to pray or what to pray for. The Holy Spirit is for you, carrying your prayers to the Father with a compassion we can't fully grasp.

So Pray

What shall we say to these things? If God be for us, who can be against us? He loved us while we were sinners, gave His Son for us, made us righteous, intercedes for us through Christ and the Spirit, supplies grace in our weakness, and secures our eternal hope. This is our God—He is for us! So, pray! Philippians 4:6 exhorts, "Be careful for nothing; but in everything by prayer and supplication with thanksgiving let your requests be made known unto God." There's no moment too small, no burden too heavy, for our God who is for us. Let us press toward the mark, as Paul did, knowing that the God who loves us hears every prayer and works all things for our good. Wow, what a God we serve!

Chapter 10 Reference List

[140] I Corinthians 6:20
[141] 2 Corinthians 12:9
[142] Titus 1:2

Chapter 11
Our Situation: A Difficult Truth to Accept

Out of Control

The inevitable conclusion of life is that we are careening through the days of our lives without a means to control anything in them. Much of our efforts in life are about trying to control what will happen. People who try to control everything are even labeled "control freaks," trying to put everything in order so that they get the result that they so desperately want. But change happens. Change is one of the true constants in life.

Many people approach relationships with a soap opera-like view of life. If I do this set of things, they will like me, go out with me, or marry me. If I control all the variables in my life, then a particular outcome will happen. We plan events and activities, trying to cover every detail, but again, we always seem to miss something. We repeatedly play scenarios in our minds on what we will do, say, or how we will react in preparation for a conversation or a meeting. We meet with financial advisors, analyze, model, and generate statistical portfolio success strategies, all seeking to find a stable, predictable future without worries and concerns. Yet the fact is that past performance does not guarantee future results. Case in point, I retired in the year 2021 to flip my life and begin full-time ministry in writing, podcasting, and serving at my home church, or wherever the Lord chose to use me. And then the year 2022 happened, marked by high inflation and plummeting markets that fiscally pounded retirement funds. No amount of planning, worry, or fear could have prevented what happened. It was indeed out of my control. But the Lord is still good all the time, so I trust Him. Everything changes except the Lord.

As believers, we have a new life in Christ, called the new man. This new life in Christ is created in righteousness and true holiness.[143] It is also true that our old man, our flesh, remains, not to be shed from us until death or the Blessed Hope, the Rapture. Until then, we will struggle with our flesh,[144] which produces fear in our lives, among other problems and difficulties.

> "For God hath not given us the spirit of fear; but of power, and of love, and of a sound mind." *2 Timothy 1:7*

This fear disrupts our walk in this life, robbing us of our strength and causing us to focus on ourselves rather than others. Fear corrupts our thinking. We worry about everything and try to control everything around us instead of trusting the one who can. If we choose to keep everything to ourselves and not give it to God, we are stuck in a cycle of fear. An inescapable, crushing truth creeps into our awareness; we cannot even control what will happen to us in the next ten seconds. In many regards, we are speeding out of control, hurtling through life with our eyes closed. We cannot change the past or stop the future from changing. The best we can hope for is to make something lasting of the moment we are in. If we do not make this moment valuable, we have squandered it, regretting it as it moves into the past and hoping for something different in the approaching moments.

Well, that seems sad, even depressing, but it does not have to be so for the child of God. We can take comfort in knowing that we are God's children and He is in control. We do not need to settle for the status quo in our lives. Our God can and does change things. At this moment, no matter how difficult it may be, we can trust our Lord, knowing that He has never been caught off guard. Hebrews 13:8 states, "Jesus Christ the same yesterday, and today, and forever." He is the solid rock on which we stand, and He wants us to trust Him and come to Him to find peace and security. And as we stand upon this firm, unchanging foundation, we can access the real power of God as we pray to our Heavenly Father, who holds all things in His hands. He can do all things. He loves us deeply and answers every prayer, making everything work together for good. He can change tomorrow. He can guard you now, and He is a giver who cannot be outgiven. Only by leaning on the One who has control can we find real peace and joy in this world.

God Says Trust Me

Trust is difficult for most. We have been burned many times in our lives by the actions of others, so truly trusting another is difficult. Many will divulge that they even have "trust issues." But God is not like man. He says what He means and means what He says. His Yea is Yea and His Ney is Ney. He is God and can do all things. And He is love, absolute love! The more that we know Him, the easier it is to trust Him. He is God, and He is for us. Here are just a few verses of many that expound the absolute truth of the necessity of trusting our God. It is more than trusting Him for salvation. God wants us to trust Him in every aspect of life. He is a loving Father who calls us to lean on Him, to rest in His presence, and to accept His power, love, and watchcare.

> "Trust in the LORD with all thine heart; and lean not unto thine own understanding. In all thy ways acknowledge him, and he shall direct thy paths." *Proverbs 3:5-6*

> "As for God, his way is perfect; the word of the LORD is tried: he is a buckler to all them that trust in him." *2 Samuel 22:31*

> "Blessed is that man that maketh the LORD his trust, and respecteth not the proud, nor such as turn aside to lies." *Psalms 40:4*

> "What time I am afraid, I will trust in thee." *Psalms 56:3*

> "The fear of man bringeth a snare: but whoso putteth his trust in the LORD shall be safe." *Proverbs 29:25*

> "Trust ye in the LORD for ever: for in the LORD JEHOVAH is everlasting strength:" *Isaiah 26:4*

> "For therefore we both labour and suffer reproach, because we trust in the living God, who is the Saviour of all men, specially of those that believe." *1 Timothy 4:10*

> "Charge them that are rich in this world, that they be not highminded, nor trust in uncertain riches, but in the living God, who giveth us richly all things to enjoy;" *1 Timothy 6:17*

Trusting Him means that we need to pray to Him, to give Him our worries and fears, our yesterdays, todays, and tomorrows. God can do exceedingly abundantly above all that we can ask or think, and He does. As young adults at church, we sang a song that asked a pointed question, **"Why worry when you can pray?"**

> Why worry, when you can pray?
> Trust Jesus, He will be your stay.
> Don't be a doubting Thomas,
> Lean fully on His promise,
> Why worry, worry, worry, worry.
> When you can pray?
> By John W. Peterson and Alfred B. Smith

And that is so true. We waste so much of our lives just churning over things instead of giving them to our Heavenly Father. Giving everything to our Lord in prayer can bring peace to our hearts and minds that is beyond comprehension and is worth far more than anything this life can offer.

> "Be careful for nothing; but in everything by prayer and supplication with thanksgiving let your requests be made known unto God. And the peace of God, which passeth all understanding, shall keep your hearts and minds through Christ Jesus." *Philippians 4:6-7*

This is a significant truth that should impact you immensely. When you pray, you become involved in the tomorrows of everything and everyone you pray for. The Lord knows tomorrow and answers each of your prayers. This is the true path to changing tomorrow: praying to our Mighty God and trusting Him. He never fails. Recall that when you pray about or for something, it becomes sanctified to God. He now takes ownership. His answer is immediate, whether you see the result or not. God is on the task of carrying out the answer that He has immediately begun. Daniel 8, 9, and 10 each prove this. Before Daniel was finished praying, God responded. Thus, you can let go of trying to control every detail of life - if you pray for them. God has made them His own, and He does have control. So, we can trust Him. Let go, He has it, and it is under control. And, as we let go and let God do His will, it glorifies and worships Him.

When you pray for someone to be saved, God is on the task of convicting, burdening, and bringing circumstances together in that person's life so that they see their need. He orchestrates circumstances and details so that the individual can choose to humble themselves to the gospel and trust. God will not overrule their free will, but He will work in the details of their life. Our God is an awesome God.

Read Philippians 4:6-7 again and then set your mind to pray for everything on your heart. Do not hold back ("be careful for nothing"). There is nothing unreasonable to pray for. Make a list and keep adding to it. When you pray for something, it is sanctified to God, and He is working on it. Suppose you pray for a new car; it is a physical thing, but now it is sanctified to God; it is now His, and He will supply what is best. It may not necessarily be that car, but it will be what is best for now and for tomorrow.

Faith and Trust

Now, let us discuss faith and trust in the context of God and who He is. We have referenced Hebrews 11:6 before, but let us examine the three critical statements it makes this time.

1) But without faith it is impossible to please Him:
2) For he that cometh to God must believe that He is,
3) and that He is a rewarder of them that diligently seek Him.

So, first, **it is impossible to please God unless we have faith**. According to Hebrews 11:1, faith makes the things we hope for substantial or tangible. Faith makes future things real to us and makes God real to us. Faith further becomes the evidence of things not seen. Evidence proves something is true or real. So, faith is critical as it enables us to find solid ground to stand upon in the unknown or as we peer into the future. The Rapture, for example, can become real to the child of God by faith, and faith enables the believer to live with that blessed Hope in view.

The second statement is **"for he that cometh to God must believe that He is."** This is precisely what we are doing when we pray to God. We are coming to God. To please God as we pray, we MUST believe that He is. We need to believe that He is God, the God of the Bible. The God who can do all things since He is all-powerful, all-knowing, and omnipresent. The God who loves you also cares for you. He spared not His own Son for you.

Sometimes, we pray with doubt and not faith. Even though we utter our prayers to God, in the back of our minds, we do not expect God to really answer our prayers. We feel that God does not think we are important enough, or perhaps we feel that what we are praying for is not worthy of God's attention, or cannot really happen. These feelings are just that, feelings, and not reality. If we grasp who God is, we will know that God values us greatly and loves us completely. God is pleased when we pray to Him, believing He is God, the creator of all things, the one who can do all things!

> "He that spared not his own Son, but delivered him up for us all, how shall he not with him also freely give us all things?"
> *Romans 8:32*

He is the God who can do exceedingly abundantly above all you can ask or think. Coming to God with faith means knowing that our God answers our prayers every time and wants to say yes and give and give again. He wants us to become engaged in our tomorrows by praying today, knowing that He can do all we ask or think, and much more.[145]

The third statement is "**and that He is a rewarder of them that diligently seek Him.**" This is broader than just seeking God by prayer and includes seeking Him in His Word. But in the case of coming to God by prayer, simply said, God answers the prayers of those who seek Him. When we come to God, it pleases Him if, by faith, we understand that He answers every one of our prayers. He rewards those who diligently seek Him. Remember, our Lord is not a genie in a bottle granting wishes, nor is He answering yes to every prayer we make. But He does answer every prayer with what is best, especially in the context of our eternal destiny. When we pray to God, we seek His work in our lives: healing for our bodies, our minds, and our emotions; His guidance and leading; His help in times of need; His protection; His intervention and authority; His giving heart; things that we need, whether physical, emotional, or spiritual. He rewards those who diligently seek Him by answering every prayer and request with what we need.

The idea of diligently is with intention and earnestness. As we have already shared, prayer is part of a relationship with God. Without faith, it is impossible for us to please Him. Furthermore, we ought to come to Him with our hearts, purposefully lifting our requests unto Him. And He will give us what is best.

Further, since praying is part of a relationship with our God where we lean on Him and seek Him, we ought to be trusting God by giving Him our requests. Trust requires letting go. Just like those trust fall exercises, where an individual must trust a person standing behind them that they cannot see. As they fall backward, they trust someone to catch them before hitting the floor. Trust implies that you have faith in the person who will catch you and that they will. Thus, when we pray and give our requests to the Lord, we should leave them with Him, trusting and knowing He is on them and has answered them. We can always pray with thanksgiving because we know that He has made what we pray for His and that He has answered our prayer. The child of God can then thankfully and patiently wait to see the mighty hand of God.

Patiently and thankfully waiting, now that is a challenging undertaking to make happen in our lives. This is where faith becomes even more critical in the believer's life. We need our faith to grow so that God and His Word become truly real to us. Our faith will make the Word become substantive and His promises real. Faith makes worry a non-issue, destroys the need to control everything, and lets God be in control by trusting Him. Trusting God is an outworking of our faith in Him.

> "So then faith cometh by hearing, and hearing by the Word of God." *Romans 10:17*

God's Word is clear that for our faith to grow, we need to be in the Word of God. We need to read it, memorize it, study it, and live it.

> "Only be thou strong and very courageous, that thou mayest observe to do according to all the law, which Moses my servant commanded thee: turn not from it to the right hand or to the left, that thou mayest prosper whithersoever thou goest. This book of the law shall not depart out of thy mouth; but thou shalt meditate therein day and night, that thou mayest observe to do according to all that is written therein: for then thou shalt make thy way prosperous, and then thou shalt have good success." *Joshua 1:7-8*

In Joshua 1:7-8, God tells Joshua to do all that the Word of God says (the law in his day). Joshua is told not to turn from it, not to veer left or right, but to meditate on it day and night. The Word of God was to be central to Joshua's thinking and attention. Furthermore, the Word of God was to be central to Joshua's actions. God told him to "do" according to all that was written, and then Joshua would have good success. Of course, doing things God's way would be best, wouldn't it? How could we think we know better? But often we do just that and ignore what God clearly commands, instead doing things our way. This results from the flesh, our sin nature, which pulls at us, just like Joshua's. So, God commanded

Joshua to be strong and very courageous. That was what it would take to live according to God's Word and do everything God's way.

It is no different today. In Ephesians 6:10-11, we are told to "…be strong in the Lord and in the power of His might. Put on the whole armor of God, that ye may be able to stand against the wiles of the Devil." That whole armor is the truth of God's Word set in motion in the believer's life. In Philippians, the Holy Spirit, through the Apostle Paul, challenges us to also make God's Word alive in our walk each day as we encapsulate our thinking in godly thoughts and then do it! It is a challenge to think and then do things God's way.

> "Finally, brethren, whatsoever things are true, whatsoever things are honest, whatsoever things are just, whatsoever things are pure, whatsoever things are lovely, whatsoever things are of good report; if there be any virtue, and if there be any praise, think on these things. Those things, which ye have both learned, and received, and heard, and seen in me, **do**: **and the God of peace shall be with you.**" *Philippians 4:8-9*

The things that the Apostle Paul lists are what the brethren had learned, received, heard, and seen in Paul. These things are truths from the Word of God, as well as truths shown in the actions of the Apostle Paul. God's Word produces faith, which the child of God can exercise in their daily life. And if we think and do these things (true, honest, just, pure, lovely, good report, virtuous, and praiseworthy), then the God of peace will be with us. If God is with us on our journey, we will have good success. This is not to say that God is not always with the child of God. The entire triune God indwells every believer.[146] However, when a child of God lives God's Word, they experience His presence and peace in an extraordinary way.

> "For this cause also thank we God without ceasing, because, when ye received the Word of God which ye heard of us, ye received it not as the word of men, but as it is in truth, **the Word of God, which effectually worketh also in you that believe.**" *1 Thessalonians 2:13*

God's Word will effectually work in you who believe it. When you or I read or hear the Word of God, and we understand that God is speaking those words to us, God's Word works in us. Hebrews 4:12 says that the Word of God is a discerner of the thoughts and intents of the heart. Yes, God's Word works in you. It changes you; it builds your faith; it makes the things of God real to you.

The Word of God and Prayer

> "For every creature of God is good, and nothing to be refused, if it be received with thanksgiving: For it is sanctified by the Word of God and prayer." *1 Timothy 4:4-5*

The Word of God and Prayer go hand in hand for the child of God. To please God, when we pray, we need faith. But faith comes through hearing the Word of God.[147] Thus, our prayer life will be strengthened and more impactful as our faith grows. Our faith grows as we spend actual quality time in the Word of God. Speak to me, Lord! When we open the Bible, God's Holy Word, and let God speak, and we listen, God's Word can then build our Faith. A conversation is a two-way dialogue between at least two parties. When we pray, we complete one-half of this conversation. The other half of the conversation with our God occurs as we spend time in the Word of God. God, the Holy Spirit, takes the Word of God that we are reading, studying, meditating on, and thinking on, applies it to our hearts, and changes us. In Romans 12, God begs us to present our lives to Him and not be conformed to this world but transformed by the renewing of our minds.

> "I beseech you therefore, brethren, by the mercies of God, that ye present your bodies a living sacrifice, holy, acceptable unto God, which is your reasonable service. **And be not conformed to this world: but be ye transformed by the renewing of your mind, that ye may prove what is that good, and acceptable, and perfect, will of God.**" *Romans 12:1-2*

It is God's Word that transforms and renews our mind, our thinking. God gave His Word with the intention that it would help us, change us, and enable us to live pleasing lives unto Him. II Timothy 3:16-17 reveals the purpose for which God gave His Word.

> "All scripture is given by inspiration of God, and is profitable for doctrine, for reproof, for correction, for instruction in righteousness: That the man of God may be perfect, throughly furnished unto all good works." *2 Timothy 3:16-17*

Thus, as we spend time in the Word of God and give diligent attention to prayer, we become engaged in a conversation with our Creator and Almighty God. Praying all that is on our hearts to Him, and then letting Him speak to us through His Word, and then doing it, our relationship with the Lord becomes real. You will begin to feel His presence. You will experience a peace and joy that you have never felt before. If you once felt close to God, but now He seems distant, He has not moved away; examine yourself. Are you spending quality and effective time in God's Word? Are you praying earnestly from your heart? Is your life where it ought to be concerning sin? Any of these can hinder you from experiencing completeness in your relationship with the Lord. Just because you have moved away in some fashion from the Lord does not mean He has stopped listening to you and answering your prayers. He still loves you, and when you pray, He answers all your prayers for your good. Your good might well mean that you go through great difficulty and end up on the ground and your back, because there, you might look up and begin to pray and trust again. That is what is truly good for you in this case.

What is best for all God's children is that they have a living relationship with their Savior and God. We tend to focus on the short span of years of this physical life, but God considers the eternity that follows. God's answers to our prayers target eternal things with temporal blessings added along the path. He can and does produce good in the here and now, but what is best is what will last for all eternity.

A strong prayer life enhances the believer's life and produces eternal fruit.

Chapter 11 Reference List

[143] Ephesians 4:24
[144] Romans 7:8-25; Galatians 5:17-23
[145] Hebrews 11:6
[146] Galatians 2:20, Ephesians 4:6, I Corinthians 6:19-20
[147] Romans 10:17

Chapter 12
Can Prayer Change What is Going to Happen?

Can Prayer Change Things?

To understand how prayer works, or as the engineer in me thinks, the mechanics of prayer, let us first ask a few questions and examine them.

- Is prayer effective?
- Does prayer change things?
- Is there power in prayer?

If we only consider the words we pray, the correct answers to these questions are no, no, and no. Praying in and of itself has no power, is ineffective, and does not change anything. Now, before you say, "What?" and throw the book across the room or delete the eBook, these questions are presented in reverse order with the intention of drawing our attention to our God, to whom we are praying. Our Heavenly Father is the effective one, the one who changes things, and the one who has power! Praying to an idol, a person, or an inanimate object has no benefit since they have no power; prayer to them is just words spoken into the air. The effect, the change, and the power are found in our mighty God, who answers prayer, and in the genuine dynamic relationship you have with Him. This relationship is what is of utmost importance.

Thus, God's response to your prayer is filled with power, which produces the effects and the changes. If you do not pray, you will not experience this power of God working in your life. This truth alone should cause believers to engage in a dynamic prayer life, bringing God's limitless power to bear on the details of life. Hence, praying becomes effective, changes things, and has power because of the one true God you are praying to and your relationship with Him as His child. This is what we must remember.

> "Now **unto him that is able to do exceeding abundantly** above all that we ask or think, according to the power that worketh in us," *Ephesians 3:20*

> "Ah Lord GOD! behold, thou hast made the heaven and the earth by thy great power and stretched out arm, *and* **there is nothing too hard for thee:**" *Jeremiah 32:17*

> "Behold, **I *am* the LORD, the God of all flesh**: is there anything too hard for me?" *Jeremiah 32:27*

More than you CAN ASK or THINK!

Furthermore, our God, the creator of the universe and of us all, does exceedingly abundantly more than we can ask or think! Wrap your mind around that. More than you CAN ASK or THINK! Our prayer taps into God's infinite power and love. It taps into the very loving relationship that you have with Him. He wants you to communicate everything to Him; your pain and joys, the hard things and the easy, your wants and desires, your needs and requests, spiritual things, emotional things, physical things…everything.[148] In praying, you can experience the power of God in your life in a genuine way. Pray, pray, pray!

> "**Pray without ceasing**. In everything give thanks: for this is the will of God in Christ Jesus concerning you." *1 Thessalonians 5:17-18*

> "I exhort therefore, that, first of all, **supplications, prayers, intercessions, and giving of thanks,** be made for all men; For kings, and for all that are in authority; that we may lead a quiet and peaceable life in all godliness and honesty." *1 Timothy 2:1-2*

> "**Withal praying also for us**, that God would open unto us a door of utterance, to speak the mystery of Christ, for which I am also in bonds:" *Colossians 4:3*

"Rejoicing in hope; patient in tribulation; **continuing instant in prayer;**" *Romans 12:12*

Fundamental Question: Does God Honestly Care What You Think?

We have seen so far that God answers every prayer that we pray, and that He answers them for our good and according to His will. So, His answer is best. We know He can say "Yes" to our request, or "No," or something completely different. But we know that it is good and the best answer possible. Let us look at this question: "Does God honestly care what you think when he answers your prayer?" Or will God answer your prayer according to what He intended, without considering the actual requests in your prayer?

When you pray, are you not praying for what you think you need or want? Aren't they your requests, supplications, intercessions, or thanks? These are from you, from your heart. This is what is on your mind, what you believe needs God's attention. Prayer is generally about what we care about, what is on our minds. Doesn't God want you to pray without ceasing, to be instant in prayer, and to be careful for nothing, but in everything by prayer, make your requests known unto God? He is commanding us to make our requests known unto Him. He must care about what you think. Otherwise, He is playing with us like puppets on a string. This would be utterly contrary to the God of the Bible, who loves us individually and personally. Scripture has ample evidence that our God cares about what we think and that it touches His heart when we lift the details of our lives up to Him in prayer.

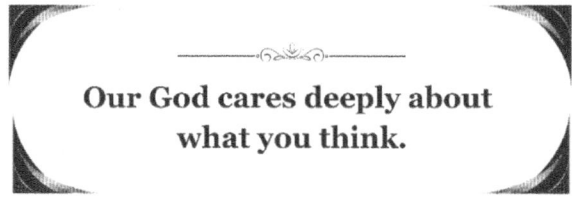

Our God cares deeply about what you think.

Can Prayer Change What Is Going to Happen or What God is Going to Allow?

This question will be central to what we are trying to understand as we go deeper into our study of how prayer works. Let me rephrase the question more directly: Does God take into account what you pray for to change what will happen in the future? Let this question sink in. Does the Lord alter the future course of events, from what would have happened if you had not prayed?

The diagram below shows what this means when we do not pray. Something is happening in your life, the "Cause." You do not pray, so it proceeds to its outcome, the "Effect." This would be God's present will

for your life. These are the regular cascade of causes and effects that we have each day when we do not pray. The Lord still promises that all things work together for good because you are His child, but the days advance without your prayers and requests. God's will is still being accomplished because He works everything according to His will. Let us look at an enlightening story of fictitious causes and effects that could be one of your mornings.

Lost Keys

You are arguing with your teenage daughter about her not putting gas in the car last night. While rushing to eat breakfast, you spill coffee on your shirt sleeve and have to change it. Your annoyed teenage daughter leaves the house early to get away from you and goes to her bus stop for school. You are late and cannot find your car keys. Your daughter gets on the school bus and is on her way to school. You remember that your daughter, who borrowed the car last night, never gave you the keys when she came home, so she has them. You angrily decide to take an Uber. You are running late. You request the nearest Uber driver, even though he only has a rating of three stars. He arrives five minutes later than estimated. The Uber driver fought with his girlfriend the day before and is distracted in his thinking and driving, continuously muttering things under his breath. He runs over a curb and blows a tire. You spill hot coffee on yourself again. You are delayed another 20 minutes until another Uber driver picks you up and gets you to work about 35 minutes late. You are written up for being late and docked an hour's pay. Your boss stares at you all day long.

This is a fictional story; however, it illustrates the small causes and effects that we each experience. Could praying to God during these various events have changed the outcome? This is the question we are asking. If we pray, can it change the effect? Does God take what we are praying and consider them to potentially change the effect, to produce a different outcome, a different future? Let us add this to the earlier diagram. Something is happening in your life, the "Cause." But this time, you pray about it. God listens and answers in some way: no, yes, or something else. A different "Effect" is the result. So, which is occurring? Does God change what will happen based on our prayer or not?

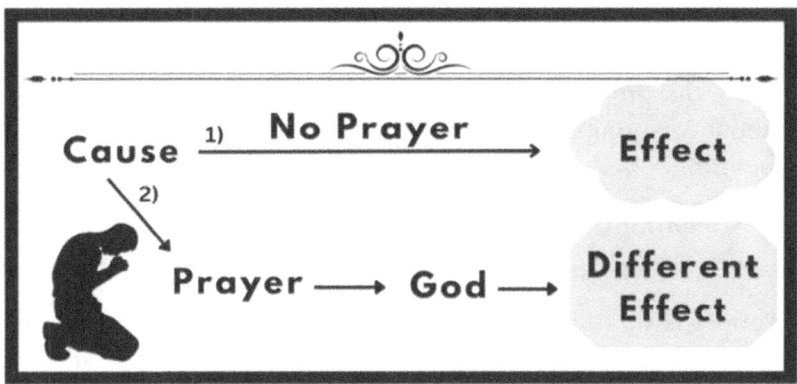

Have you ever prayed for rain or sunshine? Aren't you asking God for a different outcome? Does praying result in a different effect from what would happen if you do not pray? Some say no, as this would change your physical reality. It would change the future! However, God's Word says otherwise. Paul believed that the prayers of the saints would deliver him out of prison, out of the hands of evil men, and provide a prosperous journey. To be on point, it is not prayer that does the changing, but remember, it's the God to whom you are praying. In the Bible, there are many accounts of God altering circumstances and changing the course of events. He is sovereign and can do as He chooses. However, does God transform and change circumstances or the course of events for His children in response to prayer, or was it His intention anyway?

God's Children: Which are You?

We will examine the relationship between prayer and God's will, specifically for God's children. God has made a promise to His children that is powerful to understand. Let us look at Romans 8:28, a favorite verse for many.

> "And we know that all things work together for good to them that love God, to them who are the called according to his purpose." *Romans 8:28*

Romans 8:28, at first read, appears to be talking about one subject, God's children who love God, with a further explanation being that they are also called according to His purpose. However, if that is the case, then God only works things together for good for those who love God, who are putting the Lord first in their lives. Those not living for the Lord are left out of God's providential watch care. This would contradict the truth that Jesus Christ is the Head of the Body and that we all are part of the Body, regardless of our walk before the Lord. Our Lord cares for every member of the Body.

Hence, the proper understanding of Romans 8:28 is that this verse talks about two groups of individuals, both of which God works all things together for good.

- **Group 1** – to them that love God.
- **Group 2** – to them who are called according to His purpose.

Group 1 is those who love God. Those who love God have placed God first in their life. They have chosen to live for Him. They are actively living the Christian life. As the Apostle Paul states in Philippians, for me to live is Christ. God is a reality in their life, and they seek Him in prayer and the Word. Group 1 children are also called according to His purpose, but have also chosen to live for Christ and love God.

Group 2 is the rest of God's children. All God's children are called according to God's purpose. Every member of the Body has a calling, a gift, and a function.[149] However, these Christians are going through the motions of their Christian life. Perhaps they have even walked away from their faith. They are still saved but not living for Christ and are much like the world in their actions and daily walk.

> "But in a great house there are not only vessels of gold and of silver, but also of wood and of earth; and some to honour, and some to dishonour. If a man therefore purge himself from these, he shall be a vessel unto honour, sanctified, and meet for the master's use, and prepared unto every good work."
> *2 Timothy 2:20-21*

In 2 Timothy 2:20-21, scripture further defines these two groups of Christians. God describes His great house, the household of God, as having vessels of honor and dishonor.

Vessels of Honor: These vessels are sanctified, meet for the master's use, and are prepared for every good work. God sees them as vessels of gold and silver, doing things that have lasting and eternal value. The contextual warnings in the surrounding passage are bad doctrine and sin in the believer's life. These individuals are sanctified in their walk in the sense that they have separated themselves from the things of this world and are rightly dividing the Word of truth. They have a Colossians 3:1-4[150] view of life. Since they are God's children, they were already sanctified positionally when they trusted Christ as Savior.

Vessels of Dishonor: These vessels in God's household are God's children, saved and sanctified in their position before God, but their lives are nearly a wrecked ruin. They are consumed with the sin of this world and struggling doctrinally. They are not living for the Lord; they are doing carnal and temporal things, described as wood and earth, having no eternal value. Their lives produce valueless work, definitely not godly. Yet they are God's children, and God is still at work in their lives, but they have almost zero awareness of His work in and for them. Prayer is a distant notion in their life as they have become sensual and focused on earthly pleasures. Or perhaps, as it says a few verses later, Satan has taken them captive at his will.

The good news is that God works in every believer's life, regardless of their walk before the Lord. As Romans 8:28 states, He is working all things together for good, for all His children. This is consistent with Colossians 2:10, in which all God's children are complete in Christ, and Philippians 1:6, where we find that God continues in the good work in you, which He started in each of us at salvation.

> "And ye are complete in him, which is the head of all principality and power:" *Colossians 2:10*

> "Being confident of this very thing, that he which hath begun a good work in you will perform it until the day of Jesus Christ:" *Philippians 1:6*

Since God works all things together for good for His children, the things that happen in the believer's life must be God's will by default. At the very least, God is allowing it because He can change it if He chooses. Furthermore, the good that God is producing in the child of God's life will be quite different depending on whether one is a vessel of honor or a vessel of dishonor. In both cases, God's work in the child of God is moving us to be more like Christ. For the vessel of honor, God's work will affect positive motion in the direction that the believer is already going. However, for the vessel of dishonor, the good that God produces will work to turn around the believer from the path they are on. We will find that this is true for God's answer to prayer as well. His answers will always be to move us in the direction of being like Christ. If we are going the wrong direction, His answers will be to turn us around, which is not always easy.

For example, in the fictitious story shared earlier, "**Lost Keys**," those causes and effects could very well be the will of God for you on that day. God could be teaching you something about anger or patience or the need for love, etc. It also could be an outworking of Galatians 6:7-8, where you reap what you sow. And since God put the law of sowing and reaping in operation, it would also be His will for you.

> "Be not deceived; God is not mocked: for whatsoever a man soweth, that shall he also reap. For he that soweth to his flesh shall of the flesh reap corruption; but he that soweth to the Spirit shall of the Spirit reap life everlasting." *Galatians 6:7-8*

However, it could also be God's will to let things come hard and fast so that you learn to pray and trust God. God promises in 1 Corinthians 10:13 that He will not allow you to be tested/tempted beyond what you can handle. Again, this is God's will that He is working in your life. His will is that you respond in prayer to every circumstance. So, will you? Or will you try to do things your way and in your strength?

> "Rejoice evermore. Pray without ceasing. In everything give thanks: for this is the will of God in Christ Jesus concerning you." *1 Thessalonians 5:16-18*

Praying in every situation will make you stronger in the Lord. If, in the story, you had chosen in your free will to pray that you would not be angry when you talked to your daughter, you may have been calmer. You may not have spilled your coffee. Your daughter would not have been annoyed and perhaps would have stayed longer at breakfast, long enough to give you the keys. A simple change at one point could have altered future events. **But that would mean that what God had intended for the good that He was working in your life, He would now change because you prayed.**

To be clear, the implication is that our Sovereign God, when He answers your prayer, can change what He intended to do, His will for your life, and produce a new outcome. Hmmm. Next Chapter...

Chapter 12 Reference List

[148] Philippians 4:6-7
[149] 1 Corinthians 12:12-27; Romans 1:6; Romans 8:30; I Corinthians 1:9
[150] Colossians 3:1-4 If ye then be risen with Christ, seek those things which are above, where Christ setteth on the right hand of God. Set your affection on things above, not on things on the earth. For ye are dead, and your life is hid with Christ in God. When Christ, who is our life, shall appear, then shall ye also appear with him in glory.

Chapter 13
Prayer and the Will of God

Can God's Will Change?

When we pray, we acknowledge God as sovereign, all-powerful, and all-knowing. He is God. So, when we pray to God, are we asking God to change His will? Consider the upset Uber driver in the previous story. What if you had discerned that he was upset, and you prayed for him that God would quiet his heart and give him peace? You may have made it to work on time. Remember that God works all things (good and bad, easy and hard) together for good for the child of God. However, if the story's circumstances are God's will for you, your prayer would be asking God to change the good He has planned for you to something different —a different good. This would be asking God to change His will in response to your prayer.

So, can God's will change? We will spend this and the following remaining chapters answering this question and a much larger question: Can your prayer change God's will? This is going to be fun!

If you examined the works of theologians concerning God's will, you would discover that it is a battleground of ideas and terminology. However, scripture bears out that God's will falls into two general types. First, we find God's "sovereign" determined will, which is unchangeable and fixed, and God will bring it to pass. The second type of God's will is revealed through God's commands and instructions in His Word. We will call this God's "commanded" will. This type of God's will is also unchangeable, but mankind, in his free will, can do it or fail to do it. Because of free will, man can even choose to reject God's commanded will for a season. Man's disobedience does not change the will of God or even hinder it. When sin has finally been dealt with and that old sin nature has been left behind, in our own free will, all of God's children will do all of God's will. There will be no rejection of anything that God wills.

God's Sovereign Will

God's sovereign will is unchangeable and unable to be thwarted. His sovereign will is not something we can say yes or no to. It is not an instruction to us, or a command. It is the things God says He will do, regardless of what man, angels, or the Devil does. God has predetermined certain things, and they will not change. For instance, Titus 1:2 states, "In hope of eternal life, which God that cannot lie, promised before the world began." God will not change His mind on this. He has made a promise, and He cannot lie. Romans 11:29 clarifies further, "For the gifts and calling of God are without repentance." The word repentance means to "change the mind." Aren't you glad that when our God gives a gift, He does not change His mind? Salvation is a gift from God to everyone who believes.[151] The Lord does not make mistakes or change His mind when He gives salvation to a person who has trusted in the finished work of Jesus Christ. Here are just a few examples of God's sovereign will that God has revealed.

How Many Ways are there to Heaven?

> "Jesus saith unto him, I am the way, the truth, and the life: no man cometh unto the Father, but by me." *John 14:6*

> "For the wages of sin is death; but the gift of God is eternal life through Jesus Christ our Lord." *Romans 6:23*

> "For I am not ashamed of the gospel of Christ: for it is the power of God unto salvation to every one that believeth; to the Jew first, and also to the Greek. For therein is the righteousness of God revealed from faith to faith: as it is written, The just shall live by faith." *Romans 1:16-17*

> "Who gave himself for our sins, that he might deliver us from this present evil world, according to the will of God and our Father: To whom be glory for ever and ever. Amen. I marvel that ye are so soon removed from him that called you into the grace of Christ unto another gospel: Which is not another; but there be some that trouble you, and would pervert the gospel of Christ. But though we, or an angel from heaven, preach any other gospel unto you than that which we have preached unto you, let him be accursed. As we said before, so say I now again, If any man preach any other gospel unto you than that ye have received, let him be accursed." *Galatians 1:4-9*

God says there is only one way to Heaven today. It does not matter whether some say you need to do some ritual or that there is a different way.[152] God's Word is the authority. Only through the Lord Jesus Christ can an individual be saved.[153] And only by grace through faith. It is a gift of God.

The Rapture (the Blessed Hope)

When the Rapture will occur is also part of God's determined, sovereign will.[154] You can pray all that you want to delay it or beg that it happens now; in either case, God's sovereign will has already defined when it will occur. All we know is that it can happen at any time. God has the time of the rapture planned according to His will.

Everything Will be Gathered in Christ.

> "Having made known unto us the mystery of his will, according to his good pleasure which he hath purposed in himself: **That in the dispensation of the fulness of times he might gather together in one all things in Christ, both which are in heaven, and which are on earth;** even in him: In whom also we have obtained an inheritance, being predestinated according to the purpose of him who worketh all things after the counsel of his own will:" *Ephesians 1:9-11*

We see from this passage that God had kept part of His eternal will a secret (the mystery now revealed). Our God will gather together all things in Christ and place all under His control, both in heaven and on earth. We (the Body of Christ) also have an inheritance. The word "also" implies that our inheritance is in addition to Israel's inheritance, which is on Earth. The Body of Christ's inheritance is separate from Israel's and is in the heavens.

The Earthly Kingdom and Israel

> "For unto us a child is born, unto us a son is given: and the government shall be upon his shoulder: and his name shall be called Wonderful, Counsellor, The mighty God, The everlasting Father, The Prince of Peace. Of the increase of his government and peace there shall be no end, upon the throne of David, and upon his kingdom, to order it, and to establish it with judgment and with justice from henceforth even for ever. **The zeal of the LORD of hosts will perform this."** *Isaiah 9:6-7*

The Earthly Kingdom, with Christ reigning as King, is also part of God's sovereignly determined will. The Lord is not done with Israel. Look at the last sentence of Isaiah 9:7: "The zeal of the LORD of hosts will perform this." Nothing is going to stop God from doing this. It is part of His sovereign will for the Earth and Israel. They will reign with Christ in His earthly kingdom and during the millennium. Read Romans 11:25-29 as well.

> "For I would not, brethren, that ye should be ignorant of this mystery, lest ye should be wise in your own conceits; that blindness in part is happened to Israel, until the fulness of the Gentiles be come in. **And so all Israel shall be saved: as it is written, There shall come out of Sion the Deliverer, and shall turn away ungodliness from Jacob: For this is my covenant unto them, when I shall take away their sins**. As concerning the gospel, they are enemies for your sakes: but as touching the election, they are beloved for the fathers' sakes. **For the gifts and calling of God are without repentance."** *Romans 11:25-29*

So, in the case of God's sovereign will, God will not change it. It is fixed in the mind of God and will occur. No amount of praying will sway the mind of God in these circumstances. Other examples include the Body of Christ spending eternity in Heaven, being conformed to the image of Christ, and having new bodies that enable us to function in heavenly places.

Does Mankind Have Free Will, and If So, Why?

I know, I know, theologians and others argue, pound the table, and some stomp their feet, on whether man has free will or not. They wrestle with this verse and that verse, trying to garner the infinite musings of God into some finite visage of understanding. Yet, there is one simple, foundational truth concerning the relationship between God and His creation, an inescapable truth that affirms that man must have free will. God is love. Furthermore, because He is love, He will not overrule the free will of man; otherwise, it is not free will. Let me explain.

To be sure, there are many other arguments for the existence of the free will of man, including that God has created mankind in His image, body, soul, and spirit, as well as the attributes of His being a person. As a son of God, mankind must be able to choose, or God is a liar and the creator of sin. Titus 1:2

For the sake of brevity, we will discuss love. God is love, as stated in 1 John 4:8. It is His very nature. To exercise love, you must have someone to love. Love requires that you choose to make another person first over yourself. We see this definition of love when we look at what Christ did for us. Romans 5:8 declares, "But God commendeth His love towards us while we were yet sinners, Christ died for us." He chose us over Himself. He went to the cross of Calvary for us. Oh, what love!

Love is the reason that God has a creation. God lacks nothing, but because He is love, He wants to give and choose others first. Therefore, He created man in His image, with free will, so that He could love us. Love requires, no, demands free will. Love demands the ability to reject or accept that love. You cannot love a pencil. You may have a favorite pencil, but you cannot love a pencil because it cannot love you. It will always do exactly your will, but it cannot love you back because it cannot choose you. Without free will, God's creation could not love God back. Mankind would be a puppet, a marionette, dangling on the fingertips of God, perfectly doing His will…but without choice, without love. What a hollow creation, without choice, without love, without the ability to choose to worship or bring Honor and Glory to their Creator. A creation following a script without choice cannot please God. Hebrews 11:6 states that without faith it is impossible to please God. Faith can only exist when one can choose to trust or believe. God created us to love Him as He loves us. And so free will is an absolute necessity. Yet, free will allows us to choose whether to accept or reject God and face the consequences. One day, after we leave this flesh behind, we will no longer say no to God; we will no longer murmur or dispute against Him. We will respond in love, as our new nature is created in righteousness and true holiness. What a day that will be!

God's Will and Your Free Will

Let us examine several verses that demonstrate the interaction of man's free will and the second type of God's will, His commanded will. As mentioned earlier, God has also revealed His will in the commands and instructions that He has given man in His Word. Unlike God's sovereign will, since these are commands and instructions, mankind, in his free will, can say no or yes to what God demands. These commands and instructions are still God's will and do not change just because some of mankind reject them. Refusing what God has commanded, His will, however, does have consequences.

> "Who (God) will have all men to be saved, and to come unto the knowledge of the truth. For there is one God, and one mediator between God and men, the man Christ Jesus;" *1 Timothy 2:4-5*

It is God's will that all men be saved and come to the knowledge of the truth. If this were God's sovereign will, then everyone would get saved and come to the knowledge of the truth. Nothing can hinder God's sovereign will. However, experience reveals that this is not what happens or what has happened. This is God's will that He commands, but God has chosen in His sovereign will not to overrule the will of man. Christ died for everyone, and we are justified freely by his grace through the redemption in Christ Jesus:[155] Christ's blood paid for all mankind's sins, and Romans 10:13 declares that whosoever calls upon the name of the Lord shall be saved. However, everyone has a choice to accept the gift of salvation or reject it. God's will is for all men to be saved, but many will reject this gift. Have you prayed for someone to come to know Christ and what He did for them, and it has not happened? It is God's will that those you prayed for do get saved; that is true. But God will not overrule their free will.

In 1 Thessalonians 5:16-18, we see another instance where Scripture states that this is the will of God for each of us.

> "Rejoice evermore. Pray without ceasing. In everything give thanks: for this is the will of God in Christ Jesus concerning you." *1 Thessalonians 5:16-18*

The Lord has commanded us to rejoice evermore. That we are always in prayer with Him and thankful in every situation. This is God's will for us, yet we each have a choice to make in every moment of our lives. We can choose to rejoice, pray, and give thanks or not. When we get to Heaven, it will be our everyday experience: rejoicing evermore, praying without ceasing (continuously communicating with our God as He is Head of the Body), and we will be thankful!

In 1 Thessalonians 4:3-8, God gives three more statements concerning God's will for our lives. Scripture states, "For this is the will of God, even your sanctification."

- "That ye should abstain from fornication,"
- "That every one of you should know how to possess his vessel in sanctification and honor,"
- "That no man go beyond and defraud his brother in any matter."

This is God's will for you, but you can disobey it. You and your flesh can get in the way of living for the Lord. We have liberty and responsibility in this age of Grace. As we allow the Holy Spirit to transform our lives, and as we are in the Word of God, we will be able to do these aspects of the will of God as He commands. Even though these are God's will for all of us, He does not force us to do them. God has given his children free will to choose Him and His will, but his children can foolishly reject Him, too. As we grow in faith, we ought to make more decisions that align with our heavenly Father's will and choose God's things. Of course, after the Rapture, we will also fulfill this part of God's will. Our old flesh, that old man, will be left behind!

In discussing God's commanded will, in which God will not overrule the will of man, we could have included many other scriptural commands for our Christian walk. Bear ye one another's burdens, walk worthy of the Lord, love one another, submit yourselves one to another, weep with those that weep, be thou an example of the believers, follow after righteousness, walk in love, and so on. These and many other instructions in God's Word are God's will for our lives. And in our free will, we can obey or reject. Just because we say no to God in such matters does not change the reality that these commands are still God's will and are perfect. God's commanded will does not change.

God is at Work in Us, Accomplishing His Will.

For each of us, God is at work in our lives, working His will, filtering through circumstances, working things together for good, producing a good work in you, and ensuring that everything is for our benefit and is of value. These four verses below clearly attest to these conclusions.

"There hath no temptation taken you but such as is common to man: but God is faithful, who will not suffer you to be tempted above that ye are able; but will with the temptation also make a way to escape, that ye may be able to bear it." *1 Corinthians 10:13*

"And we know that all things work together for good to them that love God, to them who are the called according to his purpose." *Romans 8:28*

"Being confident of this very thing, that he which hath begun a good work in you will perform it until the day of Jesus Christ:" *Philippians 1:6*

"For all things are for your sakes, that the abundant grace might through the thanksgiving of many redound to the glory of God." *2 Corinthians 4:15*

God works in the details of our lives, changing, filtering, and modifying every detail. He limits what testing or trials can enter your life since He will not allow you to be tempted (tried, tested) beyond what you can bear. God knows you and knows what you can handle with His presence in your life. He also works all things together for good for you, both the easy things and the hard things. Our mighty God orchestrates good into your life from every aspect of your experiences. Furthermore, our God will not cease to produce a good work in you. He loves you and will remain an active presence in your life. What an amazing, loving, powerful, and omniscient God our God is. The good that God produces in us has positive, eternal consequences, not confined to just this life, but has promise of the next.

Chapter 13 References List

[151] Ephesians 2:8-9; Romans 6:19
[152] Proverbs 14:12
[153] John 14:6; 1 Timothy 2:5
[154] I Corinthians 15:51-53; I Thessalonians 4:13-18, Titus 2:13
[155] Romans 3:24

Chapter 14
What is Good?

What is this Good that God is Producing?

Before we go on and see how praying to God affects the will of God and the good that He is producing in our lives, we ought to spend some time clarifying what is meant by the good that God is working in the believer's life. What is this good?

> "And we know that all things work together for good to them that love God, to them who are the called according to his purpose." *Romans 8:28*

God makes all things work together for good; what does that mean? What we might consider good is not necessarily what God considers good. Our focus tends to be on the present, the moment we are in. If things are rough, not going our way, or we have severe and maybe terminal health problems or are living in turmoil, how can that be good? We live in a sin-cursed creation where everything about us decays, weakens, and falls apart, including our bodies. How can that be good? When wicked and evil people do awful, unthinkable things, and even to God's children, how can that be good?

First, the Bible does not say that all things **are** good, but it says that God works all things together **for** good. Obviously, many of the things mentioned, and many more that come to mind, are not good. Sin is not good, many of the circumstances we can find ourselves in are just not good. I have known many individuals over the years whose family situation is hard, unfair, or even devoid of godly influence. It breaks my heart every time, but God can still use even these things to bring about good through His grace. "And God is able to make all grace abound toward you; that ye, always having all sufficiency in all things, may abound to every good work."[156] And as the Apostle Paul declares in 2 Corinthians 12:9,10

> "And He said unto me, My grace is sufficient for thee: for My strength is made perfect in weakness. Most gladly therefore will I rather glory in my infirmities, that the power of Christ may rest upon me. Therefore, I take pleasure in infirmities, in reproaches, in necessities, in persecutions, in distresses for Christ's sake: for when I am weak, then am I strong.[157]"

From a human perspective, this does not make much sense. However, Paul realized that God was good and that He was at work in his life; what God produced is good. Even difficult things are valuable, as they help move us toward being more like Christ.

Scripture reveals that our all-powerful God takes the complex things that impact our lives and works them together to produce good. In Luke 18:19, "And Jesus said unto him, Why callest thou me good? None is good, save one, that is, God." Thus, God is good. Since God is good, what He does is good. We have seen before that God is love, and what He does is because of love. It is His nature. It is who He is. What God produces in the believer's life then is a nature that is like our Lord's. He is making each of us more like Him. We read in 2 Corinthians 3:18 that as we are confronted in the Word of God with the glory of the Lord, we are changed into that same glory.

> "But we all, with open face beholding as in a glass the glory of the Lord, are changed into the same image from glory to glory, even as by the Spirit of the Lord." *2 Corinthians 3:18*

The glory of God is who He is, His nature. He is gracious. He is loving. He is good. He is righteous. He is just. He is longsuffering and more. God is all of these things in infinite perfection. All these things together are His glory. And the Holy Spirit is always at work, producing all of God's nature in the child of God. "But the fruit of the Spirit is love, joy, peace, longsuffering, gentleness, goodness, faith, meekness, temperance: against such there is no law."[158] As sinners, Romans 3:23 declares that all have sinned and come short of the glory of God. This means far more than we fall short of God's righteousness. We also fall short of every aspect of who He is. None of us is as loving as God or long-suffering as God. God's will, however, is that we are conformed to the image of His Son. "For whom he did foreknow, he also did predestinate to be conformed to the image of his Son, that he might be the firstborn among many brethren." [159] And on that day, when we are in His presence, we will be like Him. We will be glorified. But until that day, our God is busy working together the details of our life, to fashion in us and through us His good.

> "For it is God which worketh in you both to will and to do of his good pleasure." *Philippians 2:13*

The good that God is producing is purposeful and directional. The purpose is to make us more like Him in thinking and action. It is directional in that the good that is produced points us in a direction toward who we are in Christ, which is our standing.[160] We are saints, holy, righteous, justified, glorified, forgiven, God's children, blessed, beloved, accepted, etc. The Holy Spirit further provides positive pressure or conviction to walk in this good that God has produced in our lives. But it is our choice to heed His conviction and will. In Romans 12, we are beseeched or begged by all that God has done for us to give our lives to God and be transformed by the renewing of our mind so that our actions and walk demonstrate God's good, acceptable, and perfect will.

> "I beseech you therefore, brethren, by the mercies of God, that ye present your bodies a living sacrifice, holy, acceptable unto God, which is your reasonable service. And be not conformed to this world: but be ye transformed by the renewing of your mind, that ye may prove what is that good, and acceptable, and perfect, will of God." *Romans 12:1-2*

God's will is that our walk[161] and standing are the same. None of us has accomplished this yet on this side of glory because we are all sinners, saved by grace. So, God orchestrates good into our lives from every aspect of our experiences. He provides a positive path forward toward being more like our Savior.

> "Not as though I had already attained, either were already perfect: but I follow after, if that I may apprehend that for

which also I am apprehended of Christ Jesus. Brethren, I count not myself to have apprehended: but this one thing I do, forgetting those things which are behind, and reaching forth unto those things which are before, I press toward the mark for the prize of the high calling of God in Christ Jesus." *Philippians 3:12-14*

The good that God produces supplies opportunities to grow and be more like our Lord and Savior, Jesus Christ. This will be true when we leave this old flesh behind at death or the Rapture. To actuate the good that the Lord has produced, we need faith. "Now faith is the substance of things hoped for, the evidence of things not seen."[162] Taking steps of faith on that path towards good and trusting our Lord along the way makes that good come alive and become a reality in our lives. When the Apostle Paul prayed to have a "thorn in the flesh"[163] removed, the Lord told him that it was needful for him and that the Lord's grace, His favor, was enough. The Apostle Paul embraced that truth by faith, and what was a burden and hardship became something good and powerful in his life. He realized that when he was weak, that was when he was truly strong. When he was weak, he relied on the Lord and His strength. "Be strong in the Lord and in the power of His might." [164]

Was Paul in the will of God? He was attacked, had numerous adversaries, was plagued by wicked men, Satan buffeted him, was in prison multiple times, was shipwrecked multiple times, and more. Hard things do not indicate in any way that one is out of the will of God. Paul was exactly where God wanted and needed him. Difficulties and hardships are recast as light afflictions and are valuable for us.[165] Because Paul had this thorn in the flesh, it produced what God wanted in and from Paul: epistles, humbleness, love, driven by the Spirit, passion about the lost, and faithfulness. And these benefited others that Paul ministered to, and even us today, nearly two thousand years later.

Of course, we can choose to wallow in the mire, blinded to the beauty that God has before us if only we trusted Him. We have free will, and as such, we can choose to live our lives trusting the Son of God, who is faithful, or we can live our lives apart from His guidance. We can reject or humble ourselves to what God is working in our lives. His Holy Spirit convicts us and empowers us to walk in the good He has created. However, we can reject what He has done and ignore our God and His goodness.

As His children, the Lord works things together for good, whether we are in obedience or disobedience. Maybe that causes you to raise an eyebrow in question? One must realize that what God does will look very different depending on the choices made by His children. The good that God produces in the lives of those in obedience to Him continues them on the path that they are on as they grow in the Lord. Peace, love, and joy accompany this path, even if there is adversity. On the other hand, the good that God works in the lives of those in disobedience is focused on stopping them from the destructive path they are on and turning them around. Their choices are actively moving them away from being like Christ, away from the good things of God. This good may not seem good to them; in fact, it might be hard, but our Lord is looking to what is of eternal value. He is chipping away at their old man, their sin nature, weakening its hold, so that they can choose to walk in newness of life. Our God does this for everything that happens in our lives. We need to wake up and begin to seek things above and set our affection on things above.

God's Good that He Works, Our Free Will and Faith Response

However our Faith Response is not always "Yes Lord." It can be totally "No Lord" or some sort of partial obedience. Let's see what that looks like and how God's working all things for good changes, but maintains it's focus to conform us to the image of His Son.

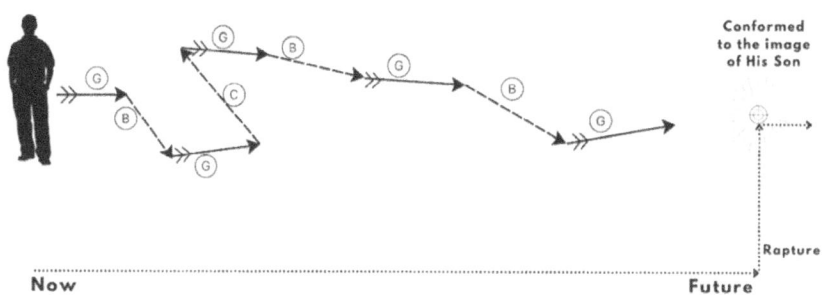

The diagram above illustrates, in schematic form, how this process works. Examine the Key, and you will see two types of arrow lines. The solid one represents God's good that He is working in the child of God's life. The arrow with a dotted line represents man's Faith response to what

God is doing in his life. Notice that it can produce positive motion in the direction that God is working, or produce negative motion away from what is good in the believer's life. The circles labeled G, A, B, and C correspond to the descriptive text. Circle G is God's producing of good from the things in our lives. Circles A, B, and C are man's various Faith responses to the good that God has produced in the believer's life.

(G) God's good that He is working, His Will for you.

God is always producing good from the things that come into our lives. For those who respond positively to God's work in their life, that good is made up of circumstances, conviction, strength, peace, love, joy, and other fruits of the Spirit. For those who are wandering or running away from God, that good is also circumstances and conviction, but with a lack of strength, peace, love, joy, and other fruits of the Spirit. In both of these cases, God is working to move the child of God to be more like Christ. For those who are growing in the Lord, the good that God is working builds on what is already there. For those who have become wayward and dishonorable children, God works to turn the wandering child back to the direction that is good, much like a bridle in a horse's mouth. These things probably seem not good to the wayward child since God is working against their will, chipping away at their flesh and misguided will. In both cases, God is producing positive pressure and conviction, always pointing us to be conformed to the image of His Son. (For those of you who know the parable of the prodigal son, he is a picture of this process.) *Philippians 2:13, 2 Corinthians 3:18, Romans 8:29; Philippians 3:10-14.*

(A) Man's Faith Response to what God is doing in his life.

This is man's faith response to the good that God works in them. In this case, we see a perfect response to what God is working in one's life. This faithful response aligns with God's Will and aims to conform them to be like Christ. This is a positive response to God's will and work. This is what honors and glorifies God the most, when we, by Faith, accept His will and walk in it.

(B) Man's Incomplete Positive Faith Response

This is a positive Faith response to what God is doing, but not in complete obedience to the good that God is working. This Faith response has leaned to the left or perhaps to the right. Possibly, there is a lack of faith, will, courage, or understanding. Consider Joshua 1:5-9 and

Philippians 4:8,9. Many times, this is our type of response, even for the willing, faithful Christian. We lean unto our own understanding. *Proverbs 3:5,6*

(C) Man's rebellious response

This is man's rebellious response that is characterized by actions that are in the negative direction, and in rejection of the good that God is producing. Perhaps, as Philippians 2:13 states, there is murmuring and disputing with God on what He is doing in their life. A Christian who minds earthly things responds this way many times as well. Consider Jonah in thinking about this.

On the next page is a diagram walking us through God and Jonah's battle of wills. By the way, God always wins. Spend some time on the diagram and seek to understand how God always directs his working in the child of God's life to point him to being more like Christ. (Even in the Old Testament.) Our faith is what is needed to engage that good in our lives.

<u>Notes</u>

Jonah Example

There are very real differences between Grace and the New Covenant, between the Body of Christ and the Nation of Israel. However, God's love for His children, Man's Free Will, and the need to respond in Faith to God is quite similar, if not the same. Let's look at Jonah and God's Will for Him and diagram it.

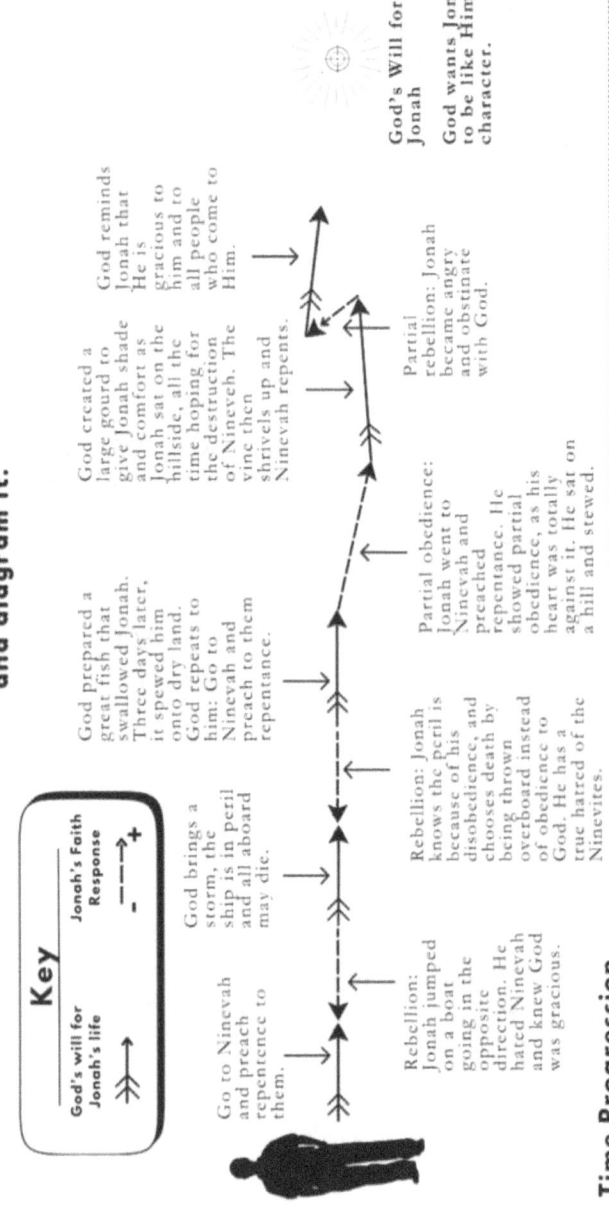

178   Praying to a Mighty God

More Complexity

Another truth of Scripture that God interweaves with His working all things together for good is the truth of reaping what we sow.

> "Be not deceived; God is not mocked: for whatsoever a man soweth, that shall he also reap. For he that soweth to his flesh shall of the flesh reap corruption; but he that soweth to the Spirit shall of the Spirit reap life everlasting." *Galatians 6:7-8*

Each act of obedience is a good seed that bears good fruit at some point in the future. However, each act of disobedience is a bad seed that bears corrupted fruit at some future time and then reaps corruption. God is accounting for these in the mix of things that He is working together for good as they bear fruit in our lives, good or bad. For the erring child, the corrupted fruit from sowing to the flesh makes it more difficult for them to see the good that God is doing. This is beyond complex, but our God, who knows the number and names of all the stars,[166] is continuously working all these things together for our good. He is God. Is there anything too hard for Him?[167]

The Apostle Paul testifies to his faith in Galatians, choosing to live by the faith of the Son of God.

> "I am crucified with Christ: nevertheless I live; yet not I, but Christ liveth in me: and the life which I now live in the flesh I live by the faith of the Son of God, who loved me, and gave himself for me." *Galatians 2:20*

The truth is that Christ lives in you and loves you. You have been "bought with a price: therefore glorify God in your body, and in your spirit, which are God's.[168] It is God's will for you and me to glorify Him. We glorify Him as we live our lives for Him by faith. He is at work in you, making you more like Him, right now.

Do not be discouraged; the believer's struggle is very real, but we can be strong in the Lord and the power of His might. The battle between the new man and the old man, the Spirit, and the flesh, is daunting and difficult. God commands us to walk in the Spirit, and we will not fulfill the lust of the flesh.[169] The fantastic thing is that our God takes all these things, good and bad, both in the Spirit and in the flesh, both in obedience and in disobedience, and works them together to produce good in the believer's life. This good is a positive outcome for the child of God in the wilderness of life, a way forward to better things. Mix this way forward with faith, and it leads to love, joy, and peace. Mix this way forward with faith, and it leads to a richer, Spirit-filled life that has victories over the everyday burdens that plague us. Mix what God is doing in our lives with faith, and this good that He produces blossoms and grows, transforming each of us and making us more like Him.

There is a chorus that we sang in church some years back that comes to my mind that seems appropriate, **"My Lord Knows the Way Through the Wilderness,"** written by Sidney E. Cox (1951). The good that God produces is a way through the wilderness, all the messy things in our lives that are happening at this moment - all we have to do is follow.

My Lord Knows the Way Through the Wilderness
My Lord knows the way through the wilderness,
All I have to do is follow.
My Lord knows the way through the wilderness,
All I have to do is follow.

Strength for today is mine all the way,
And all that I need for tomorrow.
My Lord knows the way through the wilderness,
All I have to do is follow.

God creates a way, a path to good in the believer's life. A simple step of faith, trusting Him, is all we need for that good to become a reality. He does not take away the wilderness. The hard things are still there in your life, but He is with you along the way. His grace is sufficient. He promises strength for today and all along the way. He made the way and knows the way, so follow Him. He already has tomorrow taken care of for you. What a powerful chorus and an even more powerful and amazing God we have.

> "If ye then be risen with Christ, seek those things which are above, where Christ sitteth on the right hand of God. Set your affection on things above, not on things on the earth. For ye are dead, and your life is hid with Christ in God. When Christ, who is our life, shall appear, then shall ye also appear with him in glory." *Colossians 3:1-4*

This passage summarizes God's focus as He produces the good in your life. Every child of God is commanded to seek those things that are above, where Christ sits at the right hand of God. The good that God produces leads us to seek those things above. It leads us to pray and enter the throne room of God with our requests. It always leads to seeking God first before all other things.

Every believer is commanded to set their affection on things above, not on things on earth. Affections grow as a relationship develops, as someone or something becomes more real to us. Faith is what makes the things of God real to us. The good that God produces in us will lead to growing our faith and exercising our relationship with God. It will further pull us away from earthly things, lessening their value. Our attachment to heavenly things becomes more real as our faith grows.

And finally, the good that God produces in each of us will lead us to know God's protection and watch care since we are hidden in Christ. This good path forward will lead us to experience His faithfulness and love. Our faith will grow as we follow Him. What God has in store for His child will become even more real. The good that God is producing can lead believers to victory over everything in their lives that once broke or hindered them. We need to **turn our eyes upon Jesus!**

Turn Your Eyes Upon Jesus

O soul, are you weary and troubled?
No light in the darkness you see?
There's light for a look at the Savior,
And life more abundant and free

Refrain:

Turn your eyes upon Jesus,
Look full in His wonderful face,
And the things of earth will grow strangely dim,
In the light of His glory and grace

Thro' death into life everlasting,
He passed, and we follow Him there;
O'er us sin no more hath dominion--
For more than conqu'rors we are

His Word shall not fail you--He promised;
Believe Him, and all will be well:
Then go to a world that is dying,
His perfect salvation to tell!

Author: Helen Howarth Lemmel (1922)

The Believer's Reward: An Eternal Good

There is another result of the good that God produces in our lives, and that good's impact has eternal consequences. In brief, as God's children, what we do in this life decides our reward in eternity. After the rapture, God's children will appear before the Lord Jesus Christ at the 'Bema' seat, the reward seat, and everyone will receive their reward for their own labor.

> "Now he that planteth and he that watereth are one: and every man shall receive his own reward according to his own labour. For we are labourers together with God: ye are God's husbandry, ye are God's building." *1 Corinthians 3:8*

Notice that we are laborers together with God. Our responsibility is to be faithful to Him. He is producing good in us. He always gives the increase. His Spirit renews us daily and is with us in all we do. "For it is God which worketh in you both to will and to do of his good pleasure."[170] He works in us in two ways. First, He creates a will, a desire to do His good pleasure. Second, He works in us to do His good pleasure. And then He rewards us for the good that we have done!

As we read in 2 Timothy 4:7-8, our reward is based upon the activity of our spiritual walk in this life. The good that God produces in us has positive pressure, moving us along in doing God's will when we trust God and walk by faith.

> "I have fought a good fight, I have finished my course, I have kept the faith: Henceforth there is laid up for me a crown of righteousness, which the Lord, the righteous judge, shall give me at that day: and not to me only, but unto all them also that love his appearing." *2 Timothy 4:7-8*

The "henceforth" means because of the former things, in this case: "I have fought a good fight, I have finished my course, I have kept the faith." Paul expected the Lord Jesus Christ to reward him with a crown of righteousness. He fought a good fight, being a soldier in the Lord's army, serving faithfully. He finished his course as he ran the race of the Christian life. He controlled the desires of his flesh, living a godly life, seeking to do what God had called him to do. And he kept the faith as a good husbandman, planting into the lives of others. He shared the gospel, met the hard things of life by faith, and stayed faithful to God's Word, building it into his life and the lives of others. So, he proclaims that a crown of righteousness awaits him and all those who love His "appearing." Those who love His appearing are living for the Lord Jesus Christ. They also are fighting the good fight, running the race, and keeping the faith. They are seeking and setting their affection on those things above. The believer's reward is more than the crown. It represents our reigning in heavenly places with Jesus Christ, Head of the Body. If we suffer, we shall reign with Christ.

> "It is a faithful saying: For if we be dead with him, we shall also live with him: If we suffer, we shall also reign with him: if we deny him, he also will deny us: If we believe not, yet he abideth faithful: he cannot deny himself." *2 Timothy 2:11-13*

> "Yea, and all that will live godly in Christ Jesus shall suffer persecution." *2 Timothy 3:12*

The use of 'suffer' in this verse conveys the idea of enduring difficulties and afflictions for the sake of Christ. Those who choose to live for the Lord are promised difficulties, but the Lord also promises that we will reign with Him if we do. Denying Him is choosing not to endure difficulties for the cause of Christ and to walk according to the course of this world. The result is the rejection of God's will and way in this life. He promises to deny those who live for themselves. This is not sending someone to Hell but denying that person reigning with Christ. At the Judgment Seat of Christ, the reward seat, they will suffer loss, a loss of reward,[171] and reigning with Christ.

> "Now if any man build upon this foundation gold, silver, precious stones, wood, hay, stubble; Every man's work shall be made manifest: for the day shall declare it, because it shall be revealed by fire; and the fire shall try every man's work of what sort it is. If any man's work abide which he hath built thereupon, he shall receive a reward. If any man's work shall be burned, he shall suffer loss: but he himself shall be saved; yet so as by fire." *1 Corinthians 3:12-15*

The following two verses encapsulate these ideas: the good that God is working out in our lives, the difficulties we face, and the reward that awaits the faithful child of God. The challenges of life that God is working together for good are light afflictions compared to what awaits the child of God.

> "For our light affliction, which is but for a moment, worketh for us a far more exceeding and eternal weight of glory; While we look not at the things which are seen, but at the things which

are not seen: for the things which are seen are temporal; but the things which are not seen are eternal." *2 Corinthians 4:17-18*

"For I reckon that the sufferings of this present time are not worthy to be compared with the glory which shall be revealed in us." *Romans 8:18*

In fact, the difficulties and afflictions are actually working for us and producing something of eternal value. The scripture says a far more exceeding and eternal weight of glory. This is our reward, our reigning with Jesus Christ. His glory will be revealed in us. This is the good that God is producing. "Oh, that will be glory for me…" As we, by faith, trust our Savior, the good that God makes in our lives becomes real; those afflictions and persecutions become light and valuable. They produce good and reward that goes on into eternity.

Have eyes of faith. See the eternal things. Look past the temporal details of life, trusting our Lord and Savior as we go through the things from which God is producing good.

Something Else: Does God Have a Plan for Your Life

I've heard since I was young that God has a plan for my life and that I need to discover God's will for my life, as well as what He wants me to do. As a young person and adult, I anxiously wondered what it was and if I had done anything to mess it up. While there is much truth in these statements, they give the wrong impression that it is a rigid, specific path or plan and that you could miss it totally if you fail along the way. And if you missed it, could you ever recover? However, the truth of the Word of God gives a more dynamic and fluid context to what God's plan is for your life. God does have a plan for your life. We have each been given gifts, and the exercising of those gifts is part of God's will for us, and helps define the path we are on. However, the reality of God's will for us is that it is continuously being modified by our free will actions, which also include our prayers. A better picture sees God's will for each of our lives as being dynamic and directive. God is very much focused on conforming us to the image of His Son, and this process is continually being refined…until He comes.

Chapter 14 Reference List

[156] 2 Corinthians 9:8
[157] 2 Corinthians 12:9-10
[158] Galatians 5:22-23
[159] Romans 8:29
[160] Standing – We are in Christ, that is our position. God sees us in Him. And in Him we are holy, righteousness, accepted, forgiven, justified, glorified,
[161] Our Walk – how we live in this physical life, the things we do and say
[162] Hebrews 11:1
[163] 2 Corinthians 12:7-10
[164] Ephesians 6:10
[165] 2 Corinthians 4:17-18
[166] Psalm 147:4
[167] Jeremiah 32:17, 27
[168] 1 Corinthians 6:20
[169] Galatians 5:16-18 This I say then, Walk in the Spirit, and ye shall not fulfil the lust of the flesh. For the flesh lusteth against the Spirit, and the Spirit against the flesh: and these are contrary the one to the other: so that ye cannot do the things that ye would. But if ye be led of the Spirit, ye are not under the law.
[170] Philippians 2:13
[171] I Corinthians 3:14-15

Chapter 15
The Will of God Revisited

The Dynamic Will of God for His Children

What God is doing in our lives, by necessity, is God's will for our lives. Since He is at work and producing good, that good would be His will for us. A further truth is that you could reject this good work and say no to God in your free will. You could live selfishly, walk away from Him, and follow other foolish choices.

> "For it is God which worketh in you both to will and to do of *his* good pleasure. Do all things without murmurings and disputings:" *Philippians 2:13-14*

Yes, God is at work in us, not only in working all things together for good in our lives, as we have examined, but also working in us to produce both the will and the doing of His good pleasure. So, God is producing a will in our lives to do His good pleasure, but we often fail the "doing" part. Our flesh gets in the way, and we murmur and dispute with God.

As Galatians 6:7-9 teaches, we reap what we sow. If we sow to the flesh, we will reap corruption. However, if we sow to the Spirit, we will reap everlasting life, things with eternal value.

Here is what we have concluded thus far:

- God is active in the believer's life, working all things together for good.
- This good produced is God's will for the believer.
- This would be God's will for the child of God, but the Child of God can reject it.

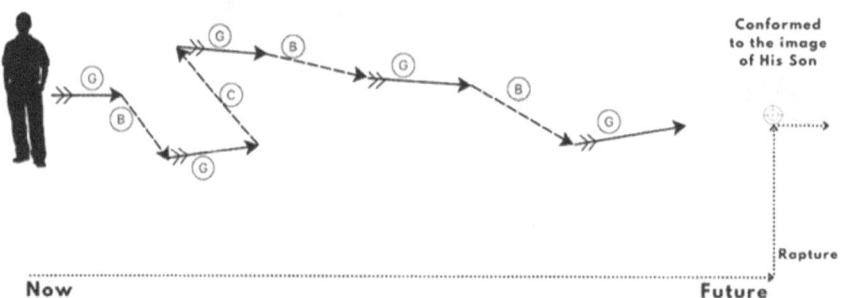

This diagram from the last chapter remains a picture of the interaction of God's will and our Faith response. As God works in us, the Holy Spirit is producing fruit in our lives, making us more like Christ.

Let us bring prayer back to the forefront of our discussion. In our free will, we can choose to pray or not. How does this impact God's will and actions? Does God take our prayers and change the good He would do in our lives to a different good in response to that prayer?

The diagram below pictures this discussion. Is this what is really happening? Can our prayer change what God's will is for us? Does God's answer to prayer produce a different good from what God initially intended? Or is something else going on?

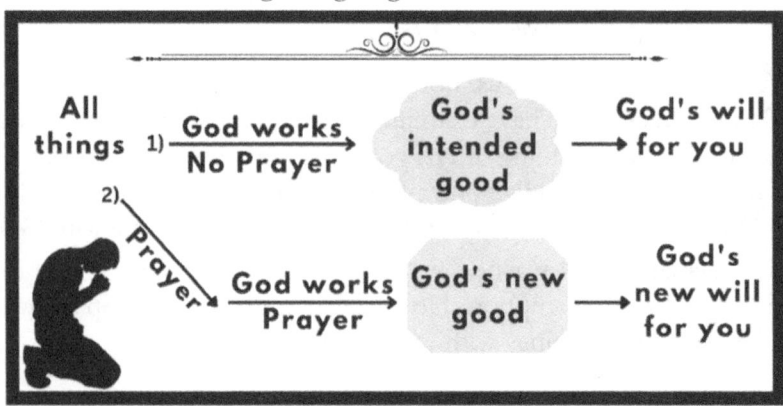

188   Praying to a Mighty God

In examining the diagram concerning the impact of prayer, Path 1 does not involve prayer. However, God is at work in the believer's life, working all things together for good, which is God's intention and will for the believer. Path 2 is for the same believer with the same all things, but instead, the child of God prays, resulting in a new good and God's will for the believer. If path 2 is true, it is also true that God has changed His will for the believer as a result of prayer.

This new response would be God's will, but not His sovereign will or His commanded will, neither of which God changes. But this will of God He necessarily creates as He works all things together for good in the believer's life. This would be a different type of God's will, a dynamic will for the child of God. This will of God can change in response to the prayer or free will actions of His child to produce a new good for the believer. As we have seen, he is continuing that good work that He started at salvation, faithfully sifting through the testings of life to only allow in what you can handle. We will find that God's answer to our prayers moves us in the direction of completing God's sovereign and commanded will. Let us examine these ideas and see whether they are so by studying the scriptures to seek answers to our questions.

> **Dynamic Will of God** – God changes His will for each believer in response to His children's free will actions to continuously produce good in the believer's life and move them in the direction of God's sovereign and commanded will.

Let Me Alone!

To understand how God's will and His answers to prayer interplay, we will examine a fascinating passage in the book of Exodus. Romans 15:4 instructs us that even though not all of the Bible is directly to us, it is all for us, and we can learn much through studying the entire Word of God.

> "For whatsoever things were written aforetime were written for our learning, that we through patience and comfort of the scriptures might have hope." *Romans 15:4*

The scriptures written to others before this age of Grace in which we live are for our learning and enable us to find comfort and hope as we read and study them. The character and nature of God have never changed. He is the same yesterday, today, and tomorrow. Of course, how He has dealt with mankind has changed, though, as we have seen. The passage in Exodus that we will examine will lead us to some fundamental understandings about prayer and God's will.

> "And the LORD said unto Moses, Go, get thee down; for thy people, which thou broughtest out of the land of Egypt, have corrupted themselves: They have turned aside quickly out of the way which I commanded them: they have made them a molten calf, and have worshipped it, and have sacrificed thereunto, and said, These be thy gods, O Israel, which have brought thee up out of the land of Egypt. And the LORD said unto Moses, I have seen this people, and, behold, it is a stiffnecked people: **Now therefore let me alone,** that my wrath may wax hot against them, and that I may consume them: and I will make of thee a great nation." *Exodus 32: 7-10*

Let us break this down and see what is going on here.

- What is God's will here?
- What is His intent?
- What does God tell Moses that He is going to do?

He tells Moses to let Him alone so that His wrath may wax hot against Israel because they have corrupted themselves, and that He could consume them, that is, burn them up. And then He would make a great nation from Moses. This is God's will. This is what He intends to do: destroy and eliminate them. If God consumed the nation and used Moses to form a great nation, He would still be faithful to His promises to Abraham, Isaac, and Jacob (Israel).

Some say that God said certain things to Moses to get him to respond and defend his people. This would mean that God did not intend to consume the nation and make Moses a great nation. He was dangling some words to cause Moses to react and answer. But for that to be true, God would be lying to Moses about His intent to destroy the people and then make a nation from Moses.

First, God cannot lie.[172] So, He is stating what He intends to do. Second, this would dictate that God is like a marionette puppeteer pulling strings on a puppet, manipulating Moses like a toy to solicit a response. This would not be a God whose very nature is love. This could not be a

God that, as Exodus 33:11 reveals, "spake unto Moses face to face, as a man speaketh unto his friend."

> "For all the promises of God in him are yea, and in him Amen, unto the glory of God by us." *2 Corinthians 1:20*

Therefore, the only consistent Biblical conclusion you can arrive at is that God means what he says. If Moses obeys God's command to "Let me alone," God fully intends to burn them up, consume them, and make of Moses a great nation. That is the "effect" or outcome God has in store for the nation of Israel for their "cause" of corrupting themselves. It is God's stated will, but it is contingent on what Moses does. God told Moses to **let Him alone so that** He could burn them up. However, we will see that Moses does not let God alone; he seeks God instead. Moses prayed[173].

The **"let me alone"** declaration is huge! It uncovers an intrinsic truth about praying to God that can transform your life if you can grasp it. You see, God wants Moses to let Him alone so He can do what He wants. The implication is that Moses, through prayer, can hinder God from doing what He wants to do, His dynamic will. Nothing can thwart God's sovereign or commanded will. But God wants Moses to let Him alone so that He can move forward with His desire to burn up Israel. That is what God is saying! He commands Moses, "Now therefore let me alone so that..." God is angry. He has had enough, and He is done with the nation of Israel. He wants to consume them, and His will is to destroy them, but He knows that if Moses speaks to Him, He will listen and respond, taking into account what Moses prays.

What? How is this even possible? Well, first, Moses and God have a relationship. Yet, it means even more than this. The even more significant meaning is that Moses' prayer has the potential to interfere with what God wants to do. That is why God tells Moses to "let me alone." But Moses did not. He opened his mouth.

Nothing can keep God from doing what He wants. The conclusion can only be that God - in his sovereign will - has chosen to listen to His children. He has further bound himself, because of love, to consider the request of the child of God in forming His answer for them, the good that He creates. He will not ignore His children. To be even more explicit, God has chosen to obligate Himself to change His will for His children in response to their prayers to Him, provided it does not violate His sovereign or commanded will, which cannot and will not change. At least, this is the case with Moses. We will see whether this extends to us today or not in a bit. Moses does indeed have a special relationship with God, though, so this could be a special case and not for us today.

Let us examine Moses' prayer and conversation with God. What did he pray that caused God to literally change His mind and thus His will for the people of Israel and Moses?

> "And Moses besought the LORD his God, and said, LORD, why doth thy wrath wax hot against thy people, which thou hast brought forth out of the land of Egypt with great power, and with a mighty hand? Wherefore should the Egyptians speak, and say, For mischief did he bring them out, to slay them in the mountains, and to consume them from the face of the earth? Turn from thy fierce wrath, and repent of this evil against thy people. Remember Abraham, Isaac, and Israel, thy servants, to whom thou swarest by thine own self, and saidst unto them, I will multiply your seed as the stars of heaven, and all this land that I have spoken of will I give unto your seed, and they shall inherit it forever. And the LORD repented of the evil which he thought to do unto his people." *Exodus 32:11-14*

First, Moses does not tell God anything that He does not already know. Moses just recounts God's promises and the mighty hand that God showed in delivering Israel from Egypt. Moses' arguments, though true, do not negate the truth that God would still be faithful to His promise to Abraham, Isaac, and Israel (Jacob) by making a great nation of Moses because Moses is of their seed.

Second, was it Moses's persuasive argument? No. God knows everything from the beginning. His thoughts are perfect the first time. Moses did not reveal to God something of which He was not aware. Yet, God, the creator of everything, listened to Moses, His creation, and changed His mind. "And the LORD repented of the evil[174] which he thought to do unto his people." That is precisely what repent means: to change the mind. He listened to Moses and changed His mind. Why? Well, it boils down to the Lord listening to Moses' heart, not the arguments, no matter how eloquent they might have been. Moses moved the heart of God to a different action and, thus, a different result. So, God answered the request, the prayer of Moses, with "Yes, I will change my mind on this."

For God to answer Moses' request to change His mind about destroying Israel, God chose to be more long-suffering with the nation of Israel. Remember that the Lord was angry and wanted to consume them. But because Moses prayed, God changed the course of events.

Thus, God says "yes" to Moses' request and changes His mind and will for Moses and the people. However, God does say "no" also. Read the following passage that describes what happens next with Israel.

> "And it came to pass on the morrow, that Moses said unto the people, Ye have sinned a great sin: and now I will go up unto the LORD; peradventure I shall make an atonement for your sin. And Moses returned unto the LORD, and said, Oh, this people have sinned a great sin, and have made them gods of gold. Yet now, if thou wilt forgive their sin--; and if not, blot me, I pray thee, out of thy book which thou hast written. And the LORD said unto Moses, Whosoever hath sinned against me, him will I blot out of my book. Therefore now go, lead the people unto the place of which I have spoken unto thee: behold, mine Angel shall go before thee: nevertheless in the day when I visit I will visit their sin upon them. And the LORD plagued the people, because they made the calf, which Aaron made." *Exodus 32:30-35*

In this case, Moses prays to God to judge him personally for the sin of the people. Forgive them and judge me in their place is his request. When Moses asks to be blotted out,[175] he tells the Lord to judge him for the people's sins, to kill him instead of them. God tells Moses "No"; in fact, emphatically, "No!" Now, what is different here? Moses again shares his heart with God and is even willing to die for the people God has given him to lead. Why doesn't God say "yes" to Moses? Well, to answer Moses' request with a "yes" to this prayer would require God to become a liar, to do something contrary to His nature. According to what God has already revealed in His Word, His sovereign will is that the individual who sins must pay for their sin. In Genesis 2:17, God declares this as the result of sinning against Him, "But of the tree of the knowledge of good and evil, thou shalt not eat of it: for in the day that thou eatest thereof thou shalt surely die." Later, in Romans 6:23, God states that "the wages of sin is death." Thus, God confirms with Moses, "Whosoever hath sinned against me, him will I blot out of my book." Everyone is responsible for their actions. This is God's sovereign will - it cannot be changed or added to. So, God says, "No." But note that God still answers Moses' prayer. He always does.

Now notice Exodus 33:1-4.

> "And the LORD said unto Moses, Depart, and go up hence, thou and the people which thou hast brought up out of the land of Egypt, unto the land which I sware unto Abraham, to Isaac,

and to Jacob, saying, Unto thy seed will I give it: And I will send an angel before thee; and I will drive out the Canaanite, the Amorite, and the Hittite, and the Perizzite, the Hivite, and the Jebusite: Unto a land flowing with milk and honey: for I will not go up in the midst of thee; for thou art a stiffnecked people: lest I consume thee in the way. And when the people heard these evil tidings, they mourned: and no man did put on him his ornaments." *Exodus 33:1-4*

The Lord tells Moses that He is going to send an angel with him. He will get Moses into the land. The angel will clear their path, and the land will be as promised - flowing with milk and honey. God shares His reasoning for sending an angel and not going with them Himself. If He were to go up with them, He might consume the people in the way because they are stiff-necked people. These are bad tidings; the people and Moses know it.

Let us ask these questions. What is God's will here? What is His intent? What is He going to do? It is plain to see that He is sending an angel with the nation into the land. God cannot lie. This is His will. And if Moses does not intercede, this is what will happen. Yes, send an angel to get the nation into the land. This will still satisfy the promise made to the forefathers. But Moses does not leave it alone; he prays to God. Moses intercedes.

"And Moses said unto the LORD, See, thou sayest unto me, Bring up this people: and thou hast not let me know whom thou wilt send with me. Yet thou hast said, I know thee by name, and thou hast also found grace in my sight. Now therefore, I pray thee, if I have found grace in thy sight, shew me now thy way, that I may know thee, that I may find grace in thy sight: and consider that this nation is thy people. And he said, My presence shall go with thee, and I will give thee rest. And he said unto him, If thy presence go not with me, carry us not up hence. For wherein shall it be known here that I and thy people have found grace in thy sight? is it not in that thou goest with us? so shall we be separated, I and thy people, from all the people that are upon the face of the earth. And the LORD said unto Moses, I will do this thing also that thou hast spoken: for thou hast found grace in my sight, and I know thee by name." *Exodus 33:12-17*

In summary, Moses reminds God that he was told to lead the people into the land, but he is unsure who will accompany them. However, he knows

God, and God knows him. They do not want to go without the Lord's presence; only then will others know that they are the Lord's. We will be like every other nation if you are not with us. And then the Lord agrees with Moses to go with them into the Land.

To answer Moses' request with a "Yes," again, God changed His mind based on Moses's prayer to Him. God has, once more, changed His dynamic will for Moses and the people. He has decided to be even more long-suffering, not because of Moses' reasoning, but because of Moses's relationship with Him. Wow, what a great and extraordinary God! Now, in this case, the Lord directly states why He answers Moses' prayer with a "Yes." **"I will do this thing also that thou has spoken: for thou hast found grace in my sight, and I know thee by name."** Can it be any clearer? The Lord answered Moses' prayer based on their relationship and His love for Moses. Moses had found grace in God's sight, and God knew Moses by name.

For Thou hast found Grace in my Sight, and I Know Thee by Name.

Let us examine this just a bit more. Moses had found grace in God's sight. Grace is God's favor. This is Moses' standing before God. He does not deserve it; he did not earn it. It is grace. Moses was a child of God, like faithful Abraham. And when Moses prayed, God listened to Him and answered Him because of this relationship. The second part of God's explanation of why He chose to respond to Moses' prayer with a "Yes" is that God knew Moses by name.

Now, our God is omniscient. He knows everyone's name, as well as the number of hairs on our heads. He knows the number of the stars and also their names.[176] This phrase means something more profound than that. God is saying, "I know you; you are part of my family; you are precious and special to me. You are mine." This is powerful to understand. God desires to please Moses and to answer his requests with yes. Just as you would want to help your children and make them happy if you can, He is love, and it is His choice to do so.

Another powerful truth is that when God listened to Moses and changed His mind, it changed the course of events solely on the input of one man, based upon a relationship of love. If Moses had not prayed to God, history would have been different. The actions of a faithful person can have far-ranging implications. In James 5:16, God affirms that "the effectual fervent prayer of a righteous man availeth much."

What About Me?

Was this just for Moses and his special relationship with God? When you pray, how does God answer you? You are a child of God, and we have shown already that God answers every one of your prayers. But can prayer change the will of God for your life? Can it change what God will allow in your life and in the lives of others?

Does God know you by Name?

> "Nevertheless, the foundation of God standeth sure, having this seal, The Lord knoweth them that are his. And, Let everyone that nameth the name of Christ depart from iniquity." *2 Timothy 2:19*

Our Lord knows us. We are part of His Body, and He has placed us in the Body of Christ as He has seen fit.[177] He has called, justified, and even glorified us, and nothing can separate us from His love, which is in Christ Jesus our Lord. [178]

> "For we are his workmanship, created in Christ Jesus unto good works, which God hath before ordained that we should walk in them." *Ephesians 2:10*

In this verse, the word "workmanship" in the Greek is the word ποιημα, poiēma. We get the word "poem" from it. We are God's workmanship, a poem, an expression of God's love, meticulously crafted with care and God's heart. Yes, our God knows us by name, and we are special and unique to Him, precious and loved. The Lord knows each of us intimately. Romans 5:8 says that He died for us while we were yet sinners, and now He lives for us. The Lord knows each of us by name; there is no doubt.

Have you Found Grace in God's Sight?

God's infinite grace has saved every child of God. And we are all children of God by faith in Christ Jesus and what He did for us.

> "For by grace are ye saved through faith; and that not of yourselves: it is the gift of God: Not of works, lest any man should boast." *Ephesians 2:8-9*

> "But for us also, to whom it (righteousness) shall be imputed, if we believe on him that raised up Jesus our Lord from the dead; Who was delivered for our offences, and was raised again for our justification." *Romans 4:24-25*

And today is a day of grace. The Apostle Paul declares that today we are in the Dispensation of the Grace of God in Ephesians 3:1-6. Grace reigns today.[179] Every believer stands in grace before God. Thus, every believer has found grace in the sight of God.

> "By whom also we have access by faith into this grace wherein we stand, and rejoice in hope of the glory of God." *Romans 5:2*

We have the same, if not greater, relationship with our God than Moses. Because of the work of Jesus Christ, we have access to the throne of grace at any time. We can come boldly before our God in prayer with all our requests and all our needs. God will never tell you to "let me alone." When God showed Moses His glory, Moses had to hide in the cleft of the Rock. He was not allowed to see all of God's glory.

> "And he said, I beseech thee, show me thy glory. And he said, I will make all my goodness pass before thee, and I will proclaim the name of the LORD before thee; and will be gracious to whom I will be gracious, and will shew mercy on whom I will shew mercy. And he said, Thou canst not see my face: for there shall no man see me, and live. And the LORD said, Behold, there is a place by me, and thou shalt stand upon a rock: And it shall come to pass, while my glory passeth by, that I will put thee in a clift of the rock, **and will cover thee with my hand while I pass by: And I will take away mine hand, and thou shalt see my back parts: but my face shall not be seen.**" *Exodus 33: 18-23*

However, according to 2 Corinthians 3:18, we, with an open face, can behold the glory of the Lord.

> "But we all, with open face beholding as in a glass the glory of the Lord, are changed into the same image from glory to glory, even as by the Spirit of the Lord." *2 Corinthians 3:18*

That glass is the Word of God. As we behold God's glory in the Word, we are changed into the same glory. God, the Holy Spirit, which lives in you, changes you and makes you more like Him. We have the Word of God today that allows God to speak to us at all times, and God calls us to pray to Him at all times. We, too, can be in a dynamic relationship with our God. Our relationship is "open face beholding...the glory of the Lord."

However, Moses was not allowed to see God's face; thus, we have more extraordinary privilege and access. Moses' relationship was remarkable, and God bound Himself by love to listen to Moses and take Moses' heart and prayer into account when Moses spoke to Him. God sought to answer Moses' prayer with a "Yes" if possible. And yet, our relationship with God is even more remarkable. So, what about our prayer to God, then?

The Conclusion of the Matter: Bound by Love and Choice

And we, too, are known by God intimately - by name - and we have all found grace in His sight. And just as God did with Moses, He answers using our requests to shape tomorrow. He dynamically works all things together with our prayer to produce a different good than if you did not pray. Moses prayed to God, and God changed tomorrow. That is precisely what happened.

Sometimes the answer is "Yes," sometimes it is "No." But in all cases, He desires to interweave our prayers with His will for us, changing the course of our tomorrows. He wants us to get involved in our tomorrow by praying from our hearts. He calls His children to live with purpose and intention, calling on His name at every circumstance. He has not told anyone today to "let me alone." He says to come boldly, with all your requests and supplications with thanksgiving. He is an awesome God, an omnipotent God, an omniscient God, and an omnipresent God. When we pray to Him, we worship Him. Praise God that we have such a loving God who works out the details with the hearts and lives of His children intertwined, blended perfectly for His glory and our good.

A Trip Analogy

We can understand this further from a trip analogy. I am sure you have planned a trip to some destination. Consider a family traveling for a beach vacation. The destination is Virginia Beach, six hours away if no stops are made. The plan is to leave Monday morning as close to 6:00 am as possible, arriving at their rented vacation home by 3:00 pm to collect the key, and then stay for one week. While there, the parents plan to visit a waterpark, for which they pre-purchased tickets, play a round of miniature golf, go to the beach, and fill the remainder of their time with relaxation. So, this is the parents' will for their family vacation. It is a fixed will. It is like God's sovereign or commanded will. Outside influences could change things since they are not God, but within the parents' power, this is their plan for their family vacation.

And now come the requests from the kids, all along the trip and during the vacation. "Dad, can we stop? I have to go to the bathroom!" "Mom, I'm hungry. Can we get chicken nuggets?" And when they get to their destination, the requests continue. As they pull into the vacation home they rented, "Dad, can we go to the beach now?" "Mom, can we buy that puppy?" "Do we have to go to the beach today? I want to go to the waterpark." "Dad, can you help me fly this kite?" "Dad, Mom, can we stay another week?"

So how do the children's requests affect the parents' fixed will for their vacation? The parents' fixed will is analogous to God's sovereign or commanded will, and the children's requests are equivalent to our prayer requests. If the children make no requests, what happens on the vacation is solely up to the parents. It will be excellent and wonderful, but the kids – if they do not make requests - have no input into their parents' plans for them on their vacation. The week will pass according to their parents' will, and they will have passively received good from it.

Now, notice how the moment-to-moment requests from the children affect their parents' fixed will and the parents' dynamic response to their children.

"Dad, can we stop? I have to go to the bathroom!"

Dad compares the request to the travel plans, the parents' fixed will for the trip. There is time available for a bathroom break, plus it is a pressing situation, so Dad says, "Yes." Dad has added this to his plans and stops at a roadside rest. The parents' fixed will has not changed, but their will related to their children has dynamically adjusted to include the roadside rest stop. The child's request has changed the parents' will for the child to a new will that now includes the roadside rest stop.

"Mom, I'm hungry. Can we get chicken nuggets?"

Mom says, "I packed lunch, but we are on vacation. We can use it tomorrow at the beach, though." Mom says, "Yes, we can stop and get chicken nuggets!" A hearty cheer arises from the back seat! The parents' fixed will has not changed; however, their will for their children has transformed. They have added a stop at a fast-food restaurant in response to their child's request.

"Dad, can we go to the beach now?"

Dad says, "We just got here and need to unpack." But he tells his two kids to go ahead and dress for the beach. They will all go as soon as the car is unloaded. They are on vacation and can put stuff away later. The parents' fixed will is still unchanged, but their will for their children is dynamically changed in response to the child's request.

"Mom, can we buy that puppy?"

Mom quickly says, "No," along with Dad. "We are on vacation; where would we keep a puppy?" The parents privately discuss getting a puppy when they return home, but they will keep it a surprise. The parents' fixed will is still unchanged. But the parents' will for their children has been modified with future plans for a puppy in response to the child's request.

"Do we have to go to the beach today? I want to go to the waterpark."

Dad says, "It is supposed to be hot tomorrow. The rest of the week looks uncertain, with rainy weather. We will go to the waterpark tomorrow. It will be the only day we can go, and we have tickets." Off to the beach they went. The parents' fixed will and the parents' will for their children remain unchanged, and it was good.

"Dad, can you help us fly this kite?"

Dad wasn't planning on it; he just sat down in the beach chair to relax. Ugh! But he looked at them both with love in his heart, and his spirit was stirred, and he said, "Why not?" It will bring them closer together. The parents' fixed will does not change. However, the parents' will for their children has dynamically altered to a new will that includes the children's request to fly a kite with their dad. Dad gave up relaxation because love always wins.

"Dad, Mom, can we stay another week?"

The answer from the parents is no. This would change the parents' fixed will of only staying a week. This is unchangeable, so the answer is no. The parents' fixed will is unchanged, and their will for their children remains unaltered.

So, we see from this simple analogy that the parents' fixed will remains unchanged. However, upon every request by their children, there is a loving obligation to listen, consider, fashion an answer, and say yes if possible. Why? Because they love their children, and it is their choice to do so. The child's request, if it is not in direct opposition to the parents' fixed will and can be fashioned into something good, results in a change from what was initially intended by the parents—a change to something different, which occurred only because the child made the request. Because of the requests, the vacation trip became the children's trip, too. The children became involved in their day-to-day experiences and their tomorrow because they brought their requests to their parents.

This limited analogy mirrors how God is at work for us and dynamically changes His will for each of us when we pray. He is already at work, continuously changing His will for us (those who love God and are called according to His purpose) with every free will action we take. However, when we pray, we become involved in the details of our days because our God listens and responds in love for each of us. We have the opportunity when we pray to affect our tomorrows through the love that God has for us. We cannot control tomorrow or the difficulties ahead, but our God knows the way through the wilderness. He will weave all those good and bad, joyful and challenging details of life into a new good that He produces in our lives because of our requests, supplications, intercessions, thanksgiving, and prayer. It is so complex that it is dizzying. But it is also quite simple. He is God. He loves you, and He loves me. There is nothing too hard for Him. So Pray! Tomorrow awaits your heart's prayer to our Heavenly Father.

> **So, what does not happen because you do not pray?**

Chapter 15 Reference List

[172] Titus 1:2

[173] Remember that prayer at its core is talking to God. When Moses besought God, or talks to God, or speaks to God, he is praying.

[174] Evil in this context is bad things, not sin.

[175] Moses is not saying send me to Hell. In examining the result in Exodus 32:35, it is physical death, and the book is the Book of the living, not the Book of Life.

[176] Psalm 147:4

[177] 1 Corinthians 12:12-23

[178] Romans 8:28-39

[179] Romans 5:21

Chapter 16
God's Answer to Your Prayer

It's All Good!

God, in His sovereign will, has chosen, in love, to not only listen to and answer our prayer but also interweave our prayer with His will for us, saying yes to our prayer if possible. This is God's choice; no one has made God do this. This is a sovereign decision of the God of the Universe, motivated by love for His children. This is the same love that drove the Son of God, Jesus Christ, to the cross for the sins of all mankind.

His decision to do this is because we have a very real, precious, personal relationship with Him. But God is faithful to who He is and His Word. As you may recall, everything is sanctified to God through His Word and Prayer.

God's Word defines the criteria upon which He bases His answer to our prayer. Recall that God answered Moses with yes and no to his requests. He answered yes when the request did not conflict with who He is and His Word. He said no when the request was against who He is or His Word. God's Word gives us insight into how God answers prayer. God answers every prayer, and today the Holy Spirit is also making intercession for each of us as we pray, since we know not what we should pray for as we ought. With heartfelt personal yearnings, He intercedes for us and aligns our prayers with the sovereign will of God.

> "Likewise the Spirit also helpeth our infirmities: for we know not what we should pray for as we ought: but the Spirit itself maketh intercession for us with groanings which cannot be uttered. And he that searcheth the hearts knoweth what is the mind of the Spirit, because he maketh intercession for the saints according to the will of God." *Romans 8:26-27*

It is God's will to do so! He has chosen this as part of His relationship with His children. Can anything demonstrate His power, grace, omniscience, omnipresence, and authority more than this? No wonder prayer is fundamentally the purest form of worship to God. When we pray, we transform the tomorrow that we live, not by any power of our own, but because our God loves us. He is for us and desires to give and give. He is always at work in us, but through prayer, we become part of the orchestration of God's hand in our lives and the lives of those about us. When we pray, we seize tomorrow. We make the most of our tomorrows by bringing God to bear on the details of our lives, all because we pray. God has chosen in His sovereignty to obligate Himself to listen and answer our prayers and, in the process, use and abide by our requests if possible. Our God wants to say yes in love.

Defining Criteria from the Word of God for God's Answer to Prayer

Now, I will not be so ignorant as to tell you that I can discern God's answer to your or even my prayers. As the Word says, we do not know what we should pray for as we ought. We really do not know what the answer should be. We are finite beings and limited, but our God is not. He knows tomorrow today. However, we do know that God will not do anything against who He is or against His Word, and He will not make Himself a liar in answering prayer. He will not do anything contrary to His sovereign will, so we can see in God's Word the criteria for how God answers prayer. We know that the Holy Spirit intercedes on our behalf in our prayer life, recrafting what we pray according to the will of God. Hence, our God always answers all our prayers, and those answers are in accordance with God's will. Below are several defining criteria for how God answers our prayers. It is far from complete, but it gives an idea of how God answers prayer.

1) **We know that the answer that God gives to our prayers cannot change His Sovereign Will (Ephesians 1)**

    "If we believe not, yet he abideth faithful: he cannot deny himself." 2 Timothy 2:13

He will not go against His sovereign will. He will not delay the day He is coming back for His children (the rapture) because of prayer. He will not save someone who has not called upon the name of the Lord Jesus Christ in faith. These are predetermined in the mind of God and immutable. So, if we were to request that God alter something that is part of His sovereign will, His answer would be no, just as the answer He gave Moses when dealing with those who had sinned.

2) **We know that the answer that God gives to our prayers cannot make God a liar**

    "In hope of eternal life, which God, that cannot lie, promised before the world began;" *Titus 1:2*

His answer will not make Him a liar. Perhaps you are tired of the world around you. I get it. However, if you pray to God to destroy the world again with water, His answer will be no. He has made a promise to never destroy the Earth again with water.

God has also promised that in the rapture, all the Body of Christ will be caught up together with Christ at His coming. This is our blessed hope and promise. We will receive our resurrection body, and so shall we ever be with the Lord,[180] reigning with Jesus Christ in the heavens. If you pray to God to spend eternity on the Earth, our God will say no to that request, as He has promised us a home in heaven. It would make God a liar to say yes. As members of the Body of Christ, our hope, our destiny is in heaven. Ephesians 2:6-7 teaches us that we will be seated in the heavens for the ages to come. Heaven is our destiny.[181]

3) **We know that the answer that God gives to our prayers cannot overrule the free will of others**

    "For this is good and acceptable in the sight of God our Saviour; Who will have all men to be saved, and to come unto the knowledge of the truth." *1 Timothy 2:3,4*

God's answer will not overrule man's free will. Pray for someone to grow up and mature, find peace, find comfort, gain victory over sin, or accept Christ as Savior. These are all incredibly important and things that we should be praying concerning the people that God brings into our lives. Our Lord will not, however, magically zap them with these things. We, as beings created in the image of God, have free will and can accept or reject. However, when we pray such things, our God will bring His power to bear on that person's life through circumstances, conviction, opportunities, difficulties, and other people. Every situation that God brings into this person's life allows that person to humble themselves to God or not. But God will not overrule their free will. They can choose to rebel, but in praying for them, God continues to convict and burden them. He brings opportunities and people into their lives that can help move them in a positive direction if they accept what God is doing. Because God is infinitely wiser than mankind,[182] how he responds to our prayer is intricate and multifaceted, potentially bringing to bear all His creation, including persons, places, and things. God does not overrule, but because of your prayer, aligned with His will, He supplies opportunities for good to become part of the person's life for whom you are praying. Perhaps God convicts you to share the gospel with the person you are praying for and then provides an opportunity for you to do so.

Interesting truth. If you pray for yourself in these areas, and you earnestly mean it, you have already humbled yourself, and God can work quickly and effectively in your life to bring about change!

4) We know that the answer that God gives to our prayers must continue God's good work in us

> "Being confident of this very thing, that he which hath begun a good work in you will perform it until the day of Jesus Christ:"
> *Philippians 1:6*

God's answer to our prayer will not stop this good work in you, but must continue it. If our prayer request would hinder this work in us, God will not say yes, but he can change it and answer it another way, with the best alternative. Perhaps you are not mature enough to handle what you are praying for. You are not ready for it yet. For example, when my son was six, he wanted a BB gun. That would not be a good idea for him at that age. Instead, I got him a Nerf gun. It was safe for him and acceptable to me.

5) We know that the answer that God gives to our prayers cannot produce a greater temptation than we can handle

> "There hath no temptation taken you but such as is common to man: but God is faithful, who will not suffer you to be

tempted above that ye are able; but will with the temptation also make a way to escape, that ye may be able to bear it."
1 Corinthians 10:13

God's answer to our prayer will not cause a greater temptation in your life than you can handle. For instance, "Lord, let me have ten million dollars. We have a great camp ministry and could do much for camp with such a nest egg." No matter how I justify it, God knows me better than I know myself. Ten million dollars may not be good for me. The temptation is perhaps more than I can handle. It could affect my ministries as others treat me differently due to my newfound wealth. I can no longer minister spiritual things to them because they see me differently. God knows me. God knows my calling and what is best for me. Sometimes, the requests we make would control us instead of us controlling them. If the prayer request would cause a temptation or testing in your life that is more than you can handle, God will say no or provide an answer that would not cause such a temptation.

6) **We know that God's answer to our prayers must be for our sake and produce glory to God**

> "Knowing that he which raised up the Lord Jesus shall raise up us also by Jesus, and shall present us with you. For all things are for your sakes, that the abundant grace might through the thanksgiving of many redound to the glory of God."
> *2 Corinthians 4:14-15*

God's answer must be for us. It must produce positive movement in our lives toward God. Everything that God brings into your life is beneficial, positive, and ultimately brings glory to God. If it does not bring glory to God or would be against you, God will not answer your prayer as you ask. But He will answer your prayer in a way that continues the positive movement He is already making. When you pray, you engage yourself in your tomorrow, as God has taken what you prayed for and produced a new effect with your input. It is hard for me to fathom how amazing our God is and that He is so intimately at work in the extreme details of our lives. But He is.

7) **We know that the answer God gives to our prayers must be faithful to our calling and produce positive motion in our growth in service.**

> "Faithful is he that calleth you, who also will do it."
> *1 Thessalonians 5:24*

God's answer to you will move you further in your calling, where God has placed you in the Body of Christ. For instance, Paul was called to be an Apostle. What if he prayed, "Lord, I want to stay at Corinth. I want to stay in one place, put my roots down, and develop this one church. I can be a great help here at Corinth. They need direction and help to walk the way you want them to." What would God's answer be to Paul? Although a good prayer with a godly purpose, it does not align with an apostle's calling. A pastor or teacher, yes, but not an apostle. As you know, Paul never prayed that prayer, as it would not be faithful or true to his calling.

What about you? What is your calling? Perhaps you need to pray to God to reveal your calling and help you do it. Each of us may have multiple callings. For instance, presently, I am called to be a husband, a father, a grandfather, a teacher, and a pastor. Each of these is special, and I strive to be the person God wants me to be in each of them. I know that God is at work moving me along in a positive way in each of them, and my prayers should also do the same. As a pastor and teacher, God is guiding me in authoring this and other books, producing solid Christian teaching podcasts, pastoring a new church plant, and serving in various youth, adult, and missions ministries. God's answer to my prayers will not hinder me in any of these callings that God has given me, but will move me along and help me grow in each, and open doors to others that I am not yet aware of.

8) We know that the answer that God gives to our prayers cannot produce a reduction or lack of anything

> "That ye may walk honestly toward them that are without, and that ye may have lack of nothing." *1 Thessalonians 4:12*

God's answer will not reduce anything positive or good in your life. It will not cause you to lose ground on your growth, on the good work that He has done in you. So, if your prayer would hinder what God is doing in your life, then God will change it. Praying to God for an increase in godly goodness in your life will yield positive answers from God.

9) We know that God's answer to our prayers must benefit the Body of Christ—individual, local, and corporate

> "And the Lord make you to increase and abound in love one toward another, and toward all men, even as we do toward you: To the end he may stablish your hearts unblameable in holiness before God, even our Father, at the coming of our Lord Jesus Christ with all his saints." *1 Thessalonians 3:12-13*

> "And above all these things put on charity, which is the bond of perfectness." *Colossians 3:14*

> "But as touching brotherly love ye need not that I write unto you: for ye yourselves are taught of God to love one another. And indeed ye do it toward all the brethren which are in all Macedonia: but we beseech you, brethren, that ye increase more and more;" *1 Thessalonians 4:9,10*

> "Owe no man anything, but to love one another: for he that loveth another hath fulfilled the law." *Romans 13:8*

This is a part of God's answer to prayer that many individuals do not consider or realize. We understand that God's answer to our prayer is based upon what is eternally good for us. This might mean that we go through a difficulty that we do not like, for our good. Recall Paul's thorn in the flesh as an example.[183]

There is another outcome to answered prayer that I have not addressed yet. God's answer to your prayer will also benefit the Body of Christ as a whole. It will produce more love and cause growth in unity, peace, and joy. God's answer to your prayer is not only best for you but for the members of the Body of Christ you impact. God's answer to your prayer will be positive for your family, church family, neighborhood, coworkers, and all that God has brought into your life.

Consider if this were not the case. God answers your prayer and produces good in your life, but others around you would receive a negative impact in their life from the answer to prayer God gave you. This is obviously not the case. God loves all His children and is the Head of the Body. We have many members, but one Body. Hence, all members of the Body benefit from God's answer to your prayer. Can you imagine how amazing God is to do this?

> "O the depth of the riches both of the wisdom and knowledge of God! how unsearchable are his judgments, and his ways past finding out! For who hath known the mind of the Lord? or who hath been his counsellor? Or who hath first given to him, and it shall be recompensed unto him again? For of him, and through him, and to him, are all things: to whom be glory forever. Amen." *Romans 11:33-36*

This passage sums it up. Our God is everything. Amen. Amen. And amen.

As an example, consider the Apostle Paul, who was imprisoned for the cause of Christ. He was also in jail for the sake of others. I am sure he thought it would be better to be active in getting the Lord's work done. He says in Philippians that he was sure he would be released because of the prayers of the Philippians. Yet Paul was in prison, and God's answer for a time was that Paul would stay there. What did Paul do while he was there? Well, he witnessed to everyone that was around him: the guards, the servants, the food preparers, everyone. We know that many were saved. Also, visitors were allowed to come and see him, so he heard good and bad news concerning all the churches he helped establish. Last but not least, Paul wrote letters, the Word of God. If he were not in bonds and had been able to get to Ephesus, Colossae, Philippi, etc., he would not have written the letters. He would have gone there and set those churches straight face-to-face.

But instead, God thought of you. He thought of all the other Christians in Paul's day and through the ages. Paul was in prison so that you would have God's Word today. God's answer to Paul's prayers and the Philippians' prayers for his release was that being in prison was best for Paul and the Body of Christ. Members of those assemblies copied the letters he wrote and shared them with other local assemblies. The churches could now have God's Word because Paul was in prison. Paul understood how God works and how He answers prayer. He saw the good that God was producing because of where God had him. Paul knew that being in prison was answered prayer and God's good for him. And God received the glory.

> "But I would ye should understand, brethren, that the things which happened unto me have fallen out rather unto the furtherance of the gospel; So that my bonds in Christ are manifest in all the palace, and in all other places; And many of the brethren in the Lord, waxing confident by my bonds, are much more bold to speak the word without fear. Some indeed preach Christ even of envy and strife; and some also of good will: The one preach Christ of contention, not sincerely, supposing to add affliction to my bonds: But the other of love, knowing that I am set for the defence of the gospel. What then? notwithstanding, every way, whether in pretence, or in truth, Christ is preached; and I therein do rejoice, yea, and will rejoice. For I know that this shall turn to my salvation through your prayer, and the supply of the Spirit of Jesus Christ, According to my earnest expectation and my hope, that in nothing I shall be ashamed, but that with all boldness, as always, so now also Christ shall be magnified in my body, whether it be by life, or

by death. For to me to live is Christ, and to die is gain."
Philippians 1:12-21

10) We know that God's answer to our prayers must work all things together for good.

> "Likewise the Spirit also helpeth our infirmities: for we know not what we should pray for as we ought: but the Spirit itself maketh intercession for us with groanings which cannot be uttered. And he that searcheth the hearts knoweth what is the mind of the Spirit, because he maketh intercession for the saints according to the will of God. And we know that all things work together for good to them that love God, to them who are the called according to his purpose." *Romans 8:26-28*

All the above criteria can be summarized in this statement: God's answer to your prayer will always produce what is good. If it cannot be good, God will do it another way. God defines the good in His infinite knowledge. It is good for you and good for the Body. It is good for you, and it is good for your family. It is good for you, and it is good for the local assembly. God is working all things together for good.

The fantastic thing is that God takes our requests, our supplications, and works it all out and answers them with another good, a better good, since now you have input into your tomorrow. Prayer results in changes in all aspects of life: physical, emotional, and spiritual. God covets your prayer requests and supplications. He wants to use your heartfelt, prayerful concerns to shape your tomorrow. He wants you involved in an active relationship with Him as your life is shaped by His hand.

When we pray, our requests are sanctified unto God; they become His, and He now takes them as His personal possession. He has obligated Himself by love to listen and answer your prayer by taking your request into account. Prayer is asking God's hand to be involved in your life and the lives of others. This glorifies and worships God. Prayer acknowledges who God is. Prayer is evidence of the faith that we have in God and acknowledges God's authority, power, omniscience, love, omnipresence, and all that He is. Prayer is a measure of our thankfulness. God wants you to be involved in your life, to sanctify all of it to Him. We must prioritize the worship of our Lord and Savior, Jesus Christ; we need to pray.

God can change your tomorrow!

And you can be part of that change.

Pray.

Chapter 16 Reference List

[180] 1 Thessalonians 4:13-18, 1 Corinthians 15:51-57
[181] Philippians 3:20; Ephesians 2:6-7; 1 Thessalonians 4:13-18; Colossians 3:1-4
[182] 1 Corinthians 1:25; 1 Corinthians 2:16; Romans 11:34
[183] 2 Corinthians 12:7-10 And lest I should be exalted above measure through the abundance of the revelations, there was given to me a thorn in the flesh, the messenger of Satan to buffet me, lest I should be exalted above measure. For this thing I besought the Lord thrice, that it might depart from me. And he said unto me, My grace is sufficient for thee: for my strength is made perfect in weakness. Most gladly therefore will I rather glory in my infirmities, that the power of Christ may rest upon me. Therefore I take pleasure in infirmities, in reproaches, in necessities, in persecutions, in distresses for Christ's sake: for when I am weak, then am I strong.

Chapter 17
Commanded to Pray

Let Us Hear the Conclusion of the Whole Matter

Many individuals have cried, "Why am I here?" "What is the purpose of life?" "Does it really matter what I do?" Questions like these freely roll off the tongue of many who do not have Christ in their life. In the book of Ecclesiastes, Solomon, the Preacher, the wisest of all men, finds that life is filled with vanity and vexation.[184]

> "I have seen all the works that are done under the sun; and, behold, all is vanity and vexation of spirit." *Ecclesiastes 1:14*

Vanity of vanities, all is vanity. All things come to emptiness and have no profit. In Physics, this is the law of Entropy, where everything in life moves from order to disorder. Everything is falling apart. The scripture refers to this as the bondage of corruption,[185] which God put into operation in judgment for the sin of Adam. Everything in this life, the things and experiences of life, all produce vanity. If our hope is only in the here and now, then we have no hope. But for the child of God, there is hope, which is found in Jesus Christ. Solomon, the Preacher, shares the conclusion of the whole matter in Ecclesiastes 12:13-14. What is the purpose of life and living? Why are we here? What is the whole duty of man?

> "Let us hear the conclusion of the whole matter: Fear God, and keep his commandments: for this is the whole duty of man. For God shall bring every work into judgment, with every secret thing, whether it be good, or whether it be evil." *Ecclesiastes 12:13-14*

Through the Holy Spirit, Solomon reveals the meaning of life: to fear God and keep his commandments, for we will stand before our God one day in judgment. If our hope is found in this life only, then there is just vanity and emptiness. If we fear God and keep His commandments, when we stand before God, He will bring to light the hidden things and give rewards to His children. Others who are not His children will stand before God in fear, judged for their sin, and given their place in the Lake of Fire.

Depending on your relationship with God, fear has two meanings. If you are not a child of God, then fear means terror. Hebrews 10:31 states, "It is a fearful thing to fall into the hands of the living God" because there is judgment. In 2 Corinthians 5:11, the Bible declares, "Knowing therefore the terror of the Lord, we persuade men;." Without Christ, the lost will remain lost and face eternity separated from God in Hell and the Lake of Fire.

For the child of God, fear has a different meaning. Fear for the believer is felt and experienced when we bow before our Savior and God, the one who died for us. It is an awe-driven reverence for the One who created you and saved you. It is the respect and honor that we give Him in astonishment for all He has done for us. It is a godly fear that we show as we are in the presence of the almighty God. It is not the fear of punishment but the fear that we will disappoint the One who loves us so much that He died to redeem us from sin.

The second aspect of the whole duty of man is to keep His commandments, for all will stand before God and receive for what they have done. Solomon was referencing all the law, as that was what he was called to do, what God told him and his people to do. Today, we live under grace, as the Law has been nailed to the cross. We have liberty as adult sons in Jesus Christ, but we ought not to use that liberty to allow our flesh to reign in our lives. We have a responsibility to live for Christ and to choose Him first in our lives.

You may think that since there is no Law, God has not given commandments to obey. However, even today, our God has given us hundreds of commandments in grace found in the books of Romans to Philemon that we are to follow as His children. There are no punitive judgments against us since all our trespasses and sins have been paid for at the cross. However, sin always separates, and if we disobey, our lives will be disjointed, and we will feel apart from God and experience vanity and emptiness. He is always there for you, but because of your sin, you will struggle to know Him in a real and living way.

To have a healthy and satisfying relationship with our Lord and Savior, we must obey His commands to the Body of Christ. As we read the Apostle Paul's letters, we find numerous instructions on how to live a life pleasing to God. Here are just a few commands or instructions found in just one chapter, Colossians 3, that are to the believing child of God today. These are grace commandments.

- Seek those things which are above, where Christ sits on the right hand of God.
- Set your affection on things above, not on things on the earth.
- Mortify your members which are upon the earth; fornication, uncleanness, inordinate affection, evil concupiscence, and covetousness.
- Put off anger, wrath, malice, blasphemy, and filthy communication out of your mouth.
- Lie not one to another.
- Put on the new man.
- Put on bowels of mercies, kindness, humbleness of mind, meekness, longsuffering.
- Forbear one another and Forgive one another.
- Put on charity.
- Let the peace of God rule in your heart.
- Be thankful.
- Let the Word of Christ dwell in you richly.
- Teach and admonish one another.
- Do all in the name of the Lord Jesus, giving thanks to God the Father.
- Wives submit yourselves to your husbands as it is fit in the Lord.
- Husbands, love your wives, be not bitter against them.
- Children obey your parents in all things.
- Fathers provoke not your children to wrath.
- Servants, obey in all things, not with eyeservice, with singleness of heart, fearing God.
- Everything you do, do it heartily as unto the Lord, and not unto men.

Our duty as His children is to keep His commandments directed to us. They produce value in a time that is full of vanity. When we live our lives as God says, we redeem the time because the days are evil. We produce value and profit within our lives and in the lives of others. In the book of Titus, we have a comparative verse for us today.

> "For the grace of God that bringeth salvation hath appeared to all men, Teaching us that, denying ungodliness and worldly lusts, we should live soberly, righteously, and godly, in this present world; Looking for that blessed hope, and the glorious appearing of the great God and our Saviour Jesus Christ; Who gave himself for us, that he might redeem us from all iniquity, and purify unto himself a peculiar people, zealous of good works." *Titus 2:11-14*

We are to live by grace and do all that God calls us to do. We will stand before our Lord and Savior one day. He is coming to take us home to be with Him. It will be a glorious day! Until then, grace teaches us to deny our flesh and to live unto the Lord. He gave Himself for us to redeem us from all our sin, but also to separate unto Himself a unique people, producing good in this world and in the lives of all around them.

How we live is critical, not only for us but for others. Your presence or lack of presence impacts your family, friends, coworkers, church family, and all you meet. When you are with others, it impacts them. When you are not with others, the void you leave behind also impacts them. It is a constant of life. Your life matters to God and to the ones He has placed in and around your life. Is that impact positive, or is it negative? We all would like our lives to impact others positively. So, pray. Pray for everyone in your life. Pray for those who make you smile and those who make you grimace. Pray for everyone in your life when you are with them, and especially pray for those in your life when you are not with them. Pray for all who are in authority. Pray for your family and each of their needs. Make specific requests. Know that God can do anything and far more than you can ask or think. Pray for those you have just met and those you have known for years. We have been commanded to pray over and over again. Our God expects and commands us to pray.

> "Rejoicing in hope; patient in tribulation; continuing instant in prayer;" *Romans 12:12*

> "Continue in prayer, and watch in the same with thanksgiving" *Colossians 4:2*

> "Be careful for nothing; but in everything by prayer and supplication with thanksgiving let your requests be made known unto God." *Philippians 4:6*
>
> "Praying always with all prayer and supplication in the Spirit, and watching thereunto with all perseverance and supplication for all saints;" *Ephesians 6:18*
>
> "Rejoice evermore. Pray without ceasing. In everything give thanks: for this is the will of God in Christ Jesus concerning you." *1 Thessalonians 5:16-18*

These are all commands to us to pray.

Prayer should be a dynamic, ever-present activity in our lives. If you do not make prayer an intention in your day, it will languish as something that happens when emergencies arise or as an afterthought. Choose to pray when you wake up. Choose not to close your eyes in sleep until you have prayed to God about the details of your day. Choose to seek God throughout the day and pray for others' needs as they arise. Your prayers can last from moments to hours in length. But choose to pray. It obeys, honors, and glorifies God.

Prayer is part of an active relationship with our God. Our Father wants us to engage with Him and share all our heart with Him. God commands us to live and pray with purpose and intention. He desires us to be in a continuous conversation with Him. In this 24/7 information-sharing social media-driven culture, it is readily apparent that individuals are seeking connections with others. Their souls are yearning to fill a void, an emptiness, a vanity. Their phones never leave their hands. Every notification interrupts whatever actual events are happening right around them. Yet, the emptiness remains no matter how many messages and posts are consumed. However, God requires no artificial device, nor has any bandwidth limitations or latency issues. He is the true satisfaction of their yearning and need to connect. He is ready 24/7/365 to provide fulfilling and satisfying answers, filling the void with His presence. We can be filled to overflowing with His love, joy, and peace. But we need to pray to Him. We need to let Him speak to us through His Word. We must connect and engage with Him in directing our lives. Seek God's impact on your tomorrow, and He will weave your prayer and requests into His will for your life.

When we pray, our God always answers. Our God receives our prayers, requests, and supplications, making them His sanctified possession. He is at work immediately for our good. Our prayers become integral to His will and the good He produces in our lives. This good has our prayers and requests embedded in it. So, the good that He has made has changed your tomorrow and is different from what it would have been because you prayed. Seize tomorrow by praying today. Stop being a passive observer in your life. Our God is not limited or hindered. He is God.

Do you want your life to be different from what it is presently? Is there something missing in your life? Are there issues or problems in your children's lives? Is your marriage what it should be? Is the government ruling well? Is your friend struggling with an addiction? Whatever it might be, pray! Our God answers every prayer. Remember, we know not what we should pray for as we ought, but the Holy Spirit makes intercession for us according to the will of God. God answers every prayer and produces good every time. So, pray. Our God knows tomorrow, and prayer allows us to participate in what tomorrow looks like. Seek God's will for your life; pray! You can be part of the change. So, what does tomorrow hold for you?

I have already prayed that this work will bless and encourage you to pray and engage with God for all your tomorrows. Glorify Him by sharing with Him all your heart and the details of your life. God loves you.

Finally, pray for me. God's best to you. Fight the good fight of faith!

> "Finally, brethren, pray for us, that the word of the Lord may have free course, and be glorified, even as it is with you:"
> *II Thessalonians 3:1*

Chapter 17 Reference List

[184] Difficulty, troublesome, hardship of both body and mind
[185] Romans 8:18-23

Chapter 18
Am I a Child of God?

So, are You a Child of God?

The most important truth you can know is whether you are a child of God. So, ask yourself, "Am I a child of God?" Some may think everyone is a child of God since He is the creator. However, Galatians 3:26 states clearly, "For ye are all the children of God **by faith in Christ Jesus.**" You see, Jesus Christ is the deciding factor determining if you are part of the family of God and whether God is your Father. In John 14:6, Jesus declares, "I am the way, the truth, and the life: no man cometh unto the Father, but by me." You must go to God on His terms and through Jesus Christ.

Now, what might those terms be? What requirements must I complete to become part of God's family, to become a child of God? Next are listed some practices that many believe are required by God for you to be part of His family and to go to heaven. Consider your thoughts as you read this list of good things and how they align with your beliefs.

What must I do to be part of God's Family and go to Heaven?

- o Obey God's law and commandments
- o Doing your best
- o Live a good life
- o Holy Communion
- o Water baptism
- o Good works
- o Trying to obey the Golden Rule
- o Church membership or attendance
- o Born of Christian parents
- o Penance
- o Prayers
- o Confirmation
- o Tithing

Perhaps you think that one or more of the above is God's requirement to be part of His family. The truth is that God does not require any of these for you to be part of His family and go to heaven. First, each involves our attempts to reach God and make ourselves worthy of God's love or heaven. It is not that these are bad things, but the problem is that all fall short of God's standards. We must ask the right question: "What does God say is required?" That is what is profoundly important. Proverbs 14:12 says, "There is a way which seemeth right unto a man, but the end thereof are the ways of death." Since this determines where you will spend eternity, you need to be sure you are doing it God's way.

The real answer to how to get to heaven and become part of God's family is not found in the things we do (religious activities, doing "good"…). God has declared that "there is none righteous, no not one."[186] "For all have sinned and come short of the glory of God."[187] None of us can make ourselves sinless. We all fall short, no matter what we do. Further, God's Word teaches that sin is a serious matter resulting in "everlasting destruction from the presence of the Lord."[188] Anyone not found written in the Book of Life will be cast into the lake of fire.[189] The wages of sin, what we earn daily because of our sinful actions, is death. And that death is more than physical death; it is eternal separation from God in Hell.[190]

What can you do about this sin problem that the Word of God says you have? Can you clean up your life, do good deeds, and hope that your good will outweigh your bad in the end? Well, you can try, and many do. But unfortunately, God's Word is clear that it will not be enough. Why? Because these things, even excellent things, are trying to get to Heaven our way and not God's way. They may seem right to you and many others, but they are not the right way to God. We are trying to do things without asking God what He wants. You see, God's way is simple. Salvation and becoming part of God's family do not come to those who work for it but to those who cease from their works, placing their trust in the Lord Jesus Christ. So, what does that mean? Romans 4:5 makes the point abundantly clear: "To him that worketh not, but believeth on him that justifieth the ungodly, his faith is counted for righteousness." God equates your faith in what He has done as righteousness. Faith = Righteousness.

This is not just faith in anything, but in what Christ has done for you. Ephesians 2:8-9 declares, "For by grace are ye saved through faith: and that not of yourselves, it is the **gift** of God, not of works lest any man should boast." Romans 6:23 says, "For the wages of sin is death; but the **gift** of God is eternal life, through Jesus Christ our Lord." It is a gift to be received. You accept what Jesus Christ has done for you. It is not about the things we have done, because, as God says, if it were based on our works, we would get to heaven and say, "Look at me, " and "Look at what I have done." This is boasting. There is no room for pride in heaven, just grace.

The issue is not what you can do for God but what Christ has done for you. "But God commendeth His love toward us in that while we were yet sinners, Christ died for us."[191] "He hath made Him to be sin for us, who knew no sin; **that we might be made the righteousness of God in Him.**"[192] You have no righteousness of your own. To have eternal life, you must have the righteousness of Christ, and here we find that God makes us righteous as a result of our faith in the Lord Jesus Christ. "To declare, I say, at this time his righteousness: that he might be just, and the justifier of him which believeth in Jesus."[193] God justifies you based on your believing in Jesus; that is, trusting that what He did for you is enough.

What, then, is your responsibility? What are God's terms for becoming part of His family and going to Heaven? God has given you free will to accept or reject what He has done for you. To have God's righteousness and to be part of His family, you must believe that "Christ died for our sins according to the Scriptures; and that He was buried; and that He rose again the third day according to the Scriptures."[194] Your response to the gospel should be to believe and trust what Christ has done for you. In Ephesians, it is clear: "In Whom (the Lord Jesus Christ) ye also trusted, after that ye heard the Word of truth, the gospel of your salvation: in Whom also after that ye believed, ye were sealed with that Holy Spirit of promise."[195] This seal is a guarantee that your salvation is eternal--you can never lose it.[196] Yes, **believe on** the Lord Jesus Christ and thou shalt be saved![197] It is "believe on" because it is about what He has done, His faithfulness, His righteousness...it is trusting your eternity to Him. And who better to trust?

That is right. Just believe what God says about Christ and what Christ has done for you. Jesus Christ is God Himself, and He paid the price of your sin: death. He died, was buried, and rose again on the third day, and now He offers eternal life as a gift to everyone who believes in Him. He died for you, and He offers you eternal life. If you are not part of God's family, you can be saved and become a child of God right now, at this very moment. If God's Word convicts you, you may want to pray something like: "Dear God, I trust You now. I know I have been a sinner. I believe Christ died for my sins and rose again so that I might be declared righteous. Thank You for giving me eternal life through my Savior, Jesus Christ. Amen."

> "Whosoever shall call upon the name of the Lord shall be saved." *Romans 10:13*

If you trusted Christ today or have questions, please don't hesitate to contact me or Impact Grace Church Ministries. We are eager to share more with you from God's Word.

Pastor John Harris
www.Facebook.com/impactgraceministries
www.Facebook.com/Everyday.wisdom.for.the.child.of.God
www.YouTube.com/@GraceTeachingToday
www.YouTube.com/@GraceBibleTeaching
www.YouTube.com/@HowPrayerActuallyWorks

Chapter 18 Reference List

[186] Romans 3:10
[187] Romans 3:23
[188] 2 Thessalonians 1:9
[189] Revelation 20:15
[190] Romans 6:23
[191] Romans 5:8
[192] 2 Corinthians 5:21
[193] Romans 3:26
[194] 1 Corinthians 15:3-4
[195] Ephesians 1:13
[196] Ephesians 1:14, 4:30, 2 Corinthians 1:22
[197] Acts 16:31; Romans 4:23

Appendix
Praying Only for Spiritual Things???

An Incorrect Teaching: Only Pray for Spiritual Things

I typically teach the truth of the Word of God and attempt to do it thoroughly and clearly. If we are established in the truth when some doctrine or teaching comes along that does not ring true to the clear teaching of the Word of God, red lights should come on and cause an alert; something does not seem right. And that is the case for a teaching falsely claiming that God only responds to spiritual prayers, that God's children should only pray for spiritual things, and that His answers are only spiritual in nature, such as love, hope, peace, joy, comfort, spiritual maturity, salvation, conviction, etc. There are variations on this theme, but that is a reasonable summary. This assertion can even rise to the level that praying for physical things, such as health, money, one's home, and similar, would be outside the will of God, since God only answers in spiritual ways. Some even go as far as to assert that since God only answers prayer for spiritual things, then praying any other way is wrong and even sin. This directly contradicts Philippians 4:6-7, which clearly states that you are to be careful for nothing, but in everything by prayer…make your requests be known unto God.

This teaching is unreasonably limiting for the child of God, especially for those who are newly saved or young in the faith. Consider the new believer just learning to walk by faith; how could such a newborn babe in Christ pray spiritually when they are a spiritual babe? It takes maturity in the Word and one's Christian walk to be spiritually minded. Paul shares the crushing reality of the battle of the flesh and the Spirit in Romans 7 and the conflict of the flesh and Spirit and how they are contrary to one another in Galatians 5:17-23. At any given moment, the believer is either in the Spirit or driven by the flesh. Access[198] to God is a truth for every member of the Body of Christ, regardless of their spiritual walk. All are commanded to be constant in prayer. All can be careful for nothing, meaning not to hold back or restrict yourself, "but in everything by prayer and supplication with thanksgiving let your requests be made known unto God. And the peace of God, which passeth all understanding, shall keep your hearts and minds through Christ Jesus."

There is no limit to what we can pray for here or anywhere in scripture. As shared earlier, the little boy's request for a wagon was actually a spiritual request, despite being a physical thing.

How did this teaching come about? The basic argument follows this general train of thought: God does not work physically today, but only spiritually. The following two premises are brought to bear on the Word of God: You are complete in Christ, and God's Word is complete. Now, these are true, which the scriptures attest.[199] However, even if a premise is true, if it is misapplied, it results in error. For example, Columbus operated on the premise that if he sailed west, he could reach the east. That is a valid premise. However, Columbus failed to apply his presumption correctly and did not get even close to where he intended.

This is a perilous approach to the Word of God. The first rule of "Bible Study Errors 101" is that you do not go to the Word of God with a preconceived idea and attempt to prove it. Many damnable doctrines have been supported in this fashion, leading countless believers astray and unbelievers to Hell. By applying these two premises to the Word of God, they have redefined clear understandings of certain words and passages to support their premise. This teaching not only has doctrinal issues regarding prayer but also limits the work of the Holy Spirit and effectively negates any unique spiritual gifts[200] for God's children in the age of Grace. There are serious errors in this teaching. It is essential to allow the Word of God to teach and change you. It is the authority, not you, not me.

They conclude by taking these two premises and applying them to God's Word, that if God reveals Himself by answering prayer in some physical way (healing someone, making it rain, not running out of gas, getting your health back, sunshine, finding the right house, etc.), then God would be revealing extra-Biblical truth. Since the Word of God is complete, this cannot be. It is inconsistent with their premise. God has revealed Himself outside the Word of God and thus revealed "new" truth by answering prayer in some tangible way. Since that is impossible according to their premise, they conclude that God's answer to prayer is limited to spiritual things. Hence, physical answers to prayer are not possible, and correspondingly, praying for physical and material things would be wrong or, at the very least, should be avoided.

This bad doctrine takes away the very purpose of prayer: to be in communion and conversation with our God. If the child of God must limit his conversation with God to only spiritual things, he only shares part of his heart with God. Our God wants all of me. He wants all of you. Sharing only part of yourself with your spouse or friend does not work in your relationships in this life, and it does not work in your relationship with God. This hinders growth in the believer's life.

Some ascribe to this teaching and attest that you can pray for whatever is on your heart, but they teach that God only answers in spiritual ways. Those who aspire to this teaching use Philippians 4:7-8 as proof for their claim that Paul says to pray for everything, but the answer is always spiritual peace.

> "Be careful for nothing; but in everything by prayer and supplication with thanksgiving let your requests be made known unto God. And the peace of God, which passeth all understanding, shall keep your hearts and minds through Christ Jesus." *Philippians 4:7-8*

The assertion is that any prayer related to physical things is basically ignored, and all other requests are nebulously dealt with by an answer of God's peace that guards your heart and mind.[201] The details don't seem to matter because God only gives His peace, more valuable than gold, to be sure, but all that you brought before Him that is of a physical need is essentially not considered. God knows what is going to happen anyway, doesn't He? And isn't it His will? He just changes how you feel about it, and you have peace. God doesn't change anything about your situation, but you feel better about it. Seems a little hollow and indifferent on God's part.

Now, I have been one-sided in making the point, leaning hard into praying for physical things. There is far more to pray about than the physical world in which we live, of course. And I agree that our prayer life should be spiritually driven and focused, and that comes with spiritual maturity. However, our God does not limit us to just those aspects of prayer, and our God's answers to prayer are also not limited to spiritual things. The very focus of this book is to encourage and equip you to be a prayer warrior on the spiritual battlefield, gaining victories for the cause of Christ. So, pray for everything on your heart!

Individuals who prayed to God in the Bible fully expected God to answer and do what they asked; they expected action. And God answered. Not always the way they wanted, but He did. Recall Chapter 3, "**What can prayer do?**" Numerous prayer examples in scripture were shared for you to think about and meditate on. All had one thing in common: the praying person expected God to do something, and most expected the answer almost immediately. Today, in the Dispensation of Grace, this is still true. When the Apostle Paul prayed, he expected God to do something. He expected to see God's hand at work around him. Paul knew a truth about God: He is a very active and powerful God who "does exceedingly abundantly above what we ask or think."[202] Every time you read the phrase "pray that," the individual praying was expecting a result. The preposition "that" grammatically starts a result clause. Hence, "pray that" has a direct expectation for an outcome in God's answer to that prayer. Look at these two examples from scripture in describing what prayer does.

> "… The effectual fervent prayer of a righteous man availeth much. Elias was a man subject to like passions as we are, and he prayed earnestly that it might not rain: and it rained not on the earth by the space of three years and six months. And he prayed again, and the heaven gave rain, and the earth brought forth her fruit." *James 5:16-18*

What more straightforward statement can be made than what is said here: the effectual fervent prayer of a righteous man availeth much. These are results related to the requests made in prayer. It is not complex; God listens to us, loves us, and answers us.

> "Finally, brethren, pray for us, that the Word of the Lord may have free course, and be glorified, even as it is with you: And

that we may be delivered from unreasonable and wicked men: for all men have not faith." *2 Thessalonians 3:1-2*

You can easily see in 2 Thessalonians 3:1-2 that Paul is praying for physical deliverance from unreasonable and wicked men. Paul also expected God to answer when he prayed concerning his physical thorn in the flesh. Paul exclaims that he besought the Lord thrice, three times, expecting God to respond. And when the Lord did answer, notice that Paul had peace about the things of life which he did not have before. He felt God's protection and grace and was ready to face life head-on through God's grace and power. We are not apostles, nor is God audibly speaking to us today. Paul received a truly clear answer. The answer is often unclear to us, and it takes time to see that God has answered your prayer. Sometimes, you may never discern it. But to be sure, as has been shown, God is or has responded to your prayer. It just may not be how you intended or thought it should be. God's Word clearly states that we do not know what we should pray for as we ought, meaning we do not know what the answer to our prayer should truly be. Nevertheless, God the Holy Spirit does and intercedes on our behalf.[203] However, every time you pray, God's answer also has an added benefit to your prayer: you receive God's peace, which guards your emotions and thoughts. God's peace is not the only result of praying, but the immediate benefit we receive when we give God what is on our hearts! The rest of God's answer is not always so immediate.

This is worth repeating; Philippians 4:7-8 trumps any rationalization of man by declaring to the child of God, "Be careful for nothing; but in everything by prayer and supplication with thanksgiving let your requests be made known unto God." So, there is nothing off-limits to pray about. Whatever is on your heart or mind, take it to God! Whether physical, emotional, or spiritual, they are all valid and important to God. We are accepted in the beloved, so everything on our hearts and minds is acceptable to take to our heavenly Father. They are all worthy of His attention.

Appendix A Reference List

[198] Romans 5:1-2

[199] Colossians 2:10; Colossians 1:25

[200] Unique spiritual gifts are effectively eliminated because of their premise that you are complete in Christ. A true premise, but in their application, the Holy Spirit giving you the gift of say teacher or pastor, would imply that others do not have the gift of teacher or pastor. That is contrary to their application of this premise of completeness in Christ, eliminating unique gifts for God's children in Grace. It is generally taught that all have these gifts, and you must learn to enable them.

[201] Those that teach this do teach that God works in His children and through the Body of Christ to produce other spiritual things as well such as conviction, joy, comfort, love, etc.

[202] Ephesians 3:20

[203] Romans 8:26-27

Made in United States
Cleveland, OH
30 September 2025

20960636R00134